SA

W9-CYT-572

Pancho Villa

T E X A S

Ft. Davis

Candelaria

naga

Castolon

Las Cruces

San Antonio

Del Rio

Piedras Negras

Eagle Pass

Sabinas

Nueva Laredo

Laredo

ulalia

Isabela

Rosalia

enez

COAHUILA

NUEVO

Rio Grande

GULF

Brownsville

tillo
Inde

Torréon

Monterrey

LEÓN

N G O

San Juan del Rio

OF

MEXICO

urango

ZACATEGAS

TAMAU PAS

SAN LUIS POTOS

Zacatecas

Tampico

ATE
OF
YARIT

Aguascalientes

san Luis
Potosí

Tepic

Guanajuato

QUERÉTARO

UZ

Veracruz

JALISCO

GUANAJUATO

HIDALGO

Pancho Villa

Col Villa in Mountains
Me

Pancho Villa

Intimate Recollections by People Who Knew Him

Edited by

Jessie Peterson
and
Thelma Cox Knoles

HASTINGS HOUSE · PUBLISHERS

New York

Library of Congress Cataloging in Publication Data

Main entry under title:

Pancho Villa.

    Includes index.
    1. Villa, Francisco, 1878–1923___Anecdotes.
2. Generals—Mexico—Anecdotes, facetiae, satire, etc.
I. Peterson, Jessie. II. Knoles, Thelma.
F1234.V697   972.08'1'0924   77-12034
ISBN 0-8038-5819-1

Published simultaneously in Canada by
Saunders of Toronto, Ltd., Don Mills, Ontario

Printed in the United States of America

This book is dedicated to
our families and friends who kept
faith with us and Pancho Villa,
and to the wonderful people who
gave us their stories.

CONTENTS

viii   *CONTENTS*

Introduction

This book is composed of interviews with men and women who tell of their personal experiences with General Francisco "Pancho" Villa. Pancho Villa's deeds, victories, defeats, are recorded in history, but there is another kind of history of those "Villa" years and events which is in danger of being lost forever as the people who lived them pass away. These are the firsthand accounts of some of those who had experience with and were affected by the actions of Pancho Villa. Their stories are personal, vivid, real, and vary as greatly as their firm opinions of Villa as a "sort of Jesus Christ saviour of his people" to a "murderous devil."

These stories, told by those who lived them, preserve a part of history that would otherwise be lost. Most of these accounts have never before been published, and many of the narrators have now passed on, leaving their precious legacy of first-hand knowledge in our hands.

Pancho Villa was born on June 5, 1878 at the Hacienda de Rio Grande, San Juan del Río, State of Durango, Mexico.

He was named Doroteo Arango by his parents, Augustin Arango and Micaela Arambula.

The Arangos, like the great mass of Mexican people at the time, were peons and worked as slaves on the ranch owned by the family of Don Arturo Lopez Negrete.

At the time of Villa's birth, Porfirio Diaz was president of Mexico and was two years into a dictatorship that lasted, except for one four-year period, for thirty-four years.

Villa's father died when Villa was only twelve years old, leaving him as head of the family, with his mother, two younger brothers and two younger sisters to support. The boy tried his best, working long hours in the field, gathering wood to sell, hunting in the wilderness of the surrounding Sierra Madres. At an early age he acquired a pony, the first of the horses that were to become an integral part of his life, and learned to shoot with deadly aim. Once for leaving the hacienda without permission he was punished by flogging that left lifetime scars on his back as well as his soul.

Villa was sixteen when he was forced to become a fugitive, taking to the mountains like a hunted animal. There are varying stories about what happened, including those told by Villa himself in later years. But the story most often told has Villa murdering the son of the patrón in revenge for the rape of his sister. Hunting, scrounging, stealing, hiding out during the day, traveling at night, Villa managed to survive. Sometimes he found work as a cowboy on the range or in Chihuahua City, but with the vengeance-bound law of his home village continually searching for him, Villa was always forced to run to avoid capture.

Finally he joined a band of outlaws led by Ignacio Parra. It was at this time that Doroteo Arango took the name of Pancho Villa. (The original Pancho Villa was a notorious Mexican outlaw of the early nineteenth century.) When Parra was killed Villa struck out on his own, accompanied by several members of the band who were to stay with him through the years.

Pancho Villa the bandit became widely known along the border, terrorizing the wealthy and sharing his plunder with the peon families he encountered. This of course earned him the reputation of being a Mexican Robin Hood.

He was a great lover, marrying many times without the benefit of divorce, having many sweethearts, not all of whom were willing. He called himself a "son-of-a-bitch with women," and was acknowledged to be *muy hombre*.

By 1908, when Villa was recognized as the chief bandit throughout the states of Durango, Sonora and Chihuahua, the stirrings of revolt against the dictatorship of President Diaz were beginning to be felt. Francisco I. Madero, a member of a wealthy and prominent family, became a champion of the people.

Madero traveled the country, taking his message of "No ninth self-elected term for Porfirio Diaz, free ballot, restoration of the stolen lands to Mexico's landless millions," straight to the Indians, Yaquis and Mexican peons, the people thronged to listen to him.

The short, bearded, unprepossessing Madero lit the spark of hope in his listeners' hearts that flared, then flamed, into the long, bloody revolution that was to engulf Mexico. The "Viva Maderos" at first were considered only a nuisance by President Diaz. However, shortly after the anti-reelectionist party nominated Madero as their presidential candidate in April, 1910, Madero was arrested and imprisoned.

One of the strongest supporters of Madero's cause was Abraham Gonzalez in the State of Chihuahua. Gonzalez, recruiting guerrilla leaders who could command a following, sent for Villa in the fall of 1910. He explained, in terms that Pancho could understand, Madero's ideals of democracy. Villa was impressed when he learned that for daring to oppose Diaz, Madero had been imprisoned. He left Gonzalez with a captain's commission and his promise to enlist the guerrilla bandits to support Madero. The meeting with Abraham Gonzalez marked a turning point in Pancho Villa's life. He trusted and respected Gonzalez, and gloried in his new status. He enthusiastically rounded up bandits, vaqueros and peons, all taking up the banner of democracy and revolt.

Meantime, early in October, Madero escaped or was released from imprisonment at San Luis Potosí. He immediately went to San Antonio, Texas. There he established himself as Provisional President of Mexico. On November 20, 1910, he issued his "Plan of San Luis Potosí," calling for an uprising through Mexico. The people responded. Their battle cry of *Tierra y Libertad* (Land and Liberty) is to this day sounded by thousands of peons demanding and seizing land in the states of Sinaloa and Sonora.

Villa had recruited several hundred followers when he received word from Gonzalez that the time had come to take the field. He immediately attacked the small town of San Andres, Chihuahua, and easily realized the first of many victories in the name of Madero and the Revolution.

In March, 1911, Villa with five hundred well-trained men met Provisional President Madero at Bustillos. Pancho Villa was greatly impressed with Madero. He was said to have declared, "Here is one rich man who fights for the people. He is a little fellow but he has a great soul. If all the rich and powerful in Mexico were like him, there would be no struggle and no suffering, for all of us would be doing our duty and what else is there for the rich to do if not to relieve the poor of their misery?"

Madero decreed that in view of the great services Villa had rendered to the cause of national independence, he should be granted a full pardon of his crimes as a bandit, as the abuses and persecution by the dictatorship had forced him into his life of crime.

There followed a series of small victories and defeats for the Insurrectionists. In April, 1911, Madero with some 2,000 men established a camp across the Rio Grande from El Paso, just northwest of Juarez. With him were such leaders as

Guiseppe Garibaldi, grandson of the famous Italian patriot, Pascual Orozco from western Chihuahua, Benjamin Vilgoen, veteran of the Boer War, Raul Madero, brother of the Provisional President, and Villa. At this camp, which came to be known as Peace Grove, Pancho was commissioned Colonel.

After a fierce two-day battle, May 9-10, 1911, with the world and El Paso as avid spectators, the Revolutionists led by Garibaldi, Orozco, and Villa, took Juarez from the Federals. The capture and possession of the important border city was enough to sweep President Diaz into exile and Madero to the presidency of Mexico.

Villa soon afterward entered briefly into private life in Chihuahua City, operating a butcher shop. However in March, 1912, at Madero's summons he took the field against Orozco who was now leading a new revolt against the Madero government. They had several encounters at Parral.

When President Madero ordered Villa to serve under General Victoriano Huerta he did so reluctantly. His misgivings proved right as Huerta, on trumped up charges, ordered Villa executed at Jiménez on June 3, 1912. Villa's dramatic last minute rescue from the firing squad was credited to Raul Madero and General Francisco Castro of the Federals.

Villa was sent to the penitentiary in Mexico City. During his months there he made friends with a young clerk, Carlos Jauregi, who taught Pancho the rudiments of reading and writing. In December of 1912, with Carlos accompanying him, Villa escaped. He made his way to El Paso, where he registered at a hotel in the section of the city known as Little Chihuahua. He used his real name, Doroteo Arango, but was recognized by a local newspaper reporter.

When the shocking news of Madero's betrayal and assassination in Mexico City on February 22, 1913, reached El Paso, Villa recognized the treachery of his old enemy, Huerta. Several days later it was reported that Abraham Gonzalez, then governor of Chihuahua, had also been murdered, thrown under the wheels of a train. Villa wept at the news of the death of the two men he had admired and respected.

Within a few days, vowing vengeance against Huerta, Pancho crossed the Rio Grande with eight followers. Six months later he had raised troops of some 10,000 in Chihuahua. This army was known as Villa's Division of the North.

Throughout 1913 and 1914 the record shows a dazzling series of victories for General Villa, as his name and bold leadership caught fire across Mexico. Other leaders appeared, Carranza, Zapata, Obregon. Huerta, never recognized by the United States as president of Mexico, fled the country in July, 1914.

Villa took Juarez by a bold, midnight sneak attack in November, 1913. Chihuahua City, Ojinaga, Torreón, Naco, knew him both in defeat and victory. Early in December General Villa and the Indian leader from Morelos, Emiliano Zapata, led a triumphant parade through Mexico City. Villa posed sitting in the presidential chair with Zapata on one side of him and his righthand man, Tomas Urbina, on the other.

For a period, in 1914, Villa, considered by many a military genius, was invited to visit at Ft. Bliss, at El Paso. He met and conferred with General Hugh Scott. Scott was to remark later that while Villa was a great sinner he had been greatly sinned against.

Villa was exciting news. Correspondents such as Floyd Gibbons of the *Chicago Tribune* covered his exploits. He was marvelous copy, earthy, unpredictable, vital. He was much more interesting than Carranza, the now self-styled First Chief of Mexico. However, Carranza was clever, highly educated, and wise in the ways of diplomacy.

To Villa's stunned amazement, on October 19, 1915, President Wilson officially recognized Carranza as head of the de facto government of Mexico. Carranza's troops were allowed to travel over United States territory from Eagle Pass, Texas, to Agua Prieta, across the border from Douglas, Arizona, where they disastrously defeated Villa, in the battles of November 1, 2, and 3, 1915. Villa turned bitter against the United States, feeling that he'd been betrayed.

Once in power, Carranza clamped strict censorship on news coming out of Mexico. His propaganda showed Villa to the world as a savage barbarian. Atrocities were committed and blamed on Villa.

On January 9, 1916, at Santa Ysabel, a small station thirty miles from Chihuahua City, a party of American mining officials from El Paso was taken from a train and murdered in cold-blood. Villa was blamed, though there was no evidence that he had any connection with the massacre. A former Villista, Pablo Lopez, was executed in Chihuahua City for the crime.

On March 9, 1916 several hundred Villistas attacked the little town of Columbus, New Mexico, murdering, burning, looting, and again Villa was widely blamed. The controversy over whether Pancho Villa was actually present, directed operations from a distance, or was in another part of Mexico entirely, rages on, with witnesses for both sides. The Columbus Raid brought on the Pershing Punitive Expedition which lasted some eleven months, and did not capture Pancho Villa.

Villa with a remnant of his band continued his challenge of the Federal government with scattered guerrilla attacks and raids. He briefly occupied Juarez in 1919, but was routed by United States troops.

The Carranza government was overthrown in 1920 and on July 28, 1920, Villa laid down his arms and signed a pact of peace, under President de la Huerta. He was given a large estate, Rancho Canutillo, generous funds to repair, stock and equip it, pensions for himself and his five hundred Dorados.

On July 23, 1923, after only three years of retirement as a gentleman farmer, Villa and his bodyguard were ambushed and shot to death as they left Parral to drive to Canutillo. There were many reasons given for his murder. It was said that as long as Pancho Villa lived there was always danger of a new uprising among the people, that they might rally around him as a challenge to the government.

The stories of Pancho Villa did not die with his death, nor the unexplained happenings. In 1926 his grave was broken into and it was discovered that Villa's head had been cut off and removed. Stories still appear in Mexico and the United States about the discovery of Pancho Villa's head. In 1961 a San Francisco paper staged a week's search in Parral for the missing head and left a standing reward of 5,000 pesos for its recovery.

For the November 20, 1976 annual celebration of Madero's proclamation of independence, President Echeverria had General Villa's body taken from the little cemetery in Parral and entombed in the Monument to the Mexican Revolution in Mexico City beside the other revolutionary heroes.

The names of those others tend to fade into history, but not Pancho Villa's. He lives on, lusty, vital, controversial, in the folklore, the campfire songs, the myths and legends, as his restless, rebellious spirit still rides the dusty winds of Chihuahua. Savior or sinner, brutal killer or Robin Hood, people vividly remember Pancho Villa.

Pancho Villa

1

Pat Quinn

Cowboy and rancher, Quinn rode the Chihuahua range with Villa when Villa was still young Doroteo Arango.

"I was working for the Nations-Newman-McElroy Cattle Company in Chihuahua when I first met Pancho in 1901. So you see, my acquaintance with him started long before the Mexican Revolution began. Maybe that's why I have a different slant on him.

"Most of the time I was with a crew down on the Mexican ranch working the cattle there. We drove the herds to Torreón where they were loaded into railroad cars and shipped to the border, crossing at Juárez. Then we took them to Nations' big spread north of El Paso.

"One cold, rainy, fall night out on the Chihuahua range our outfit was just settling around the fire to eat when three vaqueros rode up. The foreman invited them to share our grub, as was our custom, strangers or not. The young Mexicans needed no urging and gratefully dug into big plates of frijoles with tortillas and steaming coffee. The one who seemed to be the leader introduced himself as Doroteo Arango. He said they were working for one of the ranches in the region.

"As they ate we sized each other up. Arango was a stocky built young fellow with big, heavy shoulders. His eyes never missed a thing, and they never gave anything away either. He and I took to each other right off. After that first meeting we ran into each other quite often down in Chihuahua, most always out on the range. I soon learned that his cowboy work was only part time. I didn't ask any questions, maybe that's why he came to trust me. But pretty soon I realized that he was a rustler or maybe even an outlaw a good part of the time. And somewhere along there I learned that he went by the name of Pancho Villa, which I figured he'd taken for his own good reasons. Anyhow, I liked him, and our friendship was a real thing.

"Pancho never talked much about his early life. If people asked, then or later, he gave them whatever story seemed to suit best, or maybe what they expected to hear. Of course I heard the rumors around Durango about him being an illegitimate son of a Spanish don, and that he was part Indian, and other stories. Whatever he was you could soon see that Pancho was no ordinary peon. He had a fierce sort of ambition that turned loose in wild rebellion at times. He loved his family, his mother and two younger brothers and sisters. His father had died quite young, worked to death by the patron of the ranch where they lived, we heard.

"Well, the Mexican Revolution broke out and pretty soon my friend, Pancho, had joined up with Francisco Madero. I saw him a couple of times during those first years and he was really proud when he told me he was a captain in the Insurrecto army. Pancho greatly respected and admired President Madero. He told me that Madero was the first and only man of high position and education who honestly concerned himself with helping the Mexican peons. Pancho swaggered a bit as he announced that he was now carrying a gun on the side of right.

"Another thing showed up, too. It didn't take long for

Pancho Villa to prove that he was a good military man. He learned quick about strategy. Some even said he was almost a genius and that if he'd had any kind of education at all he'd have gone to the top. At any rate he rose fast in the revolutionary army and soon was the big boss of all the state of Chihuahua.

"By 1913 Villa was going great guns. That was when I had quite an experience with him in Juárez. The embargo hadn't been put on by the United States then, and the rebels could buy any supplies they wanted from us. Well, Villa came up through Chihuahua on a drive toward Juárez, and as he came he gathered a great herd of cattle, about 9,000 head, from the ranches down there. Most of the beeves came from the huge Terrazas ranch. Terrazas was rightly known as the cattle king of Chihuahua at that time, and Villa hated his guts.

"Pancho figured on selling the cattle to ranchers over here and using the money to buy ammunition and supplies. He had already made a deal with some of the big ranchers before he got here. He was going to let them have the stock for only nine dollars a head, but they were to pay the United States importation charges. Naturally the stockmen here had their suspicions about where Pancho had acquired this big herd, but they didn't ask questions.

"The deal would have all gone as planned excepting that I queered it a little. It was this way. Pancho had the herd up close to the border, about ready to cross, when I happened to be talking to him in Juárez. He told me about the deal and mentioned the names of the ranchers who were buying the cattle. One of the cattlemen was a man I'd recently worked for. This man had given me a dirty deal and I grabbed the chance to get even with him.

"It happened this way. Earlier in the year, while I was working on this rancher's Texas spread he had quite a bit of trouble with having cattle stolen. Rustlers, it seemed the same ones, were raiding the stock regularly. My boss said he'd give me a thousand dollars if I'd find the thief and bring him in. So I took off from my regular work and went on the rustlers' trail.

"It led right up into the mountains. I was miserably cold but I couldn't risk making a fire because it would give me away. I just ate cold grub out of my saddle bags and kept going, thinking of all I could do with an extra thousand dollars. Pretty soon I realized I wasn't chasing a bunch of thieves but just one tough hombre. I had a pretty good idea who it was, too, a vaquero I'd punched cows with a year or so before. I'd been out more'n a week when I found the little box canyon where he was holding the stolen herd. It looked like a good hundred head.

"I decided I'd better take my man that night before reinforcements arrived to help him get the cattle out of the canyon and across into Mexico. I lay low and that night after my rustler bedded down I jumped him. It was real easy because I took him completely by surprise. I took him straight to the ranch headquarters. Then one of the boys there went into town with me to report and the rest of them went up the canyon to bring in the stolen cattle.

"Well, you can guess how amazed I was when my boss, instead of paying me my thousand dollars, started hemming and hawing and stalling me off. He claimed that I'd had to have the help of the other cowboys to bring the cattle back, so I hadn't earned the bonus. I was mad as a hornet and I quit right then and there. But I didn't forget.

"I asked Pancho if I could contact the ranchers for him and sew up the deal on the cattle he'd brought up to the border. He told me to go ahead. I contacted them all right, all but my former boss. The others grabbed up those beeves at nine dollars a head and made a pretty profit. I got a percentage of the sales. By the time my old boss knew what happened it was all over and he was out in the cold. The money he lost amounted to a darn sight more than the thousand dollars he gypped me out of.

"Not long after that I ran into him downtown on Overland Street. He jumped me about the deal and asked why I didn't get in touch with him when I did the other fellows. I told him I'd told Pancho that he didn't want any more Mexican cattle. It gave me great satisfaction to tell him that. Well, he gave me a hard look and turned and stalked away. He was maddern' a buzzard chased away from a dead cow. I'll bet he didn't break his word again to a poor cowpoke.

"Along that time, 1913 or 1914, my friend, Pancho Villa, was pretty well thought of by the Americans. But soon after that came the Benton business, and right or not, that's when people on this side started turning against Villa. Benton was an Englishman who had a cattle ranch down in Mexico and his killing caused a big stink clear up into international circles.

"There was different stories about what really happened, but what it boiled down to was Benton came up here to Juárez looking for Villa with fire in his eyes. He got himself shot and killed in Villa's headquarters, and pretty soon all hell broke out.

"The citizens of El Paso got so riled up that they called a meeting in Cleveland Square to protest Villa's actions. Mayor C. E. Kelly was afraid that feelings would get so high that a riot might break out and he had the meeting moved to the Texas Grand Theater. There it all simmered down to a bunch of resolutions condemning Villa, and nothing much came of it after all.

"Villa had strong prejudices. He always seemed to dislike the English, especially the ones that put on high and mighty airs. Maybe they reminded him of the Spanish dons that treated his people like slaves. He hated the Chinese even more than the English in Mexico. He was strongly against Mexicans intermarrying with Chinese. He didn't have any use for half-breeds and he really persecuted the Chinese.

"Some people never seemed to admit it, but Pancho Villa did have his own ideas of fair play and honor. Take the case of Colonel Contreras. This officer was a good shot, and of course Villa was, too. Well, one night in a Juárez bar Contreras had had too much to drink and he challenged Pancho to a gunfight. Pancho was not drinking, in fact he almost never drank hard liquor. He just shrugged and turned away. That fool Contreras didn't have any better sense than to follow it up. I stepped in and got him out and away from there, pronto, before Pancho changed his mind.

"I took Contreras home, but later he went back to the bar, still drunk, still looking for Pancho. Luckily for him Pancho had left. However I heard that next time Pancho took Juárez he had Contreras executed, so I guess the poor fool never learned to keep his mouth shut. He couldn't stay lucky all the time.

"Then there was the case of one of Villa's men called Coyote. Villa trusted this man with twenty-five hundred dollars that was supposed to go to buy ammunition for Villa in the United States. Coyote liked whiskey and he liked women. His first night in El Paso he had a big time in a cantina in Little Chihuahua, in the south part of town. When he sobered up he was lying in an alley with empty pockets.

"Coyote's mother, who lived in east El Paso, sold her home for five hundred dollars and gave the money to her son to take to Pancho, hoping that he would not be too hard on Coyote. Coyote should have known that Pancho would not forgive him. He threw Coyote into jail with instructions for him to be 'dobe-walled.' As far as Pancho was concerned that settled the matter. Coyote's mother visited Pancho and begged that her son's life be spared, but Pancho told her to shut up and get out or she'd get a bullet too. There was no doubt that he meant it. It didn't pay to betray Pancho Villa.

"After President Wilson recognized Carranza, Villa felt he'd been double-crossed by the United States government and swore to get even. But I'm sure he never had anything to do with the Santa Ysabela massacre early in 1916. You remem-

ber that was when those American mining men on their way
to reopen the Cusi Mines were taken off the train and murdered. Only one young fellow, Tom Holmes, got away. It was
a terrible thing and caused a lot of hard feeling along the
border. The main reason for the hold-up was that the train was
carrying a big payroll for the Cusi Mines. First it was reported
that the payroll had disappeared in the fracas. Later I heard
another story about it.

"It seems that the minute the train was stopped and someone yelled 'Bandits,' the messenger carrying the money stuffed
the bags of silver into the pot-bellied stove in one end of the
coach. Later, when the Federals arrived and took over it was
only by pure accident that the money was found, as the messenger had been killed. A soldier lighting a cigarette opened
the stove to throw away his match and found the bags with the
sixty thousand dollars in pesos. I always wondered if the soldier got a reward, but I'll bet he didn't.

"At that time I was working at the Cusi Mines as a master
mechanic. The boss of the mine called me in right soon after
the news of the massacre at Santa Ysabela. He wanted me to
take a message to the high command at Ft. Bliss in El Paso.
He wanted the American authorities to know the real truth
about the massacre and not go off half-cocked blaming Villa.
An officer was to meet me at the Paso Del Norte Hotel. My
train was delayed because of a severe sandstorm that covered
the tracks. Everyone had to get out and shovel sand, and even
then we were three hours late getting into Juárez.

"Then when I got to the Paso Del Norte I was arrested by
the El Paso police and thrown in jail. They thought I was
a criminal that they had a poster on. They claimed I answered
the description of this outlaw even to having a broken finger.
The only difference, come to find out, was that my broken finger was on my right hand and the man they wanted had a
broken finger on his left hand. The young policeman who arrested me was a grassgreen rookie because he never even

searched me. Too excited about his big capture, I reckoned. His partner was just as careless. I had the papers the mine boss had sent to Ft. Bliss in an inside pocket. I could have really raised a ruckus but I just sat tight. Finally I asked the policeman to call the big brass at the Fort. They wouldn't listen to me, acted like they thought I was just a bum wanting to look like a big, important guy.

"I could have shown them the papers I carried but I decided to teach them a lesson. There was a young bum that was in for being drunk and they let him out soon as he sobered up. I gave this young fellow a dollar and asked him to call a colonel I knew in the Fourth Cavalry and tell him to come arunning. Just tell him that Dutch Quinn is in jail and needs him, I told the boy.

"Not more'n two hours later here came the colonel and he came cussing. He got a big laugh when I showed him my gun stuffed down inside my waistband that the young policemen forgot to take off me. If I'd been the bad man they thought I was I could have killed that arresting officer easy. He sure looked sheepish when the colonel finished with him. But the colonel was happy to have the word from the mine officials. So, Santa Ysabela Massacre was one crime blamed on Pancho that I personally know he didn't do, and I'm thinking that there were probably plenty more. I always had a sneaking suspicion that the Federals themselves were back of that killing and after the payroll.

"One time those Federals arrested me on a charge of running guns for the revolutionists. Well, my heart was with Pancho and his men, but I never run any guns for them. They had to turn me loose when they couldn't prove anything. Another time, after Villa took Juárez the second time, a Federal officer, friend of mine, told me they had orders to execute me on sight. They thought I was supplying Villa with ammunition.

"Another thing is that myth about all Mexicans being knife toters. I knew they weren't and I had a chance to prove it. I was sitting around with a bunch of soldiers camped at the border, near the old Peyton Packing Plant. There was a colonel there and we got to talking about the revolutionists. The colonel said if the Villistas were as good with their guns as they were said to be with their knives that a lot more soldiers would have been killed along the border.

"I told him the Mexicans were not so good with knives as all that. In fact most of them didn't even carry knives. Right then the colonel bet me that he could prove he was right. He said we could stop a bunch of Mexican workers just then getting off shift from the packing plant, and if more of them carried knives than not he'd win the bet. I took him up fast. The loser was to buy beer for all the soldiers on duty at the camp, which was pretty big stakes. Well, the upshot of it was that we stopped eighteen Mexicans. When I explained the bet they were good-natured about it and turned out their pockets. Well, not one of them was carrying a knife, not even a little pocket-knife. Well, those National Guard soldiers and I sure enjoyed our cold beer.

"Pancho could be savagely cruel and he had a quick, mean temper. I remember hearing about an entire family of Italians he killed. This family lived close to Columbus, New Mexico, and they sold some cattle to the American soldiers. Everyone down there had been warned not to sell or give beef to the gringos, and when word came that they had disobeyed his order Villa acted fast. He took the father, mother, two boys, and a girl out and shot them right then and there. That was to teach everyone in that part of Mexico that he meant what he said. That story came pretty straight, and I guess it was so.

"Of course that happened after Carranza's recognition when Pancho figured he'd been betrayed by the United States. He was very bitter about it. Up to that time Americans or those who dealt with them had no cause to fear Pancho Villa. Wilson dealt the blow that hamstrung Villa by allowing Carranza to send his soldiers over American railroads. Even so I

never believed Pancho led the Columbus Raid. I was always
sure he knew nothing about it till after it happened.

"Another thing, you're always hearing about Columbus,
New Mexico, being the first American town to be invaded by
troops or bandits from Mexico. Why, during Carranza's rule
there were plenty of such attacks and even though Carranza
denied that his men were responsible there's many who are
sure those raids can be laid at his door.

"There was an attack on a train twelve miles north of
Brownsville, Texas, when several people were killed. There
were raids at Red Horse Ferry, the Progreso Post Office, and
even on American garrisons. Cattle, horses, and equipment
were stolen, and American citizens were carried off across the
river. They tried to blame Villa for those incidents, as they
call them, but hell, he was busy up in the northwestern part of
Mexico all during that time. That's all a matter of record.

"I remember some little things about Pancho. He was always afraid of being poisoned. Well, you can understand that,
considering his many enemies. To keep any of his own men
from feeding him something poisoned he'd eat around at the
different campfires, never letting anyone know where he'd
light for a meal. He loved American food and ate it every
chance he got. He especially liked canned asparagus. He'd buy
it by the case whenever he could. When his troops captured a
town he'd always ransack the grocery shelves of American
food and take every can of asparagus for himself.

"I saw Villa's first wife, Juana, a time or two in El Paso.
Then later I saw her in Chihuahua City where they lived in a
big house with a nice garden. They had two little girls.

"Pancho had to have something to him to have made so
many friends among really important people. Take Todd Mc-
Clammy, brother-in-law of Dr. G. B. Calnan. Calnan became
Villa's trusted friend and served as surgeon in the revolutionary army after Villa headed it. McClammy and Calnan owned
a big horse ranch in Mexico and I heard that they gave Pancho

a lot of horses for his cavalry at the start of the war when Villa was just coming into power. Later it was said that Pancho rewarded them by giving them the rich Dolores Mines.

"Then you know General Felipe Angeles joined up with Villa, and Angeles was one of the most respected military men on both sides of the border. He was a graduate of a famous military college in France and of the Military Academy at Chapultepec in Mexico. He was a real artillery expert. Villa always admired Angeles and grieved when the Carranzistas executed him.

"The Mormon people in their settlements down around Casas Grandes got along pretty well with Villa. It was the Red Flaggers under Orozco who caused them trouble. One time I heard of when Villa's funds were low the Mormons let him have grain on credit for his men and horses. They said he always paid promptly when he had the money, and didn't forget his just debts.

"Pancho had his good points as a human being. I think his good deeds offset his bad ones. And he was respected as a man of his word. I was proud to call him friend."

2

Tom Heady

Heady, retired cattleman and ranch owner, worked for almost fifty years on Colonel William Greene's large ranches near Hereford and in the San Rafael Valley.

"Bill Greene extended his range clear over the Huachuca Mountains to the San Rafael Valley, and across the line in Sonora, Mexico, where he bought the Turkey Track outfit. At one time Greene registered under his RO brand the greatest number of purebred Herefords in the world. And I was right with Bill Greene most all the way.

"Now you take the Columbus raid in 1916. Now it never seemed reasonable to me that anyone as smart as Pancho would pull such a foolhardy stunt. I'm inclined to go along with my friend, Frank King, on that. Frank was editor of *Western Livestock Journal.*

"We were talking about Villa one time and King told me that he positively knew that Villa was not within one hundred miles of Columbus the night of the attack. In fact Villa was sick in bed at the time. He was being taken care of by Dr. G. B. Calnan who told King about it right after the story of the raid broke in the papers. Backing up his story was J. Todd McClammy, longtime American agent for Villa. Both Dr. Calnan and McClammy were well-known in El Paso.

"Then there was Tom Turner, foreman for Colonel Greene's Sonora ranch. Everyone in the country knows that Turner's word was as good as his bond. Well, Turner happened to be in Villa's camp during the time of the Columbus raid and he later told me about it. Villa's men had been killing and eating some of Greene's valuable highbred cattle. Greene told Turner to go to Villa and tell him that if he'd let the purebred stock alone he could have what beef he needed from a lower grade on another range. Turner went directly to Villa's camp in the mountains.

"He was taken to see Pancho who was sick in bed. Turner made his proposition and Villa agreed to it, but said that Turner would have to stay in camp while his story was checked. Turner was treated well enough, and when Pancho was satisfied that the company offer was genuine, he was given his horse and told to *vamoose*. And Turner says positively that the attack on Columbus took place while he was at the camp and that Villa never left. He was in bed all the time Turner was there.

"'King came up with a good explanation of how so many people, on-the-spot witnesses, thought they saw Villa leading the raid. In fact King was later asked to write a story for a national magazine, *The West,* about Villa's not being present at Columbus that night. King wrote that a man of the same build and appearance as Villa was dressed and made up to look like Pancho. Then some rebel soldiers just up from Guadalajara who had never seen Villa were ordered to follow the man pointed out as their general and yell, 'Viva Villa' as they rode into Columbus. Naturally those who were captured, and there were quite a few, said that they were led by General Villa. Of course it was dark and the substitution was good, so in the confusion many people were completely deceived.

"After King's story came out a captain with the American soldiers who'd been stationed at Columbus told the editor of the magazine that the story was correct. He had been close to the supposed General Villa that night and since he'd met the real Villa knew that it was not him. I heard the same thing from another American, Harry Willingham, who had known Pancho Villa real well and said there was no doubt that it was not Villa but an imposter who led the raid.

"We always figured that Carranza was back of it all. It was his agents who pulled the attack in order to turn the United States against Villa who'd always had some sympathy over here. In fact King told me that later in El Paso one of Carranza's men told him how it was managed, as well as many other outrages and atrocities laid at Villa's door. It was all part of a huge propaganda campaign that worked pretty well.

"I had a similar experience as Turner. This was soon after Pancho suffered a bad defeat at Agua Prieta, across the line from Douglas, Arizona, in 1915.

"The cards were stacked against Pancho there and the U. S. helped to stack them. Obregón and Calles were allowed to use American railroads to transport Mexican Federal troops from Eagle Pass, Texas, through El Paso and so to Douglas and Agua Prieta. Pancho attacked at Agua Prieta, making a fierce assault of the kind that had been successful for him before. However Obregón used a new kind of warfare which he had learned from German military experts and Pancho found himself stopped by barbed wire entanglements and trenches. He was forced to withdraw. Next he tried a massive sneak attack at night, using his Yaqui troops, but powerful searchlights were turned on the Indians, exposing them to the Federals' fire. The slaughter was brutal. The story we got was that some American soldiers, against orders, also turned machine guns on the Villistas, mowing them down. That was never official, but we heard it from good sources. It was also denied later that the spotlights were operated from the United States side, but the electricity for them sure was at any rate.

"Anyhow, Villa pulled back, leaving over 2,000 of his men dead and wounded. He went to Naco, Sonora, and then on to

Cananea. All along the way he took what he needed, provisions, horses, ammunition. His soldiers were a little rested by the time they went over the Puertacitas Pass to Nogales, Sonora. With about fifty of his men Villa camped for awhile in the Altar district, southeast of Nogales, and licked his wounds.

"That is when he sent word to me as boss of Greene's San Pedro division in Sonora that he needed horses, and his outfit would stay there and eat Greene's topgrade beef till he got them. You know fifty hungry rebels can eat a lot of beef. I rounded up sixty head of horses mighty pronto and personally delivered them to Villa. He treated me all right, as he had Turner, but I never felt real easy till I got out of his camp and back to my own territory. Pancho was feeling pretty ugly toward all gringos by that time, having learned about the Federal troops cutting across the U. S. to overwhelm him at Agua Prieta. There were rumors that he had threatened to kill every gringo in the state of Chihuahua when he got back to his own stamping grounds. You sure couldn't blame him for hating the Americans. Our government really double-crossed him.

"Pancho Villa's name had been enough to scare the ranchers along the border for years. There were numerous bandit raids from across the line, of course, and it was handy to blame them on Pancho Villa. But I always had an idea that on many of these occasions old Pancho was miles away down in Chihuahua somewhere. He really wasn't up around Sonora so much, just enough to scare hell out of folks, I guess. I recall that some of my neighbors, homesteaders, had a big old lazy horse named Nig. The kids of the family would ride Nig three at a time and they thought a lot of him. Every time there was a bandit scare they were terrified that Pancho Villa would come and steal old Nig. I don't think they ever thought of Villa as being one of Mexico's most important generals. To them he was a bogeyman. As a matter of fact, a band of Federals did get old Nig. We figured they took him because he was so fat and lazy and easy to catch.

"I was in on the very beginning of the Mexican Revolution, though I didn't realize in at the time. I had been working for Colonel Greene in Cananea, Sonora, since 1903, serving as a sort of bodyguard, as I had been a peace officer in Colorado before going down into Mexico.

"In 1906 real trouble broke out in Cananea. It started in the copper mines that Greene was developing there. Greene paid the Mexican workers good wages, as high as the government would let him. The Mexican law had set the limits. He was paying his American miners more and that made for bad feeling. Greene wanted to raise the Mexicans' wages but the government claimed that would disrupt the wage scale for the whole country.

"Outside agitators came into Cananea and got in their dirty work. It was the time of undercover German infiltration, well ahead of World War I. The agitators' object was to make trouble for Americans wherever they could. Well, they made plenty at Cananea. They passed out free mescal and inflammatory speeches till they had those poor ignorant Mexican miners all worked up.

"One morning after a row at a downtown dance hall the night before, the Mexicans started milling around in groups around town. And the groups soon became an ugly mob. They went to the company lumber yard and demanded that all the workmen there join them. When the Metcalf brothers, George and William, who were in charge, resisted and tried to drive them away with a high pressure hose the rioters became violent. They killed the Metcalfs and set fire to the lumberyard.

"That taste of blood seemed to inflame them and they began yelling, 'Muerte a los gringos'—death to the foreigners—and headed for Greene's home on the Mesa. About 150 of the American miners met and stopped them before they got up the hill. There was some shooting and rock throwing but the rioters backed down.

"Well, Bill Greene wasn't afraid of anything or anyone. Next day he took the bull by the horns and went downtown to talk to the rioters. He stood in his open car, a big red Locomobile, and faced the mob. He said he'd take care of those in front of him and told me and some of his other men to watch out for those in back. So I stood with my rifle on a corner of a loading dock behind him and watched the crowd for a good hour.

"Greene had always got on well with the Mexicans everywhere and they had always liked and trusted him. Now he talked to them, hard and fast and reasonable, speaking good Spanish. That crowd was in no mood to listen. They were sort of restless, pushing and muttering, but nothing violent happened. And so Colonel Greene held them at bay you might say till Colonel Kosterlitzky got there with his rurales. He took over then and believe me it was a great relief. Kosterlitzky's handling of the matter probably staved off U. S. intervention. The incident came to be known as the Cananea Riots and was later said to be the real start of the big revolution.

"Now take Colonel Kosterlitzky. There was an unusual man. He had the reputation for being a ruthless tyrant, dobewalling prisoners for little or no reason. He was from Russia originally, and it was said that he served with our Sixth Cavalry at Ft. Apache. I always figured that if that was true he had some good reason for deserting there and going to Mexico, as was rumored.

"I got pretty well acquainted with Kosterlitzky the years he was around Nogales. I think most of the stories about him were exaggerations, big windies about a man, a natural leader, that most of the border folks didn't savvy. He was a gruff sort of character, but always seemed a real gentleman, especially around the women. Anyhow, he was a mighty welcome sight at that riot in Cananea.

"While working for Greene in Cananea I became acquainted with Henry Flipper, one of the smartest men I ever met. Flipper was said to be the first Negro ever to be gradu-

ated from West Point. His success was resented in some quarters and the story was that he was finally railroaded out of
the army at Fort Davis, Texas. In the late nineties he was employed by the town of Nogales, Arizona, to clear up the title
to its land which came under one of the old Spanish Grants.
He won the case of Nogales and won himself quite a reputation along the border.

"That was before I met him, along about 1905. By then he
was working for Colonel Greene as a consulting engineer and
general trouble shooter. Greene sent him to company mines all
around Sonora and Chihuahua, and even down to Mexico
City, since Flipper knew the law and the country.

"Flipper was in El Paso at the time of the Columbus raid
and believe me he was surprised and plenty mad when a Washington paper published the story that he was serving with
Pancho Villa. Flipper fired back a hot denial, saying he had
never even met Villa, and that he'd never served anyone but
the United States. It didn't make much impression because
pretty soon the rumors had it that Pancho Villa himself actually was Henry Flipper. It made pretty good reading, especially as Villa did have kinky hair and full lips. However, I'm
sure old Pancho was pure peon Mexican.

"Yes, those were exciting times. With our land out at the
ranch running right up to the line there were many times
when different factions, both Federals and rebels under various leaders, would be camped close by. We'd see their campfires at night.

"I was present at some of the Naco battles. There was the
so-called siege of Naco in 1915 when General Pedro Ojeda,
one of Huerta's Federals, held out for a month there. Ojeda
was surrounded on three sides by rebels led by General Obregón, Colonel Pedro Bracamonte, and Yaqui Chief Luis Bule.
Finally, unable to get any kind of supplies, Ojeda was starved
out. That thirty days gave plenty of time for newsreel men,
photographers, and reporters to gather in Naco. Lots of folks

watched the action from Purdy's Lane, toward Bisbee. When General Ojeda saw there was no hope he had his troops set fire to the garrison and everything else they could in Naco Sonora. Then they marched across the line and surrendered to our Ninth Cavalry there.

"I'll never forget one occasion in Naco. I was standing behind the screen door at the customhouse, listening to the firing across the line, when a bullet smashed into the door. I picked slivers of screen out of my hand for days. That's as close as I ever wanted to be to the action.

"That calls to mind the stories about Naco's famous bullet-proof hotel. Reporters and photographers had swarmed to the border from the east to write up the Revolution. They about filled up the old Naco Hotel, and of course lots of them never got out of the bar. They covered the Revolution from there. Now the main building had good thick adobe walls that would stop bullets, but there was a newer frame annex facing toward Mexico. I was in the hotel one night when some pretty heavy gunfire broke out across the line. You should have seen the 'observers' staying in the annex come stampeding into the old part of the hotel carrying their blankets with them. They seemed content to bed down on the floor in the halls from then on.

"Getting back to Pancho Villa. The Naco business was one instance where he came through to help the United States. There was a bad situation in Naco. Sonora's Governor Maytorena had Carranza's Federals under Calles and Hill trapped right against the line and was closing in on them. That endangered the American citizens in Naco, Arizona. In fact by late 1914 stray bullets had already killed and wounded a number of people on this side, one shot even going through the Cavalry commander's tent.

"In January, 1915, General Scott, Army Chief of Staff, was sent to try and ease the situation. He found that Calles and Hill were more than willing to evacuate Naco, but Maytorena flatly refused as he had the Federals just where he wanted them and saw no advantage to moving or letting them move. Finally Scott sent for General Villa, who was in Chihuahua. Villa, always a great admirer of Scott, had promised that if the American commander ever needed his help he'd come. Scott and Villa met in Juarez. After two hours' talk Villa reluctantly agreed to persuade Maytorena to sign the evacuation agreement, and take his forces to Nogales. The Federal troops were to move to Agua Prieta. This was done over Maytorena's objections and only because of Villa's intervention.

"This was pretty quickly forgotten by our government, it seems. Considering that Villa sure kept his word to General Scott and to other Americans up to the time when President Wilson recognized Carranza's de facto government, Pancho Villa had every right to feel betrayed and act like he did."

3

M. L. Burkhead

*Burkhead first knew Villa as a trainer of fighting cocks
in El Paso.*

"I met Villa in 1909, before the Mexican Revolution broke
out. I'd dropped into the courthouse to see my friend, Ike
Aldarete. Ike was the district clerk there. He had bought a
Chalmers car from me and I was in the habit of stopping by
for the monthly payment. While I was waiting for Ike I noticed a Mexican ahead of me at the other end of the counter.
He was stocky and though he wore the typical clothes of the
poorer class, he had a proud look about him. He was sizing me
up as I was him.

"Ike came over and told me that the Mexican was a rooster
fighter like myself. Aldarete also told me that the Mexican was
an exile from his country and he was giving him fifty cents a
week to help tide him over. He asked me to do the same.
I agreed."

This began the association between Burkhead and Villa.
Their friendship and mutual respect endured through many
changes. Within a few years Pancho became General Francisco Villa.

The first bond between the two men was their interest in cockfighting. Burkhead came from Alabama where he was reared in the tradition of cockfighting. His mother's seven lawyer brothers were well-known sportsmen, fighting cocks for pleasure and profit. Educated in the practice of law, Burkhead got into the car business by accident. One of his early clients in a criminal case had paid his fee with a car which Burkhead sold at a profit. Immediately he decided that his future lay in the new and rapidly expanding automobile business.

Burkhead came to the frontier town of El Paso in 1907 with the Cadillac agency. Those first Cadillacs, he recalls, were cheap, one-cylinder cars; the five-passenger roadster sold for $960. At the time of his meeting with Villa, Burkhead had the Chalmers agency and half of the Studebaker agency. He was the biggest car dealer in the region and sold more cars than the others put together, including Fords.

His fame in cockfighting circles approached his success in car dealing. His roosters beat champions from both the north and the south. "Cockfighting," he explains, "is the most exciting of all sports. If you have ever seen two game cocks strutting and circling in the pit, neck feathers ruffled, red eyes blazing, steel gaffs gleaming, you know what I mean.

"Cockfighting has a noble history. George Washington was known for originating the Virginia Red strain. When Andrew Jackson was president he fought cocks on the front lawn of the White House.

"The sport was always pretty well thought of. Besides it's a lucrative business as well. I could and did make more money on a shipment of a hundred cocks than a cattle broker could make off the same number of beeves, making five to ten dollars a head. I got my stock from Louisiana and Georgia.

"It's the main sport in Mexico—more popular than bullfighting—contrary to what most people believe. I fought my cocks in Mexico City, but competed more in Juárez. I remember one fight staged in Juárez where I won five thousand dollars, the largest single amount I ever won. I was breeding, fighting and selling the black-gray Gordons. They were the grittiest, fightingest cocks I've ever seen. The strain is almost extinct now, but they won me many a dollar.

"Sportsmen from all over the world brought their cocks to the Juárez pits. The fights drew fans from the highest to the lowest. There was no trouble in taking roosters over the international line. Gate receipts were very good and betting ran high. Orders for my stock would pour in after my champions fought there. We fought our cocks an average of three times a week. There was always a fight on Saturday nights.

"I had the best trainer in the business, a Negro named Lucius Talbot. I paid him top wages, $125 a month. Soon after I met Pancho at Aldarete's office I took him around to see my pens at Second Street in the twelve hundred block. I had about three hundred game roosters there. Lucius took to Villa at once and suggested that we hire him to help with the stock. I paid Pancho three dollars a week. He proved to be very good help, cleaning pens and stalls, putting the roosters out in sun coops, and generally making himself useful.

"In fact, Pancho turned out to be an expert handler. He was a big help to Talbot and me at the cockfights in Juárez. One time a Negro over there called Villa a Mexican. Pancho laughed and said, 'No! Me American!' The Negro didn't argue with him. Pancho was always very popular with the *señoritas,* they saying he was *muy hombre.*

"Villa knew many promoters in Mexico and was soon getting me lists of prospective customers. We built up a big business in shipping fighting cocks south of the border. In the process we became good friends, Villa tried a little broken English and I matched him with my border Spanish. We developed a mutual respect that was to last throughout the next years. Villa worked for me almost a year, until shortly before the Revolution really got under way. Then he went back to Chihuahua.

"Downtown here the old Coney Island Cafe was head-quarters for news and gossip in El Paso. While the Revolution was brewing it was common knowledge there when Madero was meeting with followers and sympathizers at the nearby Sheldon Hotel. Another rich source of rumors were the many jitney drivers in town who were Díaz exiles from Mexico.

"First thing we knew Francisco Madero—he was Provisional President of Mexico then—had a camp across from the Rio Grande a little north of town. We heard that Villa had joined him there with a bunch of followers.

"El Paso citizens were very interested in what was going on at the camp across the river. Late in April of 1911, hundreds of townspeople went over the old swing bridge and stood on the banks on both sides of the Rio Grande to watch a ceremony which took place near Madero's headquarters. President Madero made speeches from his auto and was well guarded by Insurrectos, four and five deep around him. Pascual Orozco was commissioned a Brigadier General; Raūl Madero, the president's brother, a Major; Guiseppi Garibaldi, a Colonel; and Pancho got his commission as Colonel. There were speeches and band music and cheering. It was really impressive.

"Pancho had natural qualities of leadership and was quick to learn strategy. The battle in which Madero's Insurrectos took Juárez early in May brought Villa to prominence in the news. It also brought about the big split between Orozco and Villa, but that's another story.

"My wife and I had become very friendly with the Madero family. We stood together, Mrs. Francisco Madero and Madero's mother and two sisters, on the roof of the Sheldon Hotel and watched that battle of Juárez. Later I took Madero to the International Bridge in my Chalmers.

"Though he remained loyal to President Madero and continued to serve under him, Pancho ran into trouble with General Huerta. In June of 1912, at Jiménez, Villa barely escaped execution at Huerta's orders and was sent to prison in Mexico City. He escaped soon and got as quickly as possible to the border and into El Paso. I was proud to count myself among his friends during that period of his exile, in fact I was probably the best friend he had here at that time.

"Pancho was still here when the news came of Madero's assassination in February, 1913. How Pancho then went back into Chihuahua with only a handful of men and in a matter of months had raised an army of followers to challenge Huerta's Federals, is history. Also his capture of Juárez in November, 1913."

From late 1913 and into 1914 General Francisco Villa controlled the State of Chihuahua. This was the peak of his power and this was the time he repaid those who had befriended him when he needed it. From his headquarters in Juárez he sent his agent to see Burkhead, still the leading car dealer of the region. Pancho needed cars, many cars, and was ready to do business for cash. It was said that he brought with him to Juárez a solid carload of silver and gold bullion for which he received $750,000 in American money.

"Villa bought Studebakers and Chalmers, all open seven passenger cars, and later Dodges. He bought seventeen cars from me during a period of six months, paying gold for them. He was a very good customer. He personally preferred the Dodge. I remember him once saying that the Dodge just never quit, going over mountains, through mud and sand, over roads that were no more than rough trails. He was driving his open Dodge when he was assassinated in Parral.

"Yes, for a few years there Pancho was riding high. He had won the respect of our military leaders. They considered him something of a natural military genius, and he was entertained at Ft. Bliss by the commanding officer. He was photographed with Generals Scott and Pershing. Contrary to the public's picture of a guerrilla leader, Villa did not drink hard liquor and it was a rare occasion when he smoked a cigarette.

He was fond of music and food, though careful where he ate, and he kept up his reputation of being *muy hombre* with the women.

"Knowing Pancho, I met other leaders of the Revolution. There was Abraham González, Governor of Chihuahua, and General Felipe Angeles. Angeles was highly educated, gentle, brilliant, had many friends in El Paso, and for a time lived in the lower valley. The contrast with Pancho Villa couldn't have been greater, but Angeles joined up with Pancho, becoming known as 'Pancho's Angel.' Both González and Angeles believed in the cause of Madero and the Insurrectos, and both gave their lives in serving those ideals. Villa never ceased to grieve for them.

"Speaking of Villa's appetite for good food, especially sweets, many a time Villa dropped into the Elite Confectionery and had ice cream. He also was in the habit of munching on peanut brittle at most any time.

"One time, my association with Pancho brought me a lot of attention. That was when I produced one million dollars of Villa's paper money at an automobile show in Chicago. It made quite a sensation when I passed it out to the big dealers. It was given to me to take to the convention by a wealthy man from Chihuahua. Of course along the border there was a lot of such money that Villa had had printed. It rapidly lost value as Villa's fortunes declined.

"I could never believe that Pancho Villa had anything to do with the Santa Ysabela Massacre or the Columbus Raid. I had sold C. R. Watson a Chalmers roadster just before he left with the other mining men on that fatal trip to Chihuahua in January, 1916. They had been told by Carranza's government that it was safe to reopen the mines down there. However, near the little station of Santa Ysabela the train was stopped and the whole party of engineers and mine employees were murdered except for one man who escaped. It was a terrible tragedy that really shook El Paso up. By the time the

Columbus Raid took place I was in Phoenix, having gone there to take the Stutz-Bearcat agency. Villa was widely blamed for both events, but I think that he was the victim of a frame-up. He'd made lots of powerful enemies on both sides of the border.

"As it happened, I sold General Pershing the Buick he took down into Mexico on the Punitive Expedition."

4

Cleofas Calleros

Dr. Calleros, noted historian, collector and book-binder, grew up in El Paso during the Revolution.

As a boy of fifteen Calleros first met Pancho Villa before the first battle of Juárez when Villa was one of the leaders of the Madero encampment on the Mexican side of the Río Grande between El Paso and the A.S. and R. Smelter. The Mexican revolutionaries gathering there would buy almost anything the local boys carried across the old swinging bridge—sardines, cookies, candy, pop, bread, cans of fruit. Calleros and his friends made five cents a can, selling Washington State pink salmon to Villa at ten cents a can. They bought the canned goods from C. H. Lawrence, a wholesaler in El Paso. Among their customers were Pascual Orozco, Rudolfo Fierro, José de la Luz Blanco, Abraham Gonzalez, Guiseppi Garibaldi, and Jan Valjoen as well as Pancho Villa.

The enterprising young traders numbered several boys and one girl, Miss Herlinda Chew. A photograph in the *El Paso Times* of May 13, 1956, was captioned, "Pancho Villa's help-mates—During the few days that the Mexican Revolutionary army headed by Francisco I. Madero was camped opposite the El Paso Smelter in May, 1911, we youngsters would cross the foot *volante* bridge to the Mexican side to mingle with the Revolucionarios. Pancho Villa was then a captain. The three El Pasoans are Miss Herlinda Chew, mother of El Paso attorney, Wellington Chew; Ervin Howard Schwartz, and his brother, Manuel Schwartz, both Popular Dry Goods Company executives."

Villa was hard on foreigners and especially persecuted the Chinese. Several years later Herlinda, now Mrs. Antonio Yee Chew, was the head of the Chinese colony in Juárez when Villa was besieging the city. She contended that Villa was the head of the Fifth column during World War I. One day in a Juárez cafe Mrs. Chew made arrangements with immigration officials to bring every one of the hundreds of Chinese across to the United States. Many came over and then went back. Herlinda, carrying her baby, Josephine, and leading her son, Wellington, fled across the international bridge to El Paso.

On one occasion an imaginative reporter took Herlinda's picture with a banner hung around her shoulders. Herlinda didn't show many Chinese characteristics and the picture was run with a story about a beautiful *Yaqui* girl joining Villa's forces. Thousands of the pictures were sold at ten cents apiece. Calleros and his friends who knew Herlinda well got a big kick out of the incident.

Pictures were also taken of Calleros and the Schwartz boys visiting Modero's camp. Pascual Orozco loaned the boys real ammunition belts and their photos were taken wearing the picturesque *bandoleros*. Later, after Madero had taken Juarez, someone got hold of the pictures and made money on them. Calleros recalls that the El Paso youngsters would stay at the rebels' camp as late as they dared.

"I remember," Calleros says, "that when Villa was camped on the Río Grande his men, most of whom were Catholic, came across the river and worshipped in the Chapel of Santa Catalina. Some of them also went to the Sacred Heart Church where the Father Father P. Roberto M. Libertini from Italy was the Priest."

"In 1913, when Villa took Juárez in a big way, I was working for the Sante Fe Railroad. Villa opened an office in the Toltec building, taking the whole first floor. Genáro Rios del Rio was his purchasing agent. The business they did brought over a year of prosperity to the El Paso district since Villa needed a lot of supplies for his army. Every day Villa took an average of fifty carloads of coal, wood, and hay into Mexico, dealing with Heid Brothers, West Texas Fuel Company, and Palm's. He got prairie hay from as far away as Kansas. One morning a train with three engines pulled two hundred cars into Juárez loaded with this material. That was the first time I knew of that many engines being required.

"This material was transported on the El Paso Southern Railway, which was built to connect the railway lines in El Paso with the Rio Grande Sierra Madre and Pacific Railway in Juarez. The El Paso Southern, which operated only within the city limits of El Paso, was the shortest standard gauge railroad in the United States, its mainline being four-tenths of a mile long, extending from the international boundary [middle of the bridge over the river] northward up South Mesa Avenue to Sixth Street, where its office, warehouse and loading platform were located. It had tracks leading off its mainline to connect with all railroads in El Paso.

"It was my job as clerk at the Santa Fe to collect for the waybills of goods that went to the Revolutionary headquarters in Juárez. Pancho always paid in gold, and I would leave Villa's office in the Toltec with sacks of gold so heavy that I staggered under the weight. The Santa Fe watchman always accompanied me as sort of a bodyguard, but at seventeen I never realized the danger to myself.

"Villa was a lot of things to many people. To some he was a hero, to some a bandit. In all my dealings I always saw him as very friendly. In 1914 he was enjoying good relations with the American press. They seemed to generally regard him as the liberator of the Mexican people. The killing of William Benton sure changed that image.

"Benton, a longtime resident of Mexico, owned a large ranch near Gallegos. As it was crossed by the Ferracarril Central, trains of rebels constantly stopped and plundered the estate, killing cattle and stealing at will. Mrs. Benton, daughter of a Mexican hacendado, had been threatened if she refused to supply whatever was demanded by the marauders. Finally Benton went to Juárez and confronted Villa at his headquarters with the situation. He demanded that the outrages be stopped.

"There is some dispute over what actually happened. Benton was known to be hot tempered. Villa was also known to flare into a fury at any little provocation. Benton was killed. I remember the story that I heard about the killing. It created a great reaction in the press and diplomatic circles. The British government requested that the American Department of State investigate. When it was learned that Benton was dead, American officials demanded Benton's body.

"Villa's attorney pointed out to Villa that Benton should have been tried so that Villa would not be suspected and accused of killing Benton in cold blood. So Villa ordered his men to dig up Benton's body. They did so, propped the corpse against a wall, preferred charges, found him guilty of aiding the enemies of the revolutionists, especially the Terrazas', sentenced him to be shot, and buried him again. Villa never surrendered the body, and in time the story died down somewhat.

"Another incident showing the brutal side of Villa's nature was an occasion in Chihuahua when he cold-bloodedly slaughtered over eighty camp followers. These women, the *soldaderas* who always accompanied the troops, cooking, nursing, and even carrying guns at times, were causing Villa trouble and slowing up his campaign. He solved the problem by having all the women rounded up and shot. Only one of the women's baby was left living. One of Villa's men asked what to do about the baby and Villa said he wasn't doing any good, so to shoot him, too. His orders were carried out. One Mexican historian said that Villa then rode his horse over the piled-up bodies."

Calleros was still working for the Santa Fe at the time of the Columbus raid in March, 1916. "The United States had committed a political and diplomatic blunder by permitting Carranza's troops to travel over an American railway and American soil from Eagle Pass, Texas, to Douglas, Arizona. There they crossed the border and at Agua Prieta defeated and almost anihilated Villa's army. Villa's friendly feeling for the United States and its citizens then turned to hate and many think that the Columbus Raid was a direct result of what Villa considered American betrayal of him.

"It was said, and believed, that the U.S. government did not want Villa captured. It was even said that Pershing and Villa actually met during that campaign, and had been seen playing poker together in the General's tent.

"At one time there were as many as 90,000 militia camped along the Rio Grande. Camp Cotton was established where the Peyton Packing Company and later the El Paso Stock-yards had their buildings. Camp Chigas was set up on the riverbank between Santa Fe and Stanton Streets.

"The present U.S.O. had it's beginning right here in El Paso. This organization for the welfare of the soldiers was started by Joseph I. Driscoll, Joseph M. Nealon, Albert W. Norcop, Leo C. Hartford, Rev. Father Carmen Tranchere, myself, and other citizens.

"Venustiano Carranza was an atheist. He made war on the Catholics. He allowed his soldiers to enter a cathedral in Mexico and destroy rare paintings and statues. They carried a statue of The Christ away and held it 'hostage.' The Crucifix was burned and broken in the street. Nuns were ordered to leave the country. Carranza allowed soldiers to take nuns into camp, one nun to every four soldiers.

"The Hotel Zeiger stood in the spot now occupied by the Columbia Furniture Company. Villa lived there for a time. In fact he entertained Generals Pershing and Scott there, during the period when he was in their good graces.

"One of the most interesting of the people brought to El Paso by the Revolution was a young woman journalist, Edith Lane, sent here by Harpers Magazine. She was a fine reporter and gave the world firsthand, accurate news of the revolution, often traveling with Villa's army to get her stories. When the war was over she settled in El Paso where she made her home until her death about ten years ago. Edith gave me Villa's saddle-blanket which I used for one of my book bindings."

5

Julius Heins

Heins was manager of the Geneve Hotel in Mexico City when the Revolution started.

In 1908 following an apprenticeship at the Waldorf-Astoria in New York, Heins was offered the management of the Geneve Hotel in Mexico City. At this time President Díaz was still in charge in Mexico. Business was good. The investment of foreign industries was welcomed and their interests protected by the Federal Government. Well-kept streets were filled with high-stepping horses drawing beautiful carriages outfitted with liveried coachmen and footmen. There were even a few expensive imported automobiles, though mostly driven by foreigners. The sight of ragged peons squatting at the side of the road picking lice out of the hair of their young did not seem to detract from the scene. Mexican policemen with lanterns and whistles stood vigilant at street corners at night.

The world recognized Mexico as a promising nation. The pomp and glitter of its national capital were unsurpassed. In September 1910, to celebrate the Centennial of the country's independence from Spain, President Díaz declared a thirty day celebration. There was a magnificent ball at the National Palace. Six thousand guests danced in the patio which was roofed, floored, lighted and garlanded with thousands of fragrant roses for the occasion. A state dinner was served to four thousand guests at the Palace by Syvain, owner of *Syvain's,* one of the finest restaurants in Mexico City. Heins assisted Syvain. Heads of state or their top representatives from all over the world were present to honor Mexico and eighty-year-old Don Porfirio and his Doña Carmelita. Elaborate gifts were presented. Kaiser Wilhelm sent a centennial gift of a monument of Alexander Humboldt. Music from the 148-piece orchestra drowned out the rising rumble of the brewing revolution.

Heins vividly remembers Francisco Madero's triumphant entrance into Mexico City the next year in June, 1911. An overwhelming series of defeats dealt by the insurrectionists had caused Porfirio Díaz to resign as President and take the exile route via Veracruz to Spain. Francisco Leon de la Barra was named interim President. He called a national election and Madero was chosen constitutional President.

The night before Madero's arrival, Mexico City suffered one of its worst earthquakes, complete with tumbled buildings and over two hundred deaths. Heins recalls that the quake knocked the poker chips from a table where he was playing cards.

Madero's followers proclaimed the earthquake a good omen, while "The Redeemer's" enemies warned that this was proof of the displeasure of the gods. The next day the crowds that massed along the street to greet Madero were so great that it took his carriage four hours to make the short drive from the railway station to the National Palace. Mr. Heins was one of the crowd.

Because of the turbulence of the revolution, business became so poor and the tourist trade fell off so badly that Heins left Hotel Geneve. In June he returned to the United States and to the Waldorf Hotel.

By January, 1913, he felt the call of Mexico again and returned to Mexico City. Hotel business was still bad, and one of the partners of the Geneve Hotel, Charles E. Guest, had ventured into another field, dealing in iron products. He gave Heins a job traveling and selling.

However, there was still great unrest in many states. In Jalapa, State of Veracruz, while staying in a typical hotel facing the Plaza, Heins was awakened at seven A.M. by soldiers who came into his room. "They went through my room to the balcony and started shooting down into the Plaza," says Heins. "That was the end of my job as iron salesman. I didn't want any more of that and took the next train back to Mexico City."

A big oil boom was on in Tampico and, as Tampico itself seemed peaceful, Heins went there with the idea of opening a restaurant. However, he saw a greater need for an American hotel. He promoted this through Rowley and Clynes, two Irishmen who were contracting stevedores, employing 2,500 longshoremen. Plans for the hotel were made, with Heins to be manager. Building was started and Heins went to Mexico City to make the necessary purchases, planning to be back in Tampico within a few days.

However, he was caught in Mexico City in the very midst of the *Decena Trágica,* the bloody Ten Tragic Days of Mexico's history, starting February 9, 1913. This period of wholesale killing was the result of a plot against Madero, involving among others, Félix Díaz, nephew of Porfirio Díaz; Bernardo Reyes, formerly governor of Coahuila; and General Mondragón, a renowned artilleryman. President Madero's brother, Gustavo, learning that General Victoriano Huerta who was now First Military Chief was also one of the plotters against the government, warned the president, but Madero chose to believe Huerta's frantic vows of loyalty.

According to plan, Díaz and Reyes, both then imprisoned for lesser revolts that had failed, were released from their separate prisons that Sunday morning of February 9, 1913.

Joined by Mondragón and followed by several thousand rebels they attacked the National Palace, but were rebuffed by defending troops. Some three hundred people, many of them curious citizens, were killed. The rebels, numbering then about 1,800, attacked the Ciudadela, which was the arsenal.

During the bombardment of the Ciudadela, Heins, wearing a Red Cross armband, watched the battling. "I stood right beside Félix Díaz," he says. "Díaz and Mondragón were there on horseback." Around eleven A.M. the Ciudadela surrendered to the rebel forces who then entrenched themselves behind its four-foot thick walls.

Constant gun battles and fighting between the rebels in the Ciudadela and the Government troops in the National Palace continued. At the end of ten days there were approximately 5,000 dead, most of them noncombatants.

"Corpses lay in the streets until they were collected in carts, taken to a park and burned, or doused with kerosene and burned where they fell," Heins recalls.

The Madero home was burned one night and the family fled to the Japanese embassy. President Madero remained in the National Palace.

During the ten days of gunfire, a neutral zone had been set up by the government for foreigners. This zone included Hotel Geneve. The hotel was now filled with foreign ministers, professional people, industrialists and their families. It was said that the men set up a non-stop poker game which lasted the entire ten days. Players would drop out to take their turns at patrol duty, guarding against soldiers from either side entering the neutral zone, and resume their card play when their stint was up.

General Huerta was observed meeting with Díaz, but was still able to convince Madero of his loyalty. The American ambassador, Henry Lane Wilson, whom Heins knew well, openly favored the cause of Díaz and Huerta.

An embassy car flew the American flag while driving to

the Ciudadela on February 18 to transport the rebel leaders to the embassy for a conference with government representatives from the Palace. The meeting took place in the embassy, under the chairmanship of Wilson. There Díaz and Huerta signed a peace pact and planned the organization of the new government.

Madero, requested by the Senate to resign in order to end the terror and also to prevent possible intervention of the United States, replied that he would rather be the ruler of a people of corpses, of a city in ruins, than resign. Three days later, Lieutenant Jiménez Riveroll accompanied by armed soldiers went to the palace with the Senate's demand that Madero resign.

Seemingly maddened by fury, Madero shot Riveroll and then when Major Izquierdo rushed into the room Madero also shot him. General Blanquet, in command, disarmed Madero and made him and the Vice-President, Pino Suárez, prisoners in the palace.

Finally, with guarantees of exile, Madero and Suárez drafted and signed their resignation from office. Although a special train was ready to take them and their families to Veracruz, Madero and Suárez were murdered the night of February 22 while being transferred from the National Palace to the penitentiary for their "safety." The stories about that assassination had—and have—many versions.

When the *Decena Trágica* was over and things had quieted down, Heins went back to Tampico. The train was intercepted several times by rebels, but no one was harmed. Heins recalls the gruesome sight of executed rebels hanging on the telephone poles all along the route.

"Back in Tampico the building was progressing rapidly. I went to New York City to buy the equipment for the hotel. Bringing in the equipment by ship we had little difficulty in regard to Customs or with other officials, because Rowley and Clynes were well known and respected. Finally on April 4, 1914, I opened the Imperial to the public.

"Everything went pretty smooth until April 21, when President Wilson ordered the landing of our marines in Veracruz. This was to prevent the German ship, *Ypiranga,* from delivering a large cargo of arms to a Mexican government hostile to the U.S."

On that morning of April 21, the United States consul, William Canada, watched through binoculars from his office window as the *Ypiranga* waited within the breakwater for its turn to dock. The plan was to land the U.S. Marines from the nearby U.S.S. Prairie and so seize the arms after they'd been unloaded from the *Ypiranga* and just before being loaded onto waiting trains. However, when the German ship approached at noon the marines had already come ashore at 11:30 and the *Ypiranga* never docked. After waiting off Veracruz a month, the *Ypiranga* left to deliver her cargo down the coast at Puerto Mexico.

Within minutes of landing, the marines were fired upon from a lighthouse tower. A U.S. naval shell promptly took off the top of the tower and the tragic sequence of the sniping, attacking, defending of Veracruz had begun.

Nineteen Americans and one hundred twenty-nine Mexicans were killed. Anti-American feeling ran high. Hell broke loose about two hours later in Tampico. Both there and in Veracruz crowds of people filled the streets shouting "Death to the gringos."

"By four P.M. the Imperial was filled with American refugees who were rescued by the German, Captain Koehler, of the light cruiser, *Dresden.*" Heins remembers. "Most of the Americans left. After my four hundred guests were evacuated I closed up the hotel. For my own protection I wrapped a red, white and black band around my arm, indicating German nationality. My housekeeper, Isabella Smith, patched together a flag of the German colors from bunting and I hoisted it to the corner of the top of the building. We were not molested from then on.

"On May 4, 1914, I reopened the Imperial under very

trying conditions. I was told that General Venustiano Carranza was coming to Tampico and wanted the hotel opened. His request was a command. Two days after I opened up, Carranza's brother. Jesús, arrived and made his headquarters in the Imperial. His band playing in the lobby at two A.M. woke me and I hurried to open up a floor for him. There was no water available in the rooms and we had to carry it up in tubs.

"Jesús Carranza's mission was to stop and wipe out the banditry which existed on the Tampico-San Luis Potosí road. However he and his son were ambushed and killed by Villistas. Gabriel Salinas was executed for the murder. I saw Carranza in his square box of a coffin."

Pro-German feeling was strong in all Mexico. Kaiser Wilhelm had openly expressed his sympathy for and admiration of the exiled Díaz. When Díaz reached Europe, the Kaiser invited him to a great review of the German army, and in the presence of crowned heads and the highest dignitaries of Europe seated Díaz at his right, in the seat of honor.

Heins' German birth and nationality were both a protection and a cause of anxiety to him on occasion, especially during the trouble in Tampico. When England declared war on Germany, Heins' English friends thought he was pro-German because the German Colony gave a banquet at his hotel and he allowed a large portrait of Von Hindenburg to be displayed. It was a Scottish friend, an official of the Aquila Oil Company, who made it clear that the Imperial was an American hotel and neutral.

"When the French diplomat, Deladier, arrived, the French flag was nailed on one corner of the hotel and the German flag on the opposite corner. It was the first time the French colors were so displayed since Maximilian's reign," Heins recalls.

Everything was closed up tight in Tampico when the rebels threatened. Since the hotel cashed checks for payrolls, Heins was caught with $60,000 on hand. He hid the money around in the telephone boxes in one hundred rooms. It was never bothered.

When Carranza took Tampico and the Imperial Hotel was reopened the only beer for sale in town was Carta Blanca at one dollar a bottle. It could only be bought through an enterprising *aide de camp* of General Gonzales, a colonel who brought two carloads of the beer from Monterrey. At a banquet held for Carranza—who never showed up—Heins found himself sitting between a major and captain who were revolutionists. When the conversation turned to revolvers and who was the quickest draw, with the likelihood of a demonstration coming up, Heins slipped away from the table.

One of Heins' most interesting and memorable experiences at Hotel Imperial was the coming of American news correspondents, many of them internationally known, in the wake of Carranza and Villa hordes. There was Jack Durborough of the *New York World,* Frederick Palmer, and the famous cartoonist, McCutcheon of the *Chicago Tribune.* The most outstanding was Jack London, representing *Colliers Weekly.*

Heins spent an entire week with London who called him "Mine Host." London would consume two-thirds of a quart of whiskey during an evening. Heins made it possible for London to meet the leaders of the different forces in Tampico. London often told Heins of his plans for a trip around the world in his "Snark." Those plans never materialized.

Late in 1914 Heins left Mexico, joining his mother and sister who had arrived in New York from Germany. From then on his wanderings took him in and out of the hotel business in Chicago and Dallas, and back to Mexico City. He joined up with Conrad Hilton in El Paso and at one time took over the management of the Knox Hotel. He also promoted the building of the Murray Hotel in Silver City.

6

Louis Fischbein

Fischbein was a successful tailor in Parral during the Revolution. He once fitted Villa for a suit that was never delivered.

"My first memory of Pancho Villa and his activities was when a friend in the jewelry business in Parral, a Mr. Dehlberg, was killed by Villa in 1903. Villa and another man broke into Dehlberg's shop as he was closing up for the night. They cut his throat. They then took everything in the showcase, pens and watches and such items, but didn't get the better jewelry which had already been locked in the safe. They were caught a few weeks later selling the watches. They were jailed, but escaped.

"Next thing I remember about Villa was a few years later, 1907 or 1908 when I made a trip with a friend to a mining town in Chihuahua. We stopped at a little place where the mayor had a store and rooms where people could stay. A nearby rancher had sent a note to the mayor asking him to get men and rifles together to go after a cattle thief who was driving a bunch of cattle north. They thought it was Villa. The posse was eight or ten fellows armed in various ways. One member arrived with half a young goat across his saddle. I think they forgot about the hunt and just roasted the goat. I didn't wait to see.

"During those years Villa stole cattle from all around Durango and took them to Columbus, New Mexico, where he sold them. He knew the Sierras well and had many friends in that part of the country. He took an outlaw's name, 'Pancho Villa,' although he was born Doroteo Arango. The original Pancho Villa left him his horse and saddle.

"My most vivid memories of the hectic days of the revolution are as it affected Parral in 1912. The struggle for control of the city was between Pancho Villa, then in charge of some troops loyal to Madero, and Pascual Orozco, who was trying to take Parral.

"There was no garrison at Parral then. Villa simply rode into town with his men and established headquarters. He had a businessman friend there, Maclovio Herrera, also a friend of mine. Herrera was a good guy, had the same thoughts about Madero as Villa.

"Soon after Villa arrived in Parral, his secretary, a man from Las Cruces, came into my shop and told me that Villa wanted me to make him a Mexican riding suit. I said, 'Why not?' I took my samples and went with the secretary to Villa's headquarters, which was a shack on the outskirts of town.

"Villa was surprised and suspicious when I asked him to take off his 44 pistol and gunbelt. He wanted to know what for.

"I explained that I couldn't get a correct measurement over the gun and holster. So he reluctantly removed them and laid them very close at hand on a nearby table. I guess I was the only man that ever asked Villa to disarm and got away with it. I remember Villa as being about five feet ten inches tall and having sloping shoulders.

"I promised to return to Villa's headquarters in three days for a fitting. However that was the day the Orozquistos under Emilio P. Campo attacked the city and I didn't keep my appointment. I heard cannon fire early that morning and stayed inside. I didn't go out until everything was quiet. Villa had repulsed the attackers.

"I went up a hill overlooking town. There was a wall on one side where Villa's men had posted themselves, with a wide view of the country around. One of Orozco's men had suddenly appeared with a short-barrelled, eighty-five millimeter cannon pulled by two horses. He stopped forty to fifty yards from the wall. The Villistas let him fire one shot, which most likely went too high. Then they shot, one bullet catching the cannoneer in the forehead. By accident one bullet went directly into the mouth of the cannon, pressed the empty shell against the lock and stopped it. The cannon man was still alive but they had already taken his boots off, expecting him to die. The two Villa guards on hand and the children playing around seemed unconcerned. I sent a doctor up to the wounded man.

"Later when Villa was trying on his suit I heard him ask about the wounded man and saying he could use a man like that. I heard that the Orozco cannon man died in the hospital a week or so later.

"The next day I went back to Villa's headquarters. The doors were open and I could see many Mexican and Spanish merchants sitting in a row facing Villa at a desk. I saw a rancher I knew in a room opposite and asked him what Villa was doing with the people there. He said that Villa was holding them for money. I went back and stood in the door.

"Villa looked up and saw me and said, 'Why didn't you come yesterday as you promised?'

"I said, 'Yesterday too many bullets were flying around.'

"Then he said, 'Those that fly around don't hurt you. It's those that hit you that are the bad ones.' Then he tried on his coat.

"Pancho never got to see his completed suit. In a few days the Orozco troops under the command of José Inés

Salazar returned. I saw Villa and his bunch riding out of town about three in the afternoon, before the Orozco troops came in.

"I was staying at the Central Hotel. My cousin came after me about six in the morning after the attack on the city, because they were looting our place.

"We hurried to the shop. There were five or six soldiers at the store and a lot of women and children. They were going through broken show windows and grabbing up everything, piling merchandise onto bedsheets and blankets.

"I went to the Plaza and found one of Orozco's captains who I'd known in Chihuahua City. The captain accompanied me back to the shop. I asked him if he couldn't get the soldiers out of there and the captain said that he was sorry but they were not his men and so would not obey his orders. The captain said he would try to save the goods if I would show him where it could be taken.

"The Central Hotel was a short distance away, so I told the captain to have the goods put on the patio there. The captain had one of his men put in front of the hotel, and then stationed himself with me at the broken show window. When the women came out with their big bundles we sent them to the guard at the hotel. The guard had them dump the bundles into the patio. By afternoon there was a huge pile of loot, including stuff stolen from three or four other stores. About four in the afternoon I phoned the other merchants to come and pick out their goods, which they did. The soldier guard asked me if he hadn't earned a pair of new shoes and I said he certainly had, but the poor fellow couldn't find a matching pair. The looters had pushed all the shoes off the shelves with their rifles and all were mixed up. I don't know who got Villa's suit.

"Looting was bad all over town. Soldiers would go into a bar, take a bottle of any kind of liquor, break the neck off the bottle and drink it.

"Among Orozco's followers I recognized Sam Dreben.

They used to call him the 'fighting Jew.' He was sitting on some stone steps leading up from the street with about twelve other soldiers. I asked him, 'Why didn't you save our place?' Dreben said if he had known whose it was he would have done so.

"One incident occurred on the night that Parral was captured that I will never forget. My room was on the second floor of the hotel. A mining office was on the ground floor of the next house, and their safe was against the wall next to my room. At about two A.M. there was a terrific boom and an explosion that lifted me about a foot off the bed. Bandits had dynamited the safe of the mining office on the other side of the wall.

"One of the most publicized incidents of the revolution was the killing of William Benton, an Englishman, in Villa's headquarters in Juárez, in February, 1914. I knew Benton well. He was a customer and a friend. I stayed at his ranch and have pictures of the house. Benton was a long-time resident of Mexico, owning and operating a cattle ranch at Inde in the State of Durango. Benton went to Juárez to complain to Villa about his soldiers stealing Benton's cattle. Benton was killed there and the true facts of the murder have never been satisfactorily reported. Benton probably demanded that Villa pay for the cattle stolen from his ranch and trouble followed.

"Villa once maintained a home in Chihuahua City as neighbor to my brother, Max, and his family. That was when Pancho was married to Juana. From what my niece says, Mrs. Villa and their two little girls were pleasant neighbors. Villa of course was hardly ever home.

"I knew and visited the Mexican rancher who owned Rancho Canutillo long before it became Villa's retirement home. It was a typical cattle ranch of the time, where guests slept on cowhides.

"I also knew the man, Barraza, who killed Villa. Pancho had killed his brother."

Villa in 1899

The cockpit at Juarez

Colonel William C. Greene

Alvaro Obregon

Porfirio Diaz

Venustiano Carranza

Francisco I. Madero

Victoriano Huerta

F. Villa,   G. Madero,   F. Madero,   G. Garibaldi,   F. Gar

V. Carranza,   V. Gomez,   F. Madero, Jr.,

A. Gonzalez,   J. M. Maytorena,   A. Fuentes,   P. Orozco.

Villa in El Paso, February 191[?]

Rudolfo Fierro on horseback

Villa sitting in the presidential chair in Mexico City. To the right is Emiliano Zapata, to the left is Tomas Urbina.

Pascual Orozco (Photo courtesy Julia Breck)

Villa at the Elite Confectionery in El Paso

Naco Hotel in Naco, Arizona with "bullet-proof" rooms for news correspondents

7

William N. Fink

Fink was a mining engineer at the Cusi Mines south of Chihuahua city when Villa took the mine over.

"I went to Mexico as superintendent for the Cusi Mexicana Mining Company, in 1908. With headquarters also at the old town of Cusihuiriáchi was the Cusi Mining Company owned by the Potter Palmers of Chicago. This old mine had been worked since the 1860's, producing silver ore with some lead and zinc. There were no American families at the camp.

"It was very quiet around there till about 1911. There was a little trouble on the ranches but everything was well under control. For a period in Chihuahua after the revolution was going Villa was in control of the state government. He came up around the mines often. We got along fine operating under him. He said to keep the mines running and people working. They had to work to eat. We were there to run the mines and the way to operate was to get along with Villa.

"I remember shortly after he was in control he called all the mining operators to a meeting in Chihuahua City in the government office. We were accustomed to that, often meeting with state officials of the government, prior to Villa's time. He got thirty or more of us in there, all the representatives of mining, smelting, and so forth from all over the state.

"Villa came in. He was a strong, good-looking man. He looked at us with those piercing, Indian-black eyes—eyes that anyone would remember.

"He said, 'You afraid of me?'

"We told him that we weren't afraid of him or any other bastard.

"And Villa said, 'Fine, we understand each other.'

"We made an arrangement where the payroll money was exchanged for dollars—33 dollars to a peso. On the black market it was cheaper, but we had no part of that. Villa was a man of his word and we wanted to impress him with the fact that we would also keep our word. Normal Mexican money wasn't used at that time. Villa was to all intents the state government and what he said went. He didn't fool around or try to nick us. We went to the state treasury and bought the pesos with dollars at a certain fixed rate to pay our men. We didn't go out on the street and buy at half, as could have been done. We expected Villa to keep his word and we kept ours.

"At one time Federal troops were in charge of the City of Chihuahua, and Villa, heading the revolutionary government then, was camped fifteen miles outside of town. Special passports were needed to get into each of the camps, Villa's or the state government's. Everyone kept them to use each way. Afterward it was laughable, but at that time it was not funny. I was there when Villa took Chihuahua. All we did was keep hidden.

"Early in the revolution a washerwoman came up from our camp and said a lot of men down there were going to take our horses and mules. Like a fool I went down. I thought I'd talk them out of it, but I soon saw that I was off on the wrong foot. I should have kept out of there. They were Villa's troops, and the man in charge was Tomás Gonzales who'd worked for the mine for years and who I knew as well as anybody. He begged my pardon and said they needed a lot of things, especially horses as many of their men were afoot. They took my beautiful Kentuckian bred horse. It had been brought down there by my predecessor. I loved that horse. He was named Alazán, which means bay. They said they needed him when I asked for the horse back.

"Gonzales told me that they needed money to they held me for ransom. I told them we hadn't had any money for weeks. We'd been running the crew to Chihuahua on Saturdays to pay them, with everyone paid in Mexican money. I told them they could take what little was in the safe.

"Then Gonzales says, 'You stay with us and send to the company for money. They'll pay all right.'

"I didn't know if the company would pay. Nothing like this had happened before that we knew of. This was very, very early in the revolution, about 1910. We didn't know of anyone else that had been held for ransom. I may have been the first person kidnapped by Villistas.

"We argued all afternoon. Gonzales arranged to send word to the head office in Chihuahua City. When it got dark we started to travel. This was in November and the weather was rotten—raining and snowing. They gave me a half-dead old crowbait to ride with a bum saddle. Halfway up the rocky trail we were following the horse slipped. I jumped off just in time. The horse fell over a cliff and was killed. The saddle busted off. Gonzales told one of the men to give me his horse, which he did. It wasn't any good either.

"We rode till about midnight when we camped. Meantime they got word to the mining camp and the boys from camp came out and took the demand for $50,000 ransom and left. I had to stay. Next morning we rode farther south from Santa Eulalia.

"Riding along I said, 'What if we run into Federal troops? What if they start shooting at us? What would I do? I'm in a bad fix here.'

"And the man in charge said, 'Here, take this rifle.'

"I refused, saying if I had a gun I'd be considered one of them and be shot with the rest.

"They laughed and said that the Federals shoot but never hit anything. And away we went.

"We rode all day and came to a big goat cave on the large Horcasitas Ranch below Chihuahua. It was big, holding several hundred horsemen getting out of the rain and was a terrible smelly place with goat manure a foot deep.

"We were all hungry, so a gang went out to get some beef. Cattle were everywhere. That's what made the revolution so easy. Cattle and horses were to be had for the taking. Revolutionaries and Federals alike would ride till a horse was worn out and then take another. They got away with it. There was really no danger. Most of the battles were lots of noise and not much killing. We didn't like it, of course, not being sure what to believe or what to expect.

"The ransom was sent back for me. In the meantime my captors sent to Santo Domingo to get the rest of the mine crew. They told me I'd have lots of my friends with me. They figured on getting money on everybody. Villa was not present at this incident. Another man called Sánchez was in charge. I didn't know who he was. Anyhow we landed at the old Cusi Mexicana Camp, near Santa Eulalia, fifteen or twenty of us there.

"And here came Villa to take care of a man who had made the mistake of double-crossing him. This was Antonio Cabello Siller, who had been sort of a partner of Villa's. He had lived in the village of Santa Eulalia many years and bought tools, powder, and so forth for Villa. That was his business.

"Villa had grabbed a carload of coffee which he gave to Siller to sell, also several carloads of sugar, which Siller sold for him. When Villa needed supplies for his men he sent to Siller for them. Siller thought he'd make some money and like a fool told Villa's men nothing doing, reneging on Villa.

"That was too bad. They brought Siller into camp to face Villa. Villa gave him a tongue-dressing. Called him all manner of ingrate and told all he'd done for him and so forth.

"Siller wasn't a coward. He said, 'Yes, that's true,' to it all.

"Then Villa said, 'Take him out and hang him.'

"They took Siller out to the tramway tower behind our house. Siller thanked Villa for his courtesy, and then shook hands with all of us. They hung him from the post of the tramway then and there.

"Villa said to the young American boys and engineers there, 'That's what I ought to do with all of you.' The Americans misunderstood and thought he was going to hang all of them.

"The company owned a Simplex chain-drive car. Jed Newkirk from New York was the chauffeur. It was one of the few cars that could make the trip into the mine. The Simplex was strong and expensive. It broke an axle that was made of nickel steel. Replacement for the axle came from Europe special made and cost $3500.

"There was one time when I thought we'd lost the Simplex for good. The Federals had retaken Chihuahua City and Villa was getting ready to take Juárez. We were coming from Chihuahua when we met Villa and some of his men. What Villa didn't know was that the Federals had evacuated Chihuahua and moved out beyond the city. When he asked how things were in Chihuahua I told him the town was abandoned.

"Villa stared at me with those piercing eyes and said, 'Lend me your car.'

"He took the Simplex and the chauffeur and headed for Chihuahua City. He met his troops part way toward Juárez and headed them back to take Chihuahua. In a couple of hours Villa returned with the Simplex. He had looked over the groups of his soldiers, accomplished his mission, and decently returned the car with his thanks.

"He was the best liked Cavalry commander anyone could imagine. He would get in and make them go. When he was down on his luck Villa would camp around on the plains of Chihuahua and rest. I used to see him around quite often.

"Early in the revolution a couple of Villa's men came from a village in western Chihuahua and told Villa all he had to do was work a certain mine in western Chihuahua and he'd have all the money he needed for his army. Donald B. Gillies, Manager for Cusi Mexicana Company, a big man in Chihuahua, and the company lawyer, Aureliano Gonzales, got word about this. Villa decided to see if the story about the mine was true, and Gillies and Gonzales decided that I, a kid engineer, should go look it over for Villa.

"The two Villa men and I went down to Parral through Valleza and from then on it was four days on horseback. It was November with rain and snow—wet all the time. We finally landed at a little Tarahumara Indian village. We found the old chief and all the villagers drunk. The chief, very friendly, gave me a gourdful of strong tezwine from the bottom of the barrel. When the tezwine was gone we went out and looked at the mines.

"I saw at once there couldn't be any value there, only a very few stringers of rich silver. It was still raining and I was miserable, but I gathered two big sacks of samples.

"We started the long trip back through rain and snow. Finally we reached the Mesa de Sandía end of the Parral-Durango Railroad. There was no regular train service. They were using the railroad to haul wood for fuel at the mines and on the railroad.

"We got to Chihuahua on that train to find the town dark excepting for an occasional candle light. There had been no fuel for weeks. When I got off the train a little Chinese joined me. He took my bag and we walked on down the road to the middle of town, a mile from the depot.

San Pablo Balleza (West of Parral)

"From the hotel, Old Robinson House, I got word to the lawyer, Gonzales, that I was back in town. A couple of days later they sent word that Villa wanted to see me. So I went into the capital.

"Villa asked me about the mine and I told him that it was worthless.

"Villa turned to the lawyer and said, 'Didn't I tell you? We had to send a gringo to learn the truth.'

"A couple of days later he had the two Mexicans shot. They had lied to him. I had worried all the way into town about what to tell Villa about the mines. I was glad I had decided to tell the truth.

"I knew the 18 murdered victims of the Santa Ysabela massacre of January 10, 1916, and Tom B. Holmes who escaped. For several months the mines had closed down because of the revolution's turmoil and Villa's threat to kill every gringo who fell into his hands. Villa had just suffered defeat at Agua Prieta. We had let the Federals use our railroad to cross troops which defeated him badly. He felt that the U.S. had double-crossed him. This was the reason for the Columbus raid as well as the Santa Ysabela killing. Villa's commanders had a meeting near Madera and agreed there to kill all the Americans in Chihuahua. Then they scattered, burning bridges to make it hard for Federal armies to move.

"Most of the mine operators and many of the Mexican employees had waited the time out in El Paso. However it finally seemed as though the Villistas were whipped and their danger a thing of the past. At a banquet here in El Paso General Alvarado Obregón assured the mine operators that the Carranza government was in complete control and invited them to open up the mines and smelters under the government's protection.

"Armed with passports from Juárez officials the group got on the train in El Paso for Cusihuiriáchi via Chihuahua City. I being with a small company didn't go on that trip, but stayed in Chihuahua. I was at the station when they changed trains and left for Cusi on the Mexico-Northwestern. We were all happy that the mines were to be opened up.

"Our happiness turned to horror when the news came to Chihuahua by wire of the murder of the mining party. Nothing much was known then about the killing. No one knew where the bodies were or just what had occurred. Excitement ran high in Chihuahua. Fifty or sixty Americans planned to go and see about it and we got up a special train. When the time came to go only eighteen of us actually went.

"It took all day going very slowly to get out there, as no one knew what to expect. At Santa Ysabela we were stopped by Federal troops. After a big argument they finally sent a machine gun and group on a flat car with us. We then began hearing more about what had happened.

"Seven miles out of Santa Ysabela the train had been held up by a band of Villistas led by Pablo López and Rafael Castro. They were shouting, 'Death to the Gringos!' and 'Viva Villa!' Then the bandits forced the Americans off the train, shot them, then robbed and stripped them of their clothing.

"When we finally got out where the shooting was it was already dark and cold. Bodies were piled in a heap by the track. There was a lot of tension. We got out and searched around in the brush in the dark. We found eighteen bodies. I knew all of them.

"We couldn't find Tom Holmes. We learned later that he had escaped. He was on the back platform of the train when the shooting started. Watson, he was the manager, shouted 'Run' and Tom and another man jumped down and ran down the track. The other man was shot. Holmes fell, rolled off the roadbed into a creek and got under a bush where he hid crouched in the icy water. It got dark and the killers kept busy looting the bodies. When they left, Holmes managed to make his way to a Mexican ranch where the rancher let him take his burro to ride to Chihuahua, a long way. Later Holmes operated a little mine near Cusi. He retired several years ago.

"When the news of the massacre reached El Paso feeling ran high. A special train brought the mutilated bodies into the city. They had to put the town under martial law. A deadline was established along Overland Street north of which no Mexican could pass and south of which no American could go till things quieted down."

8

Susan Knotts

Revolutionists forced Mrs. Knotts and her family to
flee their mining camp homes in Guanajuato, Mexico.
Villa held Mrs. Knotts' husband's cousin for ransom.

"Villa terrorized the American families living at the mines
and mills in Mexico. He kidnapped my husband's cousin,
Frank Knotts, from the Erupción Mine down there and held
him for a large ransom.

"The mines and mining people had for several years been
threatened and harrassed by the revolutionists and bandits.
Our first experiences dated from the beginnings of the revolution, back as far as 1909. My husband, Arthur, at that time
was a metallurgist with the Guanajuato Mining and Develop-
ment Company and we lived at Guanajuato.

The district of Guanajuato is famous as being rich gold
and silver mining country. There are records of the mines
being worked in the 1500's. Guanajuato is itself a beautiful
town situated in a hollow of the surrounding hills. I'll never
forget the gorgeous flowers that grew there. There was always
a plentiful water supply and the climate was wonderful.

"The soil has a high mineral content, mostly lime-sulphur,
and it caused bodies buried in the cemetery to become petri-

fied. One of the curiosities of the district was the catacombs where you could see many mummified bodies, standing in rows. Some of the mummies were of the Spaniards who came to the region more than three hundred years ago. Others were natives. There was talk of moving these petrified bodies to a special museum where they could be viewed and where they would be safe from souvenir hunters who were vandalizing them.

"We lived at Guanajuato from 1909 to 1914 and loved it there. We left then because we were driven out by the Revolution.

"In 1915 we went to Guanaceví, one of the mining camps of Durango. There my husband became a partner with his cousin, Frank Knotts, who owned the Santa Anita Mill. There was a rich concentration of ore at Guanaceví. Durango was Villa country and we were often threatened and bothered by Villa. He was constantly needing money, arms, horses and supplies and regularly put the bite on the mine owners. It was considered wise to keep on as friendly terms as possible with him.

"I especially recall one frightening day when Villa rode up to our house as we were sitting on the long verandah. Villa asked where my husband, Arturo, as he called him, was. I told him truthfully that I wasn't sure, but that I thought Arthur had gone to check on one of the smaller properties. Villa didn't believe me, muttered something and gave me a dirty look.

"I was afraid that he was planning to search our house. The thought of such a thing made me weak and still does. His men, a rough looking bunch, just sat on their horses and watched Villa. They seemed eager for his order to ransack the house. Why Villa thought Arthur was hiding from him, I don't know, because my husband had always been friendly and was certainly not afraid to face Villa or anyone else. Just as Villa turned to his men we all saw Arthur come riding from around a house that stood near the trail up the mountain. The sight of my husband was a blessed relief.

"Arthur took in the situation at a glance. He must have noticed that I was angry and frightened, but he didn't show it. He jumped down from his horse and threw the reins to the Mexican boy who worked for us.

"Arthur greeted Villa and went forward with outstetched hand. Villa hesitated and then held out his hand. You'd have thought my husband was Pancho Villa's best friend. Arthur then told the *mozo,* who had come out of the house, to bring out some food and something to drink. Then he asked Villa to sit down on the verandah.

"Villa and Arthur settled themselves in porch chairs. But I was so nervous that I made some excuse and went into the house. I realized that Arthur had acted wisely. We couldn't risk Villa's hatred or even his dislike. We had to live in Mexico. This was where our living was.

"When Villa finally left Arthur tried to calm me down. He reminded me that as long as Villa was friendly with us the other bandits in the area would not have the nerve to attack us. Our only chance of survival, maybe, and certainly our only chance of keeping the mine from being looted, was to keep Villa's uncertain friendship. I had to agree with him. But I kept seeing that mean expression in Villa's eyes when he stared at me and I'd never forget the rough way he spoke.

"Shortly after that experience it was decided by my husband and the other mining officials that it was not safe for the American families to remain in Mexico. Also Arthur and I thought it was time that I took our three daughters, Eloise, Margaret, and Ruth, back to the States so that they could go to school.

"That was a very harrying trip out from Guanaceví. Several of our servants and some of the trusted helpers from the mine went with us. We had to travel horseback for two days to Rosalía to get to the railroad. There we took the train to Parral and on to El Paso.

"At Parral Joe Knotts, another of my husband's cousins, had gotten seats for us on an overcrowded train. Refugees from all parts of northern Mexico were fleeing. This was during the time when Villa had turned against the United States. There was no food to be had on the train. Occasionally we stopped at a village; watermelons were brought onto the train and we could buy them. That was our only food and I worried that we'd get sick from having only watermelon, but we didn't suffer.

"We finally got to El Paso and settled down in a house on Missouri Street to wait out the Revolution. We all missed Mexico. The country around where we'd lived in Guanajuato and Guanaceví was so beautiful and the climate so mild that we loved it. The children always seemed to be well and happy there. And there was the matter of help. Servants were so inexpensive that we had two or three all the time. We really became dependent on them. Our maids and *mozos* were happy, goodhumored people and we liked them and they liked us. I remember many of them yet with real affection."

Susan Knotts and her daughters were still living in El Paso in 1918. By that time her husband and his cousin, Frank, were at the lead-silver Erupción Mine near Villa Ahumada, in the State of Chihuahua. Frank's wife, Emily, and family were also living in El Paso when Frank and another mine official, D. B. Smith, were kidnapped by Villistas and held for ransom. From the moment that W. D. Greet, a close family friend, brought them the news of the kidnapping, it was a time of great worry and suspense for all members of the Knotts families.

"From October 22 till November 16, when Frank returned to El Paso, we all feared for his life," Mrs. Knotts says. "As it happened Arthur was not with Frank and Mr. Smith when they were taken."

It was about a week before the kidnapping was reported in the El Paso papers. The stories were sketchy and contradictory and offered no comfort to the anxious families and friends of the captured men. One news story, dated October 29, states that E. F. Knotts, D. Bruce Smith and A. M. Tinney, American mining men of El Paso, were being held prisoners by a band of Mexicans, headed by a well-known Villista, Epifánio Holguín. The location of the kidnapping was said to be somewhere in the neighborhood of the Mexican Central Railroad, eighty-one miles south of El Paso. The information came from an announcement made by Charles A. Kinne, associated with the Americans at the Erupción Mine.

On October 31 another story reported that two men recognized as D. Bruce Smith and E. P. Fuller were taken from Villa Ahumada to Chihuahua City under Mexican military guard. Fuller was said to be a California cattleman who went to Villa Ahumada to make an effort to obtain the release of Knotts, Smith and Tinney.

A news story on November 2 stated that according to Charles A. Kinne, Smith and Tinney had been released by the Villistas but that Knotts was still being held. On November 3, the paper reported that Smith and Tinney had been freed to obtain the $50,000 ransom money demanded by Epifánio Holguín. Smith and E. P. Fuller, who had interceded in behalf of Knotts had been taken to Chihuahua City under guard on a charge of aiding the enemies of the Mexican government. Knotts was supposed to have been liberated at a point on the Northwestern Railroad line and was expected to reach the border the next day.

However, Frank Knotts' wife, Emily, had received no word by November 5. She was quoted as saying that although feeling ill she had waited up till two o'clock in the morning for her husband, but he did not come.

"We were frantic with worry during all this time." Susan Knotts recalls. "Arthur had managed to arrange for the ransom and had sent it to the designated place, but Villa refused to accept bills and had demanded gold.

"Anyhow, when it was finally settled and the ransom paid

to that bandit, Pancho Villa, Frank came home the early morning of November 16. I remember a big party was held in the Hotel Paso del Norte to celebrate. Frank told us all about his terrifying experience."

✗ On the morning of October 22, 1918, Frank Knotts and his mining partner, David Bruce Smith, left El Paso and went down into Chihuahua to their mining property about eighty miles south, in the Villa Ahumada district. The Americans inspected drilling operations close to the mine and then made ready to go on to the Erupción at Los Lamentos.

However, as they were trying to start their old Ford touring car, a band of about twenty Mexicans rode through the mesquite and surrounded the men and car. Knotts recognized them as Villistas.

The bandits tied Smith's hands and pushed him over by the driver and the cook, Maria, who had been going to ride to Villa Ahumada. Knotts demanded to see the commanding officer of the group. A Colonel Pinones stepped forward and demanded to know Knotts' business there. Knotts explained that he was a photographer taking pictures of the country and had also planned to do a little hunting. When Smith gave his name the leader seemed to recognize it.

Knotts and Smith were ordered to get into the car and drive to the mine. The raiding party accompanied them, some crowding into the Ford. At Los Lamentos, Smith and Knotts were imprisoned in an adobe shack. They were told by Pinones that they were waiting for the arrival of Epifánio Holguín.

Knotts was familiar with Holguín. He was a Villista, at least when it suited him to be, and had robbed and harrassed the mining company for over a year. Holguín was a tall, big man, and when he came through the door of the little shack to confront the two prisoners they felt that there was little chance of mercy for them.

Holguín appeared to know Smith and brusquely demanded of Knotts what his position was with the mining company.

Knotts reluctantly admitted to being president of the company, as he was quite sure that Holguín was already aware of that fact.

After a little discussion with his men Holguín announced that the Americans would have to take a little trip with him. Along with A. M. Tinney, an associate who had been taken prisoner at the mine, they were then taken back to the place where they'd been captured. There they spent the night, all three prisoners sharing a single bedroll. Holguín and his men sat around a bonfire while Holguín boasted to the others about the murders and atrocities he had committed. His followers applauded loudly and egged him on.

The next day, three guards accompanying the Americans in the Ford, and the rest of the guerrilla band surrounding them on horseback, the whole band traveled to a spot known as Well Number 2. On the way Holguín informed the captives that he expected a ransom of $50,000 American money or he planned to turn them over to Pancho Villa. Knotts told him to take them to Villa as there was no way to raise that much money.

Holguín forced Knotts to write out an order requesting the mining company's supply truck to bring all the supplies of food and clothing it could carry to the camp. When the loaded truck came the supplies were swiftly divided and the band moved on. For six days they traveled, raiding and looting ranches on the way. On October 29 they stopped near the Candelaria Mountains. A scouting party was sent on ahead. When the scouts returned they all went on into the mountains.

There they encountered Pancho Villa at the head of a company of followers. Villa started off by asking if Knotts didn't know that he, Villa, was killing all gringos. He accused Knotts and Smith of being of the rich robber class, stealing mines from the peons and making them work for nothing and robbing the land of gold and silver. He stated that it was his duty to execute them. With nothing to lose, Knotts argued.

When Villa got on the subject of President Wilson he became so wrought up that he actually began to cry. Suddenly, however, when Knotts fell silent, Villa said that if a ransom of $300,000 were paid the men could go free.

When Knotts protested that the huge sum could never be raised no matter what might happen to him, Villa came down on his demands. Finally he agreed to $20,000. A note was written to the company treasurer in El Paso. From then on the captives were treated with more consideration. Villa even let Knotts ride his own mule when Knotts' animal played out.

That evening Smith and Tinney were sent to the railroad station of Ranchería with Holguín as guard and escort. Smith was to go to Villa Ahumada for supplies to be sent to the Villistas and Tinney was to take the ransom note to El Paso. Villa then took his band and Frank Knotts to a campsight in a mountain canyon.

There, Knotts became truly well-aquainted with Pancho Villa. Sitting by the fire they talked for hours. Villa often expounded on his hatred of President Wilson. He blamed Wilson for all the injustices done to Mexico and Mexicans. Villa told Knotts that he had known nothing of the Columbus Raid or Santa Ysabela Massacre and that Pablo López was to blame.

During this time and those long conversations Villa informed Knotts that he had no desire to be President of Mexico, but would like to be Secretary of War. He stated that Carranza and his followers were a bunch of thieves. He called the Carranzistas monkeys. He even told about his early life, saying that when he was seventeen he became an outlaw. He had been struck with a whip by a rural policeman for trespassing, though he had only been riding through a pasture and meant no harm. Blinded by rage Pancho shot and killed the policeman. He then robbed the officer and fled.

Knotts said that Villa was one of the best shots he had ever seen. One day in camp Villa pulled his gun and hardly seeming to aim he shot off the head of a jackrabbit streaking through the brush. Knotts let Villa see that he was properly impressed. Though Villa watched him closely and stayed at his side, Knotts enjoyed the freedom of the camp. He shot a deer one day and, when Knotts finally left, Villa gave him the deerhide. Knotts always claimed that was the most expensive hide in existence, as the hide and a ring which Villa presented him on parting were the only tangible things he could show for the ransom. In later years a school friend of Knotts' daughter recalled that Miss Knotts wore that ring to school, calling it her $20,000 ring. It was quite a conversation piece.

Knotts observed that Pancho never spent two nights at the same camp. They lived partly off friendly ranchers, mostly eating tortillas and game that they killed as well as occasionally appropriating beef on the hoof. The weather was bitter cold but they all had enough blankets to keep warm.

On November 1 they rode back to Well Number 2. There Villa sent Candelario Ruiz, a trusted employee of the mining company, to Villa Ahumada to see what had happened to the supplies and the ransom money expected. Ruiz went and returned with his burro loaded with corn for Villa's prize Kentucky-bred racing mare. Ruiz told them that Smith had been arrested and taken to Chihuahua City by Federals and it was said that Tinney was in a hospital at El Paso.

Villa, apprehensive and nervous, decided to move camp. They traveled south and finally stopped near the ranch of Ojo de San Antonio. There, during the long night of waiting for a messenger with the ransom, Villa demanded that Knotts tell him some funny stories.

Desperately Knotts tried to think of something that might amuse and distract the bandit leader. Finally he remembered an incident that occurred when he was living at Guanaceví. The Knotts had a bathroom built onto their home there, containing the usual facilities. They had a new *mozo,* a young boy from a neighboring ranch, working in the house. This boy was smart and eager to please, but knew nothing of bathroom conveniences. Mrs. Knotts asked the boy, Jesus, to fill the bathtub with warm water so that she could bathe the baby. She saw Jesus make trip after trip carrying buckets of warm water from kitchen to bathroom. Finally she called to him, asking if he hadn't yet filled the tub, knowing he'd carried in enough water to fill it many times. The boy replied that though he kept pouring water into the *little* tub the water kept disappearing. Villa appreciated that joke and roared with laughter. He woke his men and told them about the boy pouring the bath water down the toilet and laughed again with them. For a little while anyhow the tension had been broken.

When they rode back to Ojo de San Antonio a soldier came to meet them shouting that Knotts' friends were there. At the ranch was Knotts' good friend, George Holmes, from El Paso, with a Mexican guide. They'd ridden a hundred miles over the desert, even passing through Carranzista lines, but had finally arrived with the ransom money.

However, the money was in $100 bills instead of the gold Villa had specified. Knotts had to do some fast talking to convince Villa that it was worth American gold. He pointed out the fact that Holmes could not have carried all that gold with him. He assured Villa that an agent could be sent to El Paso to collect gold in exchange for the currency. Holmes backed Knotts up, adding his assurance. Villa finally agreed to accept the ransom. However he declared that he would keep Knotts a prisoner until the exchange was made.

He then sent Knotts, accompanied by Holmes, Colonel Pinones and five guards to Bosque Bonito, a point on the Río Grande about one hundred fifty miles from El Paso. Villa embraced Knotts as they parted. Knotts had the feeling that Villa would miss his company. "I talk very little with my men," Pancho said. "With you I have been a regular parrot."

Knotts had to wait at Bosque Bonito through November 15. There, finally, George Holmes, who had gone on, returned with several wagon loads of supplies and the precious gold. Some Mexicans and a company of American soldiers waited on the far side of the Río Grande. Always thorough, Colonel Pinones relieved Knotts of his watch, blanket, bedding and the few pesos he had left, before allowing him to leave. George Holmes and Frank Knotts then crossed the river, returning to the United States.

"Frank told this story many times in the years to come," says Susan Knotts. "He was a very lucky man to come out of that experience alive, and we never ceased to give thanks.

"I remember the things that happened at Guanaceví. One time when we were sitting in our patio a little girl came up and asked if we had seen Señor Villa lately. 'He has many jewels,' the child said, 'very beautiful jewels. He got them, they say, at Santa Rosalía.' I shudder to think how the bandit had obtained those beautiful jewels, and how nearly he had come to pillaging my own home. I always felt he had lots of treasure hidden around, jewels and gold that he'd stolen. Perhaps even at Canutillo. I remember Canutillo as a beautiful place. There were wealthy people around Durango. Villa used to ride his troops into and through their splendid homes. However, there was one little shrine out from Guanaceví that was never disturbed. There were many young boys forced to become followers of Villa who did not wish to follow his orders, especially in some of the cruel things that he did. They would come to my husband with their complaints, but he couldn't do anything to help them."

"Yes, I remember Villa," Mrs. Knotts said firmly. "He was a brutal, vicious monster."

9

Roy Hoard

Villa was convinced that the Mexico North Western Railway owed him $350,000. Hoard, as president of the railroad, was continually harassed by Villa for the money.

When Hoard was only ninteen years old he was hired by the Lufkin Land and Lumber Company in the tough town of Lufkin, Texas. Because they employed some Mexicans who spoke no English the company had Hoard tutored in Spanish.

In 1909, Hoard developed tuberculosis of the intestines. And in 1910, the company, thinking the climate would benefit him, sent him to Mexico as assistant manager of the Madera Company, one of the largest lumber mills in the world at that time and a subsidiary of the Mexico North Western Railway. This company owned 500 miles of railway in a large half circle from Juarez to Chihuahua City and two million acres of timberland.

When Hoard began work at Madera there were 400 Americans employed by the company. When he retired there were only two. He never discharged a good man, but as the Americans left he replaced them with Mexican help, a policy which proved its merit. Hoard got on well with the Mexican people and even Villa claimed to be his friend in the early days. However, Hoard was always wary of him.

Hoard's good friend, Maximiano Márquez, in his later years as manager of the million acre Hearst Ranch adjoining the timberland of the MNW Railway, near Madera, warned him, "Villa is as dangerous as can be. I have known him to kill a good friend on impulse and then cry like a baby because he had killed him." So, evading the unpredictable Villa, Hoard managed all his contacts through Villa's officers, cultivating their friendship.

"The Revolution began in December, 1910," says Hoard, "along the MNW Railway near Chihuahua City. Villa seized cattle and horses as well as feed. Every large ranch except the Hearst Ranch was devastated. Maximiano Márquez, in charge of the Hearst Ranch at the time, had known Villa for some years. He suggested to Villa that, he, Márquez, would become Villa's Chief if Villa would take only a small amount of cattle from the ranch. Villa accepted the offer. Márquez joined up with him with the understanding that when Villa had all of the State of Chihuahua under his control Márquez would be permitted to leave Villa and return to the Hearst Ranch. When the arrangement was fulfilled Márquez returned to the Hearst Ranch. The ranch was never bothered."

In 1912 the revolutionary situation became so dangerous that the U.S. government ordered all Americans to leave Mexico. Hoard was in charge of the train that brought out seventy-eight Americans, one hundred Mexican citizens, and seventy-five Chinese refugees. All bridges between Juárez and Madera had been burned and many bridges had been burned between Madera and Chihuahua. However, work equipment and materials were taken along on the train and temporary repairs made the bridges usable. Eleven days were required for the entire trip to Juárez.

After leaving the refugees in Juárez, Hoard returned immediately to Madera, making the trip by handcar in four days, crossing over eighty-seven burned bridges. At Madera he inventoried all possessions of his company as requested by the U.S. government. This included one hundred million board feet of high class lumber which could only be realized on by remanufacture at the El Paso plant. Hoard then returned to Juárez over the same eighty-seven burned bridges. Section men had in the meantime wired the rails together and a light gasoline motor car was used over the railroad, cutting the trip to Juárez to three days.

The Madera plant was reactivated in 1914 with Hoard as General Manager of all Madera company affairs including those of Chihuahua City, Torreón and Monterrey, and with G. U. Armendáriz as manager at Madera. Hoard was also to handle matters with government and revolutionary heads.

Early in 1914 Máximo Castillo, a revolutionary general opposed to Villa and believed to be financed by agents of the Federal Government, went on the rampage, destroying sawmills of the Madera Company, and railroad cars of the MNW Railway, and shooting the officials, mostly Americans, at the Madera company town of Pearson. The name of the town was later changed to Mata Ortiz.

"Then," Hoard recalls, "there occurred one of the most cruel of the tragedies of the Revolution. Castillo's band ambushed a MNW train near Pearson. They robbed the fifty passengers, locked passengers and crew in the train, and then sent it through the five-eighth mile long Cumbre Tunnel which they had set afire. All died a horrible death. I will never forget that I was on the last train to go through the tunnel before the disaster."

During the Revolution there was almost no law or order at Madera for months at a time. There were only a few Americans and Mexicans loyal to Hoard that stayed to protect the town against fire. There was nearly always a discordant note of some type from the outside, with frequently neither police nor communications either by rail or telephone.

One incident involved an American gunman named Harry Roberts. He had killed several people in Arizona and fled to Mexico where he married a Mexican woman and became a Mexican citizen. Roberts operated a gambling house at Madera until he caused so much trouble, including stealing, that Hoard had him run out of town. However, at one of the times when Madera was isolated, Roberts came back. He threw out the people running the gambling house and took over, threatening daily to kill Hoard. For a week Hoard stayed at home, making his plans. He had a friend draw a plan of the inside of the gambling place and established where Roberts was in the habit of putting his gun when he came in.

Hoard waited patiently, then one night he followed Roberts into the bar, pistol ready. When Roberts laid his gun down behind the bar at the base of a large mirror and started out to the tables, Hoard stopped him. He ordered Roberts to get out of town and not come back. Roberts didn't argue. The next morning he was gone from Madera.

Villa heard about the incident and sent word by Major Librado Acosta, Villa's man in that vicinity, that he would kill anyone Hoard wanted out of the way. In fact, he was angry with Hoard for not letting him take care of Roberts.

Acosta then told Hoard that an American cattle buyer, Mel Wormer, would be buying cattle in Madera for Villa. Hoard was asked to assure the people with whom Wormer would deal that his checks were good and to be honored. When the owners had still not been paid for their cattle months later they complained to Hoard who sent world to Villa. Soon after, it was reported in an El Paso newspaper that Wormer had been seen entering Villa's Juárez headquarters and was never seen thereafter. A Villa officer later came to Madera and paid for the cattle.

"That was a good example," says Hoard, "of the way Villa operated. He kept his word, and those who tried to take advantage of him learned fast and hard."

Late in 1915, MNW officials in El Paso learned that General Obregón had been given permission to transport three troop trains over U.S. railroads from Eagle Pass, Texas, to Douglas, Arizona, across the border from Agua Prieta, Sonora. Knowing that Villa would immediately seek savage vengeance on all Americans for what he would consider betrayal by the U. S., the company sent instructions for Hoard to move all American women and children from the Madera plant to Juárez. Hoard was in Monterrey but arranged for a train over the MNW to take the fifty American women and children to the international border and they reached Juárez safely. Villa was known to be on the way to Madera, but Hoard was back there before Villa arrived. The fifty male employees of the company voted to remain at Madera.

Obregón troops, taking Villa by surprise by traveling over the American railroad, had almost annihilated his army at Agua Prieta. Villa took the pitiful remnants of his troops over the Sierras and headed for Madera. Not equipped for the freezing cold or stocked with provisions, many of his followers died on the rough mountain trail.

Hoard's friend, Maximiano Márquez, on friendly terms with Villa, rode horseback over the Sonora trail and met him at the "Half Way House." Villa told Márquez that he planned to confiscate all MNW Railway and Madera Company property and give it to the Mexican employees. Marquez reported this to Hoard who told his employees to agree with anything Villa wished as long as none of them, Mexican or American, was harmed.

On December 11, the second day after Villa's arrival in Madera, he sent for Hoard. Hoard found Villa surrounded by some fifty to seventy-five Madera Mexicans. When he reached the edge of the crowd two officers, whom Hoard knew well, joined him, one on each side. Hoard approached Villa and saluted.

Villa, playing with his two pistols, stared coldly at him

and finally said, "Some of your men have not been paid and if you do not pay them immediately you will be killed."

Hoard explained that there were no banks in Madera and the company maintained only a small amount of cash. By agreement the merchants cashed all pay checks, but because of Villa's arrival with his army they had all left town temporarily. Villa then told the two officers guarding Hoard to take him to the company offices and have him open the safes. He added that if Hoard did not do so, not to bring him back.

At the office Hoard had to send out for one of the staff to get into the vault and safe. While they waited a small, cocky Villista came in, drew his pistol, punched Hoard in the stomach and slapped him.

"I blew my top," Hoard says. "I grabbed the pistol, turned it away from my body and struck the man with my hand."

The guards then intervened and advised the gunman to treat Hoard decently. When the safe and vault were opened only a small amount of cash was found. Hoard was taken back to face Villa.

"Take him home," Villa said. "Let him have dinner and then bring him to the railroad offices at eight P.M. We'll take this crowd *of* Americans to the penitentiary in Chihuahua."

Then he spoke of how badly he had been treated, bitterly condemning the American government for allowing Obregón to move troops through the U.S. to defeat him. He said he should have sent his soldiers into El Paso to rob the banks there and escape to the mountains before the lazy American soldiers could catch him.

When Hoard returned to the railroad office that evening, Villa, seemingly in high good humor, said, "Kid, you came near being killed twice this evening. You owe your escape to your Mexican friends. When you are released go directly to the U.S. and do not return for one year. Then look me up. Many people will be killed during that time."

Hoard learned from the train dispatcher that Villa had

wired the railway offices and the U.S. government that if he was not paid $350,000 U.S. currency which he said the MNW Railway owed him, he would kill Hoard and all the Americans with him.

Hoard had never heard of the Railway company being indebted to Villa. However when Villa had come into power in Chihuahua in 1912 he had issued a large amount of fiatt currency. When the MNW Railway along which Villa was always strong was not able to operate because of burned bridges and no funds with which to make repairs, Villa gave the MNW Railway some of this fiatt currency with which to make repairs and get the trains rolling to serve his needs. This fiatt currency lasted only a limited time and the railway later destroyed an enormous amount of it. Later when Villa encountered difficult situations, he claimed that the MNW Railway owed him the sum of $350,000 U.S. currency, but there had never been such an agreement.

The train took three days to reach Chihuahua City. Hoard had arranged so that his group occupied two box cars, known as outfit cars, fitted up with cookstove and living accommodations, and inaccessible to the Villistas who rode in the passenger cars. At the depot at Chihuahua Hoard recognized a friend, Vaca Valles, one of Villa's executioners. He asked Valles to see Villa and ask if the Madera employees couldn't stay in one of the hotels Villa had confiscated instead of in the penitentiary. Permission was granted.

Vaca Valles, the Villa officer and professional killer who got the Americans into the hotel instead of the penitentiary in Chihuahua City, was later executed in Juárez and his body put on exhibition there by the mayor.

Valles took Hoard and the fifty Madera employees to the Hotel Grande. There with their own Chinese cooks and the Madera Company furnishing their own food and necessities they stayed under guard for thirty days. According to Lee Saunders, one of the Madera party whom Hoard delegated to keep order, everyone except Hoard played a lot of poker to pass the time. Everyone had plenty of money and nothing to spend it on. Nine other Americans from near Chihuahua City were forced by Villa to join them.

Hoard knew from his friend Márquez that Villa often took walks in the streets of the towns he had captured and talked to the people. He decided to talk to Villa personally and one morning walked downtown with his two guards. He found Villa near the center of town, telling some twenty-five people about how badly he had been treated by the United States. When he paused Hoard addressed him. "General, as an American, I regret very much that my country has interfered with your plans. I came to your country six years past with tuberculosis and have had nothing but kindness and cooperation from your people and have regained my health and hope to make my home here. Good luck."

The English Consul, substituting for the American Consul, visited the hotel frequently. He reported that Villa continued to demand $350,000, saying that the Americans would be killed if he did not receive it.

At the end of thirty days, when Federal troops threatened the city, Villa released all the hostages except Hoard whom he planned to hold for the ransom he still demanded. Hoard had kept in touch with the two Villa officers on guard, having no trouble with them, and when at the approach of the Federals Villa sent one of these officers with a saddled horse to take Hoard to meet him in the mountains near Chihuahua City, Hoard was prepared. He bribed the officer to take him instead to another hotel which had been closed; however, the hotel accepted the Madera Americans as guests as soon as Villa had left the city.

Hoard arranged passage for the party on the first train to Juárez. Two of the Madera Company employees remained in Chihuahua City, having accepted employment in an American owned mine at Cusihuirάchi. Obregόn had just visited El Paso and stated that the Mexican Revolution was under control and that it was entirely safe for the Americans to return and re-activate their business under Carranza's rule. The Mexican government was very anxious that the mines and smelters reopen.

C. R. Watson, General Manager of the Cusi Mining Company, and a friend of Hoard, arranged for a train to be operated on the MNW Railway from Chihuahua City to Cusijuiriάchi, where he owned and had operated a successful mine. Shortly after the trains were running again a train was held up by a band of Villistas a few miles out of the village of Santa Ysabela. Shouting "Death to the Gringos" and "Viva Villa" the bandits forced the entire party of engineers and mine employees off the train. They robbed, stripped and murdered the eighteen men, leaving them for a rescue train from Chihuahua to pick up later. One American, Tom Holmes, escaped when the firing began and made his way with the help of a Mexican rancher to Chihuahua City where he told the grim story. This happened while Hoard was still at the hotel in Chihuahua. "I knew the murdered men," Hoard says.

"Most of the bandits," relates Hoard, "after leaving their victims, seized the train and headed for Madera, burning bridges after crossing them. However Mάrquez, my friend at the Hearst Cattle Ranch, had been advised by the railway officials of the Santa Ysabela massacre. With eighty tough and well-armed cowpunchers Mάrquez burned the railway bridge closest to Madera, waited there for the train, and killed every Villista on it."

A short time later General José Rodríguez, celebrated Villista cavalry leader, with several Villistas, reached Madera with instructions from Villa to Mάrquez to aid Rodríguez in destroying all MNW Railway and Madera Company property. Instead, Mάrquez disarmed the group and held them until he got in contact with Federal military headquarters in Mexico City. He was instructed to execute the entire group, which he did. Soon after Márquez was made a Colonel on detached service in the Federal Army.

Later General Pershing stated that Maximiano Márquez of the Hearst Ranch was the only Mexican who showed him any courtesy or cooperation.

Hoard says, "I have often wondered why the story never leaked out before as to the debt the American forces owed Márquez for his lifesaving courage in daring to stand up against Villa's power." In 1969 the *El Paso Times* gave such information through their newspaper at Hoard's request.

Hoard left Mexico on a year's leave of absence in 1916, becoming General Manager of Champion Lumber Company of North Carolina.

He returned in late 1917 to Mexico when conditions seemed more normal for business and in 1918 became President of the MNW Railway and subsidiaries.

During the next few years Hoard managed to avoid personal contact with Villa by always knowing where the bandit-general would be. Villa however never gave up on trying to obtain $350,000 from Hoard in some way. Several of Villa's officers visited Hoard when they were in Juárez, and he in El Paso, and they would deliver messages from Villa.

In June, 1919, while approaching Juárez with an army, Villa sent this message to Hoard in El Paso: "I will attack Juárez and retreat along the MNW Railway to Mata Ortiz and instruct you to enter Mexico near Columbus, N.M. One of my staff will meet you there and bring you to me." The messenger was captured by the Federals as he returned to Juárez. When asked what Hoard's reply to Villa's demand had been, he answered, "Mr. Hoard refused to give answer."

Villa attacked Juárez at four A.M. and was repulsed. He retreated along the MNW Railway with his soldiers, all riding horses. Three trains of Federal troops were sent to Mata Ortiz over the MNW Railway. Villa annihilated them and wired Hoard if he did not send him $350,000 he would destroy all of the wooden bridges on the Chihuahua Division of the MNW. He did not get anything and destroyed all of them. He then sent Hoard another telegram stating that the next time he would destroy the largest and most expensive structure on the railway, a three hundred foot steel viaduct with a seventy-five foot center which experts had told Hoard could not be replaced for less than $350,000 and in not less than several months' time.

Hoard and Vice President Clark of the MNW who spoke excellent Spanish and also had friends in the Mexico City government offices, prepared to go to Mexico City to consult with them regarding Villa's demands. Hoard remembered then that Villa was operating along the National Railways between Chihuahua City and Juárez, occasionally stopping the daily passenger trains, seizing some enemy and hanging him to a telegraph pole. He decided to take the Southern Pacific Railway from El Paso through Laredo, Texas, and the National Railways to Mexico City.

The ticket agent at Nuevo Laredo was an old friend. Just before the train left he informed Hoard and Clark, who had the one drawing room on the only Pullman car, that the train was carrying a quantity of silver bullion and it was anticipated might be held up by bandits, probably Villistas. The train carried a small armed escort of soldiers, one Pullman car, and two ordinary passenger cars. Hoard and Clark were the only passengers in the Pullman. Both carried their old Railway Labor Union Cards. They talked with the conductor, brakeman, and porter on their car, and it was agreed that if the train was attacked, they would lock the door to the drawing room and make no noise.

The train was stopped at a water tank near Monterrey at four A.M. by a group of Revolutionists or bandits who had taken up a rail. They knocked repeatedly on the drawing room door where Hoard and Clark were and were told by the attendants that it was empty. The small escort of soldiers and a number of passengers were killed and a quantity of cash taken.

When the train reached Mexico City, Hoard and Clark, having established fraternity with the crew of the train, left from the baggage car and the newspapers never knew they were on the train.

Both Hoard and Clark had valuable friends in government circles in Mexico City and were advised that if the MNW gave Villa money, the Federal government could justifiably cancel the Railway Federal Charter under which the MNW operated. Hoard returned and advised his superiors that he recommended "sitting tight," which he was instructed to do.

Immediately after his return to El Paso, Hoard, accompanied by Hilario Aguilar, in charge of Maintenance on the MNW surreptitiously visited the steel viaduct which Villa had threatened to dynamite. Between them they devised a method of repairing the steel viaduct, which the engineers had not considered. They returned, ordered through outside people the materials needed, stored them in Juárez without anyone knowing what they were there for nor that they were with the MNW.

Shortly thereafter, Villa visited Mata Ortiz and sent Hoard a telegram that if he did not immediately receive the $350,000 he would dynamite the steel viaduct. Hoard gave no reply and the viaduct was dynamited. According to Hoard's plan the viaduct was then repaired without molestation and the trains were soon operating over it.

In July, 1920, one of Villa's principal officers came to El Paso and called on Hoard. He said, "Well, Kid, you have worn Pancho out. He is going to ask for amnesty." Shortly after that Villa had come to terms with the Mexican government and was given the large hacienda near Parral, Chihuahua, where with a couple of his wives and his special followers, the *Dorados* or Golden Ones, he retired to the life of a gentleman farmer.

Villa never forgot Hoard though, and about two weeks before he was assassinated, he was in Chihuahua at the same time Hoard was and sent word to Hoard that he wanted to see him. Hoard, with memories of the demand for $350,000 haunting him, left town immediately.

In 1948 the MNW was sold to Mexico City and New York bankers, with Hoard representing the company in the negotiations. Hoard then made his home in El Paso and devoted his energies to a very full program of civic affairs.

"I'd have seen Villa in hell before I ever gave him a nickel," said Hoard.

10

William Liggett

Liggett and his father ran a jitney service and carried mail between Cananea, Mexico, and Naco and Bisbee, Arizona during the Revolution.

"From my personal encounters with Pancho Villa, I would say he was a man people either respected and admired or feared and hated. I remember his liking good horses, cockfighting, soda pop and ice cream.

"My father and I operated a stage line between Bisbee, Arizona, and Naco and Cananea, Sonora, from the early 1900's right through the Revolution years.

"My father first established his transfer business in Naco. Business was so good that I quit my job in the Bisbee mines and joined him. The fact that I barely missed being killed in a mine cave in speeded my move to Naco. At first we used horses and mules for our stages and jitneys, but as soon as automobiles came in we bought them and added them to our line.

"Our first car was the 1910 EMF '30 Studebaker, and our finest, I always thought, was a seven-passenger Pratt 40. I felt like a king when I drove it. The sight of my automobile got everyone excited when I drove through those Mexican villages. The natives, especially the Tarahumara Indians, would stare like hell.

"When our business increased to the point where we needed an office and stables in Cananea, I was given the job of opening there. I was only nineteen but was keen on being a full partner and manager in the business. We called it Liggett and Son Transfer and Bus Company.

"Jim Kirk, he was superintendent of the Cananea Consolidated Copper Company which was a part of Colonel Greene's organization, gave me official permission to operate my stages in Cananea. The whole town, I might say, was practically owned and run by the mining company.

"I was there during the Cananea Riots of June, 1906. One evening I had just dropped my passengers at Chivatera, that's a part of Cananea near the mine, when the miners came off the night shift. Suddenly they started yelling and throwing bombs. When dynamite exploded nearby I jumped out of my rig and ran. That was the very beginning of the bloody trouble, and many people think, the beginning of the Revolution.

"Hard feeling had been growing among the Mexican workers because the American miners were paid higher wages. The trouble was made worse by outside agitators who had gotten the people riled up.

"When the trouble was over, six Americans had been killed, including the two Metcalf brothers who worked for the mining company. There were many Mexican casualties. I counted thirty-five of the dead rioters laid out near my livery stable. Many Americans left Cananea soon after that, but most remained. Things sort of settled back to normal, though there was never again quite as good feeling between the gringos and the natives.

"With about nine thousand Mexicans and some twenty-three hundred Americans working for the mines, and great demand for our stages and jitneys, Liggett and son were sit-

ting pretty. Then the Revolution got hot and really messed
things up for everyone.

"For a while after the Revolution broke out, the Americans, trying to stay neutral, just continued working and living
as they had been in their parts of town. They were pretty self-
sufficient. Most of them, including the mine officials, lived in
a colony of what was known as La Mesa or Ronquillo. Others
were at Chivatera, nearer the Capote Mine where they worked.
The mining company maintained a first-class hospital staffed
with American doctors for the benefit of its employees. The
babies born to American families had only to be registered by
their parents at the American consulate in Cananea.

"It was a joke around town that Cananea changed hands
so rapidly between Federals and Rebels that often the town
was taken while a dance was in progress, and when the Americans came out of their dance hall they wouldn't know whether
to 'Viva the Rebels' or 'Viva the Federals.'

"As I said, the Americans tried for some time to go about
their business and ignore the Revolution, but when a bullet
went through someone's kitchen, the American families decided it was time to leave. They packed up, took their babies
and left by train. Most of them went to Bisbee, Arizona, where
the men went to work at the copper mines there. Yes, that was
the end of much of the pleasant, friendly closeness of the
Cananea crowd. Many of them though have kept in touch
through the years.

"One occasion I'll never forget. I was going from Bisbee
to Cananea. At Naco, on the American side, I picked up two
Mexican women carrying babies on pillows. They were going
to Cananea and paid their fare in advance. At the crossing
point into Naco, Sonora, it was customary for the passengers
to get an okay from the Mexican Custom's officer. This day
I was surprised to see Federal General Ojeda himself come up
to the car. I knew the general and we exchanged greetings.

He didn't pay much attention to my passengers but had my car thoroughly searched. All that seemed to interest him was a large bundle of El Paso newspapers. I usually did carry such a bundle of papers and usually they were confiscated. That day General Ojeda personally set fire to the papers. He laughed as he watched them burn and said, 'Nothing but a bunch of damned lies!' I understood that that was his way of protesting news about the defeat of his forces which he felt was surely coming and in which he was right.

"After his little demonstration the general waved us on. We navigated the Rebel lines successfully a little farther on and I was congratulating myself when we had car trouble. By the time I got the Pratt 40 running again it was almost dark. Just after we started on our way, someone shot a gun over the car. I stopped as quickly as possible, wondering what the hell now.

"A group of Rebel soldiers came up and told me to follow a side road leading to the old Key Dairy. There we all were ordered out of the car. The leader began to question the two Mexican women passengers that I had picked up in Naco. Their pillows were ripped open. The Rebels found what they were looking for. Inside the pillows were documents to be delivered to Federal General Moreno at Cananea. I was released, but I'm afraid the poor women were not so lucky. I understood then why General Ojeda had ignored them and why he personally waved my car on that day.

"The battles for the border towns went something like a tug of war, first one side holding the advantage and then the other. Both sides had some good generals and equipment. The Federals had Generals Ojeda, Obregón, Calles and Colonel Kosterlitzky and the Revolutionists had Generals Maytorena, Angeles and Villa. I remember seeing General Ojeda run the Revolutionists out of Naco and into the San José Mountains.

"Another time Cananea fell to the Rebels who then concentrated all their attack on Naco. Naco was practically burned to the ground. The death toll was very large. No one ever gave a true account of it.

"On the way to Naco one day I heard the Revolutionists were preparing a cavalry attack from the east on General Ojeda at Naco. I was alone excepting for my little dog Venice. I knew that I wouldn't be allowed to go on through town, so I found a two story building and Venice and I went up there for a view of the battle. Several other people joined us there.

"Through my field glasses I could see Ojeda's cannons on all the embankments and his men placed in strategic positions. Ojeda waited till the Revolutionists were within firing range. Then he gave the signal and all hell broke out. The noise from the artillery fire was terrific. Cavalrymen, horses, saddles, and sombreros were flying in all directions. Several days after that the tables were turned and the Rebels set fire to the town. During these two battles the American side of Naco suffered casualties as it was built right up to the line.

"On the Mexican side the wounded of both sides lay all over. No effort was made to help them. I guess the fighting was too fierce. Anyhow, the sight was too much for Cochise County Sheriff Wheeler. He swore in some special deputies to keep sightseers out of the danger zone, tied a white flag to his car, and taking Percy Bowden of Bisbee to do the driving, crossed over and picked up the wounded. On the U.S. side, American volunteers took over and gave what help they could to the victims.

"I witnessed many battles in Cananea and Naco. I'll tell you those were hectic times. When I left Cananea on a run to Douglas or Naco or Bisbee I never knew whether Federals or Rebels would be occupying the town when I returned. It paid to have friends on both sides.

"One time shortly after both Naco and Cananea had fallen to Rebels, I was hired for a special trip from Cananea to Nogales. My passengers were a bullfighter and his girl. The bullfighter kept drinking mescal out of his supply in his traveling bag and he was getting to be a nuisance both to the girl and me. He sobered down mighty quick though when we passed close to several bodies of soldiers dangling from the limbs of a bunch of oak trees beside the road. They had been there for some time and the sight was pretty gruesome. We didn't stop to see if they were Federals or Rebels.

"I remember very well the first time I actually saw Pancho. It was in Cananea one afternoon. He rode in with a handful of his men. I was standing in front of my office at Ronquillo and I had a good look at him. I moseyed on down the road when I saw that Villa was stopping at a drug store. By the time I went into the store, Pancho and his men were standing around drinking bottles of cold soda pop. I had always heard that he was not a drinker of hard liquor and that he didn't want his men to drink while on the warpath. I ordered a pop and then walked up to Pancho and held out my hand. 'I've been wondering when you would pay our town a visit,' I said. 'You should have alerted us and we could have had the welcome mat out.'

"Pancho gave me a big grin and shook hands. He had a firm, hard grip. We chatted for a few minutes while he drank another pop. When he left the store I walked out beside him. I told him about the stage and mail lines that my father and I ran. Villa said he had heard about our business.

"He had a fine horse, a beautiful big black, at the hitching post. He seemed pleased when I complimented him on the horse. Pancho vaulted into the saddle in a way that showed he was more at home there than on his feet. He might have looked awkward and squatty when walking, as some people said, but on horseback Villa was great, looking like part of his mount. He waved to me and then was off down the street in a cloud of dust.

"The storekeeper, a friend of mine, came to stand beside me and people began to fill up the street again, all of them wearing relieved expressions.

"My friend said, 'There goes a real nice Mexican. He paid for the drinks with gold and waved away the change.'

"I confess that I was glad that Pancho, even though friendly, liked Chihuahua better than Sonora.

"He pretty much stayed in his own territory. But I did lose some of my good horses to Villa's army. It was when Villa was on his last legs. President Wilson had recognized Carranza's de facto government, wrongly I always thought, and had even put on an embargo that prevented Pancho from getting supplies from across the border. That was when Pancho started losing out.

"Villa was badly defeated at Agua Prieta after our government allowed Mexican Federal troops to pass over U. S. railroads and cross there at Douglas. I owned Our Cafe in El Paso at the time and watched those loaded troop trains go through town. I thought then that it was bad business as we were supposed to be neutral.

"Villa's forces were badly defeated by Obregón's Federal troops and he had to get out of there the best he could. He retreated over the mountains, getting to Cananea in bad shape. About then he went over a narrow gauge railroad through the Puertacitas Pass to Nogales, Sonora. The engineers refused to run the train for him, so Villa shot them and ran the train himself. He was desperate. He went on down to the Altar district below Nogales and rested while his men recuperated.

"In Cananea, scrounging supplies every way, he stole my fine, duty-paid horses from the company pastures. I had come to El Paso, leaving all I had built up in Mexico. I never did get my property back or damages for it as most Americans did, as the papers I needed to prove my claim had been destroyed. I came out with nothing to show for my years in

Mexico but my Pratt 40 and Studebaker cars and plenty of memories of close calls and excitement. I did hear that my pet horse Baldy had gone back to Cananea and I even thought of going down there and riding him back to El Paso, but I knew that was a crazy idea and didn't go.

"There were many incidents along the border here that have never been publicized. When Villa made his last stand in Juárez, his men demanded that my friend, C. P. Simpson, manager of the Kentucky Distillery, turn over to them some 300 barrels of liquor that the company had there. Bill Simpson flatly refused and the Villistas were at the point of shooting to enforce their order when the American Negro soldiers arrived and the guerrillas took off. That rescue came in the nick of time.

"I saw Villa a number of times around El Paso and Juárez. We often sat together at the horse races in Juarez. I guess he liked the races about as well as cock-fighting, at which he was an expert. He was always friendly, remembering me and speaking of the times he had visited Cananea. He had many friends in El Paso and when he was at the peak of his power and popularity he even associated with the big brass at Ft. Bliss. He always spoke admiringly of General Scott. One good place to encounter Pancho was at the Elite Confectionery downtown in El Paso. He would eat big bowls of ice cream and drink quantities of soda pop while he visited with his friends.

"I always thought the story about Emil Holmdahl being responsible for digging up Villa's body and cutting off the head was pretty far fetched. I knew Holmdahl quite well. He drove for me when I opened my Driv-Ur-Self Company service in El Paso. He hung around the old Shelden Hotel with a bunch of young soldiers of fortune, Sam Dreben, Tracy Richardson, and others. There was also a rumor that Richardson had stolen Villa's head and buried it on Mt. Franklin, right here in El Paso. Curiosity seekers like to have dug up the whole mountain looking. I wouldn't know the truth but I don't think neither Holmdahl nor Richardson had anything to do with that business.

"Pancho Villa really got a dirty deal from the United States, in my opinion. They shut off his flow of ammunition and firearms, but let the Federals have all they wanted. If they hadn't done this who knows but what the Revolution might have ended differently. And you have to give him credit for starting to pull the bonds from the peons of Mexico. I'd say he was neither all villain, murdering and dobe-walling people just on a whim, nor the noble liberator of his fellow Mexicans. You couldn't peg him."

11

Mariano Castro

*Castro grew up in Chihuahua during the Revolution.
His father was Francisco Castro, a General in the Federal Army.*

"As a thirteen-year-old I was really not very impressed.
For one thing Villa wore ordinary paisano clothing, though
at that time—it was 1913—as head of the Revolucionarios,
Villa was in complete command of the State of Chihuahua."

Mariano's father, General Francisco Castro of the Federal
Army and a personal friend of President Porfirio Díaz, was a
career soldier and a graduate of the Mexican Military Institute
of Chapultepec College. He had several crucial encounters
with Pancho Villa. In 1912 he had saved Villa's life.

On June 4, 1912, at Jiménez, Chihuahua, Villa faced a
firing squad, under the then Colonel Castro's command. The
order to execute Villa had come directly to Colonel Castro
from General Victoriano Huerta, Commander in Chief of
President Madero's Federals. Huerta, with 20,000 troops
under him, including Villa's, had just completed a successful
campaign against Orozco and his Red Flaggers. He had
reluctantly accepted Villa's support because of President
Madero's orders. At the first opportunity, claiming that Villa

had stolen a valuable mare from a wealthy Jiménez man, had shown insubordination for refusing to return the mare, and had not obeyed Huerta's order to report to him, he ordered Villa executed.

"My father," says Mariano Castro, "though always a brave leader and good soldier, had a kind heart. He hated to give the order for Villa's execution. Besides he knew that Villa was intensely loyal to President Madero."

Colonel Castro held up the order as long as possible while Colonel Raúl Madero, General Emilio Madero, Colonel Rubio Navarette, the Commander of Artillery, and Lieutenant Colonel Garcia Hidalgo conferred. Madero sent a telegram to his brother, the President, notifying him of what was about to happen. They tried to persuade Huerta to reconsider his decision, but he refused to change the order. By five A.M. of the day of execution there was still no word from the President and Madero was frantic with anxiety. Up until the last moment Villa seemed to think that the whole thing could not be serious, that it was a bluff run by Huerta to intimidate him. However, when the firing squad actually leveled their guns on him he resigned himself to death.

Villa turned to Colonel Castro and said, with tears in his eyes, "Señor Colonel, permit me to give you a last embrace. The National Army, if it has any honor, will repudiate this act."

Colonel Castro replied with great feeling, embracing him, "It is by higher orders."

Villa then handed his pistol, his watch and his dagger to Colonel Castro who later gave the pistol to General Joaquín Telles. Colonel Castro still didn't give the order to fire.

In the very last minutes, as the six rifles aimed at Villa, Raúl Madero rode up, shouting and waving a telegram from President Madero. It was the stay of execution that saved Villa's life. Among the sighs of relief that rose none was more sincere than Colonel Castro's, as he recalled when telling the story to his son.

Villa was sent immediately to prison in Mexico City where he served a short time and then escaped to make his way to El Paso where he went into hiding until after Madero's assassination.

The roles that General Castro and Pancho Villa played in another episode of the Revolution were very different. By November, 1913, Villa, now with a large following, attacked Chihuahua City, but retreated after losing several hundred men. When it was reported that Villa planned to attack Juárez next, General Castro, then in command of the Federal Garrison there with a total of 580 troops said, "Villa is too badly licked. Let him come—we are prepared."

However, a week later, in the dead of night Villa made a sneak attack and captured Juárez in a military stroke of strategy that has been compared to the Trojan horse incident. Villa, with Rodolfo Fierro and some 1,500 troops, had appeared at a small railroad station north of Chihuahua City and replaced a frightened telegrapher with his own man, Major Carlos Moreno.

Villa sent this telegram to Castro: "Villa in full retreat to south. Am sending you reinforcements with ammunition and supplies by returning train. Signed, Mercado." The reference is to General Salvador Mercado, chief of the Federal forces in Chihuahua.

Villa's men cut the wires in both directions, and then, using the Federals' code to identify the train, they sped through all the stations. General Castro had sent that freight train to Chihuahua City with open gondolas filled with coal. Villa unloaded the coal and filled the cars with his soldiers.

A little after one A.M. on the morning of November 15, the freight returning from Chihuahua City rolled into the Juárez station and unloaded Villa's troops. With cries of "Viva Villa" the barracks were quickly taken and armed Villistas flooded the streets, clubs and buildings. Machine-gun fire was heard in El Paso across the river.

At the Black Cat Cafe in Juárez, on the corner of Calle

Commercial [now Avenue 16th of September] and Lerdo, Otto Schuster of El Paso and the cast of a play being performed at the Crawford Theater were being royally entertained by some Federal officers. Schuster had just sat down at the piano and, with two of the Mexican officers singing with him, began to play an operatic number when they heard shouts and running. The place suddenly was full of armed Villistas. The Americans were told to stay quiet but that they would be safe. The Federal officers with them were ordered to step forward with hands raised.

Castro, however, was not among those at the Black Cat Cafe that night. Two hours before Villa appeared in Juárez, Castro was at the English Consulate. He left the English Consul and went to his house in Juárez with some of his staff. When the English Consul heard the "Viva Villa's" and shooting in the streets he knew what was happening and sent someone to look for Castro at his home.

General Castro was safe.

According to his Memoirs, Villa says: ". . . just before we arrived (at Juárez) I called Col. Juan N. Medina and said, 'Amigo, you are my chief of staff. You will keep order, with an eye to international relations. And there is another thing. The Huertista chief in Juárez is Gen. Francisco Castro. When Huerta wanted to shoot me in Jinénez, he befriended me. If he is taken, save his life and let him escape.' "

Villa says farther along, "Gen. Castro fled that morning to the home of the lawyer, Urrutia. I gave orders not to molest him. That night he crossed the canal and went to Los Partidos to the home of Máximo Weber, the General consul. I knew this also and ordered that he be allowed to leave and go wherever he wished."

Max Weber III of El Paso confirms the story that his grandfather gave refuge at that time to Castro. It was said that Castro fled so fast that he came across the bridge barefoot, leaving behind most of his personal belongings, including uniforms, decorations and sword, and that Villa kept many of the items. Villa was later photographed wearing Castro's uniform cap.

The Federal officers captured that night were not so fortunate as Castro. Following the sacking of Juarez, seventy-four of them were executed by Villa's firing squad, in spite of pleas for clemency by American friends. Charles Seggerson, the chauffeur for Otto Schuster who remained in the car in front of the Black Cat Cafe instead of joining the diners was found shot to death in the car. Accidentally killed, it was said.

When Villa took Juárez he got additional men and enormous supplies for his troops, buying much of it in El Paso. With the increased ammunition and stores he was able to go back and set siege to Chihuahua City. The wealthy citizens of Chihuahua City in anticipation of Villa's attack, loaded baggage and goods onto eleven Orient Railroad trains and, accompanied by Federal troops, fled as far as Falomir. From there they set out for Ojinaga by every means available, traveling in a few imported automobiles and carriages, on horseback and burro back, and on foot. This was said to be probably the largest body of people, between 9,000 and 10,000, ever to travel in one group over the Old Chihuahua Trail. The little town of Ojinaga was flooded with refugees, which included some of the wealthiest families of Chihuahua. Don Luis Terrazas, among them, was reported to have brought 5,000,000 pesos with him.

On December 8 the advance guard of the Federals, under General Mercado and his staff, including General Pascual Orozco and General Caraveo and other generals arrived in Ojinaga and began to fortify the town. Castro went from El Paso to Presidio and crossed into Ojinaga to join Mercado's army there. For ten days the Federal forces and Villa's Rebel Army fought, but neither side won.

On January 10, 1914, Villa himself, impatient to drive

the Federals entirely out of the State of Chihuahua, was reported approaching with a large army. Panic struck Ojinaga. Civilians fled across the Río Grande by the thousands, seeking safety in Presidio. The border patrol on the American side of the river was increased. Villa, having given orders for his men to wear their hats down their backs for identification, and that any man who turned back was to be shot, attacked furiously in three directions.

Fighting was heavy. The outnumbered Federalists, including Castro, were forced to flee across the bridge over the Río Grande and take refuge in the United States. The War Department ordered that because of the danger no Mexicans were to be turned back across the river.

Fewer than 500 U.S. soldiers guarded the refugees who gathered around huge fires to dry out. Many had plunged through the icy river to reach safety.

Approximately 5,000 Federals were taken into custody, Castro among them. Those who still had weapons surrendered them. The refugees marched by foot to Marfa where they entrained for Ft. Bliss. They were interned at Ft. Bliss for three months, and then taken to Ft. Wingate, New Mexico, for six months and were released from Ft. Wingate on September 27, 1914.

Mariano, his mother, and two brothers and a sister came up from Chihuahua City to join their father at Ft. Bliss. Mariano remained in the United States, became a citizen, and made his home in El Paso. His father returned to Mexico in 1925 and died in Chihuahua City in 1939.

Among the hundreds of well-kept pictures and letters and mementoes of his father's experience in the Revolution, Mariano Castro cherishes his father's magnificent uniforms. The black dress uniform of rich, soft wool is in remarkably fine condition, with heavy gold epaulettes and silk embroidery of the proper insignia. Mariano also displays his father's long, gleaming Toledo sword, made in Spain, in its special casing of metal with the beautifully wrought eagle, snake, and cactus emblems, and the one of similarly decorated leather that was worn in action.

"I can't help but wonder what the outcome of the Mexican Revolution, including that capture of Juárez in 1913 and the battle of Ojinaga a month later that ended my father's forty-eight-year career as an active general in the Federal army, would have been had my father not been so kind-hearted as to hold up Villa's execution back in 1912."

12

Stephen E. Aguirre

Aguirre, who later became a consul-general for the United States in Juárez, was captured, along with four companions, by Villa when trying to cross the border in April, 1913.

"We were brought before him in his office at the Hidalgo Hotel in Santa Rosalía. He didn't ask us to sit down," Aguirre recalls. "He just sat there and looked at us."

Aguirre stared back and tried not to appear nervous.

Aguirre wondered if Villa would find the 3,000 pesos he was taking to his mother in El Paso which he had hidden in a belt under his clothing. Villa looked at the "Safe Conduct Pass" that was given Aguirre by the consul in Durango.

"How do you, a blonde, blue-eyed gringo, have the name Aguirre and speak our language like a native?" Villa asked. "Who are your people?"

"My father is Stephen Monroe Aguirre. He has a grocery store in Durango."

"*That* Aguirre?" Villa shouted. "But why didn't you say you were his son? I know him well. I knew your father last year in Juárez, when he was working for the railroad. He was my Customs Broker and cleared some shipments for me at El Paso. Tell me about conditions in Durango now."

Aguirre relaxed, but he had been warned before he left Durango not to talk about military or political matters. At that point in his life he could honestly plead ignorance about such affairs. He found himself explaining how his father happened to settle in Durango, Villa's home territory.

A friend of the senior Aguirre, a Mr. Leach, manager of a lumber mill in Durango, had advised Aguirre to open a grocery business there to supply the two hundred or so Americans in the district. Mrs. Aguirre stayed in El Paso till conditions were safer in Durango, and Stephen and his brother, Ben, joined their father.

Stephen went to work for the lumber company, connecting telephones in their camps in the Sierras west of Durango. These mountains are high and very rugged, going in fifty miles from an altitude of about 4000 feet to as high as 10,000. They produce some of the finest stands of Ponderosa pine in the world. Constructing a railroad up to the camps was very difficult. At one point there is a cantilevered bridge, supported by two large steel pins, with the weight of the train causing the halves of the bridge to go down and lock onto the pins. This bridge was blown up during the Revolution, but is again in use. Much of the pine lumber received in Juárez today comes down over that bridge.

When Madero was assassinated, February 22, 1913, there was an immediate upsurge throughout Mexico of strong anti-American feeling, as it was felt and newspaper stories indicated, that the American Ambassador, Henry Lane Wilson, could have used his influence with Huerta to save Madero's life. Therefore young Aguirre's helpers woke him in the middle of the night and told him he'd better leave at once, that all gringos were in danger. Stephen rode down out of camp on the last train of logs.

Late in April he left Durango with four other Americans, one of them a giant Negro. They headed for the border on a work train sent out to repair the bridges that had been blown up. Not far out of town the conductor spotted a band of rebels approaching and stopped the train. Aguirre and his companions borrowed a handcar and went on, pumping hard toward Torreón. Four would pump while the fifth rested, and the big Negro often took over for young Aguirre when his hands became too blistered.

The first rebels to stop them was an advance group for Pancho Villa, led by Tomás Urbina. They were able to read Aguirre's consular credentials, impressive with red wax seal, ribbons, and official signatures. The Americans were allowed to proceed, after reluctantly sharing their food and clothing with the Villistas. However, they didn't answer any questions about military conditions in Durango, pleading ignorance.

Night fell and they pushed on. Three or four more miles of laborious pumping brought them to a burning bridge. They stopped and the next morning found that the rails were only bent and that they could proceed on their handcar, finally reaching Torreón one week later.

Aguirre and his companions rested from their trip at a nice hotel in Torreón. They were advised to call on George Carothers, the American consular agent. He suggested to the group that they go to Mexico City, that the American Embassy would repatriate them to New Orleans via Veracruz. Enthusiastic for more adventure they purchased tickets to Mexico City, traveling in style on a Pullman. The train left Torreón early one morning, but about one hour out of Torreón the engineer saw a burnt bridge ahead, stopped and backed his train into Torreón.

This ended the adventure to Mexico City. The boys borrowed the old handcar and headed north from Gómez Palacio, adjacent to Torreon.

The longest tangent on any railroad in Mexico is from Gómez Palacio to Escalón, a distance of forty-five or more miles. This trip over the desert took them three days and

nights to complete. Had it not been for the good people of
the section gangs along the route who gave them water and
food they would have perished.

They left Jiménez on a freight and passenger train, still
headed for Juárez. At Santa Rosalía, about sixty miles from
Jiménez, Aguirre and his companions were taken off the
train by Villa's orders. They learned later that Villa had kept
track of them all the way, constantly being informed by
runners of all activities, especially of foreigners in the region.

Having told his story to the rebel leader and discussed
general conditions in Durango, Stephen Aguirre waited to
learn his fate, trying to conceal his anxiety. He had always
heard that if Villa were your friend he never forgot it, also
that if you were his enemy you could expect savage treatment
if you fell into his hands. Pancho Villa was now known to feel
bitter personal grief for Madero's death, and a fierce desire
for revenge on all parties to his assassination.

"You can go no farther north by train," Villa said abruptly
now. "I will send you on to Chihuahua City by coach when
you are ready."

He shook hands with Aguirre and dismissed the young
gringos, to their great relief. For several days they explored
Santa Rosalía, enjoying baths at the famous mineral springs
nearby. Villa furnished them, at a good price, a buckboard
with horses and a driver, and so they journeyed on to
Chihuahua, a distance of some eighty miles.

From there they took the train to Juárez, arriving late in
May. They learned that soon after they had left Villa took
Chihuahua City.

"It is my opinion that Villa was always friendly to the
U.S. until President Wilson recognized Carranza as head
of the government in Mexico on October 19, 1915," says
Mr. Aguirre. "It was then that Pancho turned hostile to our
country and it would seem with some justification. The often

heard description of Villa as the 'Robin Hood of Mexico' is borne out by many true stories of his stormy career. Also it is no myth that he was a man of his word."

"As to the true picture of the Mexican Revolution," Mr. Aguirre says, "a newspaperman told me in 1940 that it was too soon then to write the real story, and I think he was right. I think we're just now getting the proper perspective of those exciting events and their leaders, and Pancho Villa may yet emerge as one of the greats of his country."

13

Carmen Visconti Abel

*Mrs. Abel's family had several tragic encounters with
Villa while living in Santa Rosalía, Mexico.*

"Pancho Villa kept my family on the run for ten years.
He caused us great suffering and terror. We have never truly
felt safe from him or his followers, not even yet.

"My family lived in Mexico for many years. My father,
Vicenti Visconti, was a merchant in Santa Rosalía, doing im-
port and export business. We never had any trouble with the
Mexican government or the people until the revolution broke
out. Then from 1910 on the revolutionists, mainly Villa, continually harrassed and stole from us. Our family has kept
itemized records of what we lost.

"Our family was finally forced to flee the country in 1912.
On December 14, at Chihuahua City, my mother, my three
younger sisters, two brothers and I boarded a refugee train
with about 2000 foreigners and came to El Paso.

"I'll never forget that date because our family had a ter-
rible fright the day before. That day a train carrying mostly
Spaniards had left Chihuahua. One of my youngest brothers,
Arcangel, still in his teens, was among the passengers. Just

before the train was to pull out, General Villa came up to the station with some of his men. He stared in at the people on the train and my brother said that he will never forget the feeling of danger and threat that went through him. Archie was sitting in the midst of a group of Americans in the mistaken idea that he would be safer there. He tried not to look back at Villa or to attract his attention in any way. Believe me, every person on that train was praying for it to leave as fast as possible.

"Villa looked over everyone. Then he said something and pointed right at my brother. He hustled poor Archie off the train.

"There in front of the depot he demanded $10,000 ransom before he'd let Archie go. He threatened to have my brother shot then and there if his demands weren't met. It was a terrible moment. Then the Italian consul who was in charge of the Italian refugees went over to Villa. He told him that no one could stop my brother from leaving because he was an Italian subject and all foreigners had been promised safe departure.

"Villa started to argue, but the consul was a brave man and he knew he was right. He even grabbed Villa and shook him by the arms. To everyone's surprise Villa stepped back and turned away, growling something at his men. The consul hurried my brother back onto the train which got under way at once.

"The passengers collected some 2000 pesos which they gave to the conductor and engineer to get to El Paso as quickly as possible. A little way out of Chihuahua the train stopped and the telegraph wires were cut so that Villa couldn't wire ahead to have it stopped. Villa was known to change his mind and it was feared that he would not let my brother escape that easily. Archie didn't drawn a free breath till he was across the border.

"I remember that our train got into El Paso about two in

the morning. We were cold, tired and frightened. There was no place for us to stay as the refugee train of the day before had brought in about 5,000 people. We finally got lodging for the rest of that night on the Roof Garden of the Paso Del Norte Hotel. The next morning we looked for a place to live. We bought the house at 507 East Yandell Boulevard that was to be my family's home for twenty years.

"We were not through with that incident at the Chihuahua depot. Within a few days of rescuing my brother the Italian consul, I think his name was Galin, began to receive threats on his life. He appealed to my father who furnished money to send the consul and his family to Germany. At that time there was the triple alliance of France, Germany and Italy, and the Italian consul seemed to feel that he'd fare well in Germany. My father was very glad to help Mr. Galin as the family felt he had saved my brother's life.

"A little later my father and another brother came with a Mr. McCollum to El Paso. In all we heard that there were about 12,000 people forced to flee to the United States from the State of Chihuahua during the Revolution. General Luis Terrazas was with the group that came with my father. Terrazas' younger son, Luis, stayed behind and was put in prison for several months, held by the revolutionists who hated the Terrazas family.

"The harassment of my family, the Viscontis, became worse. In March, 1916, a terrible thing happened to my uncle, Enrico Visconti, on his ranch near Santa Rosalía. There were stories in the papers about it."

The clippings in Mrs. Abel's scrapbook read:

ITALIAN RANCHMAN SLAIN BY BANDITS
FAMILY OF ENRIQUE VISCONTI LEFT
PLACE SHORTLY BEFORE TRAGEDY

El Paso, Texas, March 18, 1916—Enrique Visconti, an Italian subject, owner of the large Encinillas ranch 100

miles south of Ojinaga, was murdered by Mexican bandits
late Wednesday afternoon. His family, consisting of a wife
and two grown sons, escaped his fate several hours before
the tragedy. Mrs. Visconti and the sons started for Santa
Rosalía, eighty miles southeast.

The story of this most recent depredation was brought
here today to Vincente Visconti, brother of the dead man.
He said:

"Wednesday afternoon a band of horsemen rode up to
the ranch and found my brother. The leader asked for
money, which was given. The bandit asked for more, a
demand that could not be complied with as Mr. Visconti
had given them everything of value he possessed. Several
of the band then entered the house and sacked it of food,
linen, and bed clothing which they loaded on waiting pack
mules. The bandit chief ordered my brother to walk ahead
down the road and, as he did so, the band emptied their
rifles into his body."

Mr. Visconti has taken up the matter with the Mexican consulate in this city to see if it is possible to recover
the body and bring it to this city for burial. He will file a
complaint with the Italian consult.

Enrique Visconti was well-known in the southwest
and was a member of the Texas Cattle Raisers' Association.

OWNER OF 75,000 ACRES IN MEXICO
SLAIN BY BANDITS
BROTHER OF MURDERED ITALIAN SAYS
RELATIVES HAVE BEEN HELD FOR RANSOM.

El Paso, Texas, March 19, 1916—Enrico Visconti, an
Italian subject and one of the best known foreign ranchers
in Mexico, was murdered by Mexican bandits on his ranch
at Encinillas, Chihuahua, last Tuesday. News of the murder reached here today in a telegram sent by Vincenzo
Visconti, brother of the murdered man. The telegram was
sent from Presidio.

Visconti's ranch was 75,000 acres in extent and located 100 miles south of Ojinaga, and about an equal distance east of Chihuahua City. The bandits who murdered him seized his cousin, Juan Bilbao, a Spaniard, on his ranch, sixty miles southwest of Encinillas, a week previously, and held him for $1500 ransom, which was paid from El Paso.

It is supposed Visconti refused their demands for money, but no details have been received here. A grown son of the ranchman is thought to have been with him on the ranch, but nothing is known as to his fate.

The murder of the ranch owner aroused deep indignation in the Italian colony here, where he was well-known. He had lived twenty-five years in Mexico, never having been molested before. His brother, Vincenzo Visconti, sent the following telegram to the Italian ambassador in Washington:

"I am sorry to notify your excellency that my brother, Enrico Visconti, an Italian citizen has been murdered on his ranch in the State of Chihuahua, Mexico, by revolutionary soldiers. I beg your excellency to protest to the State Department against this outrage of crime, which is like many others committed daily on foreigners in that country."

Visconti said that his telegram would be followed by a joint protest to Secretary Lansing by the leading Italians here.

"I have a large number of relatives in Mexico," he said, "and there is not one of them who has not been held to ranson or otherwise maltreated. Some of them I have been unable to get in touch with at all and do not know whether they are dead or alive."

"We heard more about the tragedy from a neighboring rancher of my uncle's, a Mr. Ross, who came to El Paso to tell my father more about what happened. Mr. Ross was at my uncle's ranch at the time. He said that my uncle asked Villa to let him go to Mexico City to send a telegram to my father asking that he send money for ransom. Villa said it was all right, but when my uncle started to leave Villa took out his pistol and shot him seven times in the back.

"After Villa and his men left the ranch, Mr. Ross buried my uncle, piling rocks over the grave. Then he and the other ranchers went back up into the mountains as they were very afraid that Villa would return. They were all afraid of him, with good reason. Mr. Ross returned to Encinillas a few days later. There he found that the rocks over my uncle's grave had been scattered and animals, most likely coyotes, had dragged out the body and even eaten one of the legs. Mr. Ross reburied my uncle, and this time made it impossible for the grave to be disturbed. My uncle was a good man and had been loved by everyone.

"There was another horrible incident of the revolution that affected us. That was the Cumbre Tunnel disaster in February, 1914. My husband's cousin, Pedro Abel, and his wife and little boy were on that train that was trapped and burned in the tunnel. We had all thought that their bodies were lost to us."

The *El Paso Herald* of February 10, 1914, reported:

"That the terrific heat in Cumbre tunnel destroyed all the bodies of the passengers upon the North Western train wrecked and burned in the tunnel last Wednesday evening is the theory of W. S. McLaughlin, one of the rescuers. He does not believe that any more bodies will be recovered, but if all were not completely burned, he says it will be days before the debris can be dug away."

In 1935 this newspaper item appeared:

El Paso friends were advised today that the bodies of Mr. and Mrs. Pedro Abel and their 4-year-old son, Raúl, have been buried in a Chihuahua City cemetery, 21 years after they died.

It was in the days of bitter strife between Pancho Villa and Don Venustiano Carranza, that Mr. and Mrs. Abel and their son, a wealthy and prominent French family of Chihuahua, were victims, with 300 other passengers, of an attack by Mexican rebels who set fire to the train in which they traveled near Cumbre, Chihuahua, March 4, 1914 [wrong date], 160 miles southwest of Juárez.

The rebel troops halted the train inside a tunnel near Cumbre, setting fire to it, their objective being to exterminate political enemies.

The rebels, to shut off all means of escape, set fire to the tunnel exits, making the underground passage a blazing inferno.

Inside the victims suffocated or burned to death.

Only a few survived.

A number of bodies were recovered, and buried. Some never were found.

Mrs. Abel was the sister of Don León Johanis, prominent Chihuahua City merchant, who yesterday buried the bodies of the trio in a Chihuahua City Cemetery.

León Johanis' daughter, now Mrs. Matilde Johanis de Guajardo of Chihuahua, made a business trip to the railway express warehouse of the Mexico Northwestern Railroad in Pearson, Chihuahua, a few days ago, and made the gruesome discovery of the bodies.

The Johanis family and friends believed Mr. and Mrs. Abel and their son had perished in the fire, and that their bodies had never been found.

But Mrs. Guajardo's visit to the warehouse unraveled a 21-year-old mystery. At the station warehouse she asked an employe about the "three boxes in that corner."

"They are the bodies of three gringos who died in the fire of Cumbre 21 years ago," responded the man.

Mrs. Guajardo's curiosity aroused, she walked to the three boxes, and looked at the tags, which to her horror, identified the dead persons as her aunt, uncle and little cousin.

Since a little girl she had heard of the tragic deaths of her uncle and his family in the Cumbres fire, but she could not believe that those were the bodies of Mr. and Mrs. Abel.

Immediately Mrs. Guajardo advised her father at Ascensión, District of Galeana, Chihuahua, who went to Pearson.

The coffins were opened and after an examination of the three bodies Mr. Johanis made formal identifications of the bodies of those of his sister, his brother-in-law and their son.

The bodies were taken to Chihuahua City for burial.

"There are other memories I have of Pancho Villa. You would have thought he'd have felt more friendly toward the family. My cousin was godmother to Villa and his wife Luz's baby, a little girl who died very young.

"Pancho always had an eye for the girls and women. I remember once he sent two soldiers to escort my sister and me to a dance. Our family was warned in time and kept us hidden until the soldiers left the house.

"I knew one of his last wives, Austreberta, slightly. She was a very pretty woman. Villa met her when she was a seamstress for Luz and used to come to their house to sew. For a time Austreberta was at the Hidalgo Hotel in Parral. She and Pancho had two sons, one called Panchito.

"My family was finally all forced to give up their holdings and leave Mexico, all that is, excepting Archie who still lives in Parral. Our homes, our possessions, some of our very lives were lost because of Pancho Villa and the revolutionists."

14

Kate Taylor

Mrs. Taylor's family lived for eighteen years in Chihuahua City and were for a time neighbors to Villa's family when he was married to his first wife, Juana.

"It was during Villa's reign of Chihuahua in the fall of 1913 and early 1914. He had taken the city from General Mercado and was in control of the whole State of Chihuahua at that time. He and Juana and their daughters moved into a house, Quinta Prieto, which angled across from our home.

"There was roof-tall shrubbery which stayed green all year around, and the patio was filled with other flowers and wall-covering vines, and had a pool flanked with stepping stones. We liked Juana. She was petite and pretty. Her little girls were dark-eyed and favored her. General Villa awed us. He wasn't so tall, but was very broad-shouldered. His mustache was black though his hair was a brownish-red, as I remember.

"Mrs. Villa was such a good neighbor that when she was delivered large blocks of ice she would have the wagon driver bring a like amount to my mother. Ice in those days was a great luxury. She also gave us hard-to-get fresh fruits and vegetables. There were bananas and grapefruits and oranges, and I especially remember the large, luscious strawberries. Another of Mrs. Villa's kindnesses was to have the water-sprinkling wagon wet down our street every day when it sprinkled in front of the Villa house. In those days the city streets weren't paved, at least in the residential section and the dust was very bad. I remember we had lovely roses and many other kinds of flowers in our patio, and lovely shrubbery around the front.

"Our father, Max Fischbein, and our uncle, his brother, Louis, had tailor shops in Chihuahua City and Parral where we lived when I was five years old. Our stores always carried fine cloth and quality brands of clothing. When Villa took Chihuahua City he allowed his men to ransack the stores. He also extracted 'taxes' from all the merchants. If they didn't bring their contributions willingly he sent soldiers around to collect with force. Our father and Uncle Louis did business in Chihuahua and with the many large mining camps around the city.

"One of the most exciting days of my childhood was the day that great wagons began moving the Villa possessions from their big house. Our mother told us that General Villa was leaving town and taking his family to a safer place. Federal troops were moving toward the city and a battle was expected. Villa was retreating without any resistance.

"Mother gave me a pretty, ribbon-tied package and asked me to take it to Juana Villa, a present to her for her many kindnesses to our famliy. It was expensive perfume that father and Uncle Louis sold in their store. I was pleased at mother's thoughtfulness because I liked Juana Villa and the two girls. I dashed over to the Villa house, taking in the activities of the workmen-soldiers as they packed the big wagons with household furniture. There was no one in the patio, not even the girls. I was standing there hesitating about what to do when General Villa came striding into the patio. He stopped when he saw me. I was so frightened of him that I could hardly speak. I thrust the package into his big hand and mumbled, 'This is for Juana.' Then I fled, out of the patio and for home. I never saw the girls again or their pretty, dainty mother."

15

Emma Powers

Mrs. Powers and her husband, Charles, first moved to Mexico in 1893. At the start of the Revolution, Mr. Powers was with the Kansas City, Mexico and Orient Railroad in Chihuahua City. They moved to Columbus, New Mexico in 1915.

"I was riding my beautiful horse, Billy, in Chihuahua City, at the *paseo* when Pancho was riding there too, and he noticed us. Villa was riding a fine new thoroughbred he had just bought in the United States. He was very proud of his horses and always got the best he could, by many different means, I'm sure. Anyhow, he was showing off this horse and stopped to ask me how I liked him. Of course I told him he had a fine horse, but my Billy was faster.

"Pancho was surprised. He stared at me and the watchers along the road suddenly became very quiet. I wondered if I'd been too impulsive again, as my husband was always telling me. I looked right back at Pancho Villa.

"A big smile broke out on his broad face. 'All right, Señora,' he said, 'we'll see about that right now. You want a race we shall have a race.'

"Well, I surely couldn't back down then. Before I realized what was happening Villa shouted some orders and the boulevard, really a dusty road, cleared off. Out of the corner of my eye I could see people running to see the show. I leaned forward and patted Billy's neck. I knew he couldn't fail me. And he didn't.

"Billy streaked down that road as though his pride was at stake as well as mine. For a bit we were neck and neck with Pancho's mount, then as we neared the end of our half-mile course Billy pulled ahead. We had won. As we came to a halt there was a silence all around us.

"I turned to look at Villa. He was staring at me again. Then he swept his sombrero from his head and yelled, 'The lady wins!' He looked around. 'Give her some applause!' Immediately the hand clapping and bravos broke out.

"I nodded to Villa and rode over to where I saw my husband, Charlie, standing. 'Mottsie,' Charlie said—using his nickname for me—'You are a fool for luck. Don't ever scare me that way again!' I gave him a rather shaky smile. I didn't want to admit that I was trembling now that the incident was over.

"Right after this the revolution began spreading and became a real menace. At first the rebels and then the Federals would seem to be the victors. We and other Americans in Chihuahua tried to remain neutral. For a time it seemed that we could.

"Charlie had to be out on his job much of the time, as the railroads were having trouble with both factions. I was often alone, but I was never really afraid. One time I had a frightening experience while on the train on the way to Madera to join Charlie.

"A bunch of rebels stopped the train and were ransacking the freight cars up ahead. I was looking out the window, in fact craning my neck to see better when someone shouted at me to keep my head down or I'd get it shot off. When I turned around I saw that all the other passengers were crouched on the floor, some even under the seats. I joined them.

"I'll never forget another time I was on a train that had just come from Juárez, filled with federal soldiers. Villa and his men stopped the train. They made all the federals get out and lined them up. While we watched in horror the Villistas began shooting the captured, helpless men, one after another. I tried not to look but for a few minutes I was just frozen and couldn't hide my eyes. Just as a Villista raised his gun to kill one Federal officer, Villa himself came up and stopped him. I let out my breath in relief.

"I shouldn't have. Villa said something, and the executioner stepped back. Then Pancho Villa, *General* Villa, lifted his own gun and nearly shot the officer's head off. I almost fainted. I heard that more than a hundred Federal soldiers were murdered there that day.

"I had several experiences with my horses being stolen. I was alone at our place in Chihuahua City one time when I found that a rebel band had stolen my favorite horse, Jerry, during the night. I couldn't wait for Charlie to come home to help me, because if I didn't find Jerry and get him back right away I'd never see him again. I went right away to the nearest livery stable, hired a rig and had the owner drive me to the rebels' camp at Aldama, about sixteen miles east of town. He was frightened and didn't want to make the trip, but I was so insistent that he had to take me.

"I found the camp of the Villistas, with the officers eating at a table under the trees. I recognized the captain in charge. I went straight to him and told him that I wanted my horse back right then.

"He was startled, and I could see him wondering what to do. Maybe he remembered seeing me race with Pancho Villa, and wasn't sure how his commander wanted him to act in this situation. Finally he said that he didn't have any saddle for me. I told him that I had a saddle at home and didn't need one now. Then he decided to have a little fun out of me. He said if I could pick out my horse, straddle him and ride away from there bareback I could take him.

"I didn't even answer. I walked over to the corral where there were lots of horses milling around. I spotted my Jerry right away. He stood out among those other poor nags like the star he was. I called his name and whistled. Jerry came right to the fence, whinnying and stamping. That captain couldn't do anything else but have Jerry let out. Believe me, I was on Jerry's back and riding away before the surprised looking officer could change his mind. Back of me I could hear the livery stable rig pounding along, the driver doubtless anxious to be safely away.

"We were living in Madera where Charlie was agent and telegrapher for the railroad when Villa took over the town. He commandeered a train that had just drawn into the station and put soldiers in the engineer's cab to direct the engineer and fireman. He also ordered Charlie and his relief telegrapher on board.

"Fortunately I saw what was happening. Just as Pancho himself was climbing onto the train and shouting orders for it to pull out I got to the station. I called to Villa and breathlessly demanded to be taken along.

"Villa looked down at me. He said, 'No, no señora, it is not necessary for you to go. I will not harm your husband.'

"And I cried, 'I know you won't! But where he goes I go too!'

"I made a grab for the handrail of the steps and caught it just as the train began to move. There was nothing for Villa to do except let me go along. He couldn't very well throw me off but he looked as though he would like to. I was taken to the coach where my husband and his helper sat.

"Villa had us taken to Chihuahua City where he imprisoned, or rather had held, all the American railroad officials and some workers from Madera, and even some mining men, in the Phillips House. That was a hotel ordinarily patronized by Americans. He let the American women go, right away, but held the men for six days.

"As soon as I was free I demanded to see Villa. I wanted

to try to get him to release the Americans. I was told that he was at his headquarters near the depot. I was also told that Villa would shoot me on sight if I bothered him, since he wasn't feeling at all kindly towards gringos. That didn't stop me. I hired a hack and had the driver take me to Villa. The driver protested all the way that General Villa was too busy to see me.

"I found Villa busy all right. I witnessed a scene that I'll never be able to forget. Villa was in the middle of a group of soldiers on the depot platform. As I approached I saw that he was glaring down at a poor wretch, an important man who I knew had been undersecretary to the Governor. He was now on his knees, begging not to be sent into exile. He didn't want to leave his family behind in Chihuahua City.

" 'You want to stay here?' Villa demanded. He looked down at the man at his feet and I never saw such a cruel, almost gloating expression on a human being's face. I hope never to see the like again. 'Bueno,' Villa said. 'You will stay in Chihuahua.' Even while the poor man's face began to show hope Villa pulled out one of the big revolvers he carried and emptied it into the prisoner.

"I backed away. But when Villa went into a nearby building with his men I gritted my teeth and followed. I did manage to speak to him, and when I left he had agreed to let the Americans leave Chihuahua City under safe conduct and an escort to the border. However, he said we could take nothing with us. He seemed in a hurry and I didn't linger. As I left I thought that this vengeful man was far different from the genial Pancho I had raced one day.

"When I got back to the Phillips House I learned that Obregón was reported entering the city with a large force and that Pancho was getting ready to clear out. Perhaps that was why he was so willing to let us go. At any rate, our people were soon released.

"I often wonder why I had such success in my encounters

with Pancho Villa. I have come to the conclusion that the man was afraid of American women. He simply didn't understand them. And, also, I always heard that he respected anyone who stood up to him.

"At any rate that was the end of our life in Mexico. I had to sell my beloved Jerry for $100 or let him be taken for nothing, and I cried as I parted with him.

"We went to El Paso, but didn't stay there long. Charlie was contacted there by a Captain Van Ghoik of Army intelligence, with the result that we were sent here to Columbus. This was shortly before the Villista raid in 1916. Charlie operated as head of intelligence for the government for this entire area, with two operators under him. That of course was not known at the time. Buck Chadborn, a rancher and deputy sheriff, and Dick Rodríguez, a Columbus man, worked with my husband.

"Every night Charlie would ride along the international line, searching for some signs of entry or activity of either rebels or federals. One night while Charlie was out on this mission the telegraph operator for the intelligence section, a young sergeant, came to our door. It was very late and it gave me a fright because I thought right away that something had happened to my husband.

"It turned out that he had two telegrams that he thought Charlie should know about. One was from General Pershing, down in Mexico leading the Punitive Expedition, stating that he had Villa cornered and could capture him in twelve hours. The other telegram was from President Wilson telling Pershing to stop the campaign and pull back from Mexico. No wonder the young sergeant looked bewildered.

"I'll never understand it as long as I live. Here it was President Wilson who made Villa turn against the United States in the beginning by recognizing Carranza and letting him transport troops across our country, and on our railroads, which really led directly to Villa's downfall. And here was the same

President Wilson interfering with General Pershing when he practically had Villa captured!

"I have my personal opinion about what happened. I think Villa bought his way out of that mess. I told that writer, Westbrook Pegler, about it when he was down here interviewing people in Columbus. I told him about the Villa colonel I knew who later told me that he personally carried a large sum of money to a representative of the United States Government. This same colonel told me that there were American army officers with Villa all the time, serving as advisors. Pegler never said a word about that in his story, and *that* would have been real information. Well, that is all in the past, but there was something funny going on about that campaign from the beginning.

"Anyhow, when Pershing pulled out of Mexico, in February, 1917, a lot of Mexicans wanting to get out of their country came along. And this is where I had quite an experience. Captain Van Ghoik came to me and offered me a job at five dollars a day to supervise the delousing of these aliens. This took place at a little wooden shack at the port of entry where the refugees waited. I watched awhile and then I took over the scrubbing myself. It wasn't being half done and I couldn't bear to think of those lice crawling around and maybe getting into my home. When the captain saw what I was doing he paid me ten dollars a day, and believe me I earned it.

"After the troops left Columbus it got very dull here. Of course Charlie's intelligence work was over. We decided to open a drug store as Charlie was a college trained pharmacist before we were married and before he became interested in mining in Mexico.

"Charlie ran the drug store till he died in 1930. Then I continued to live in the back and to operate the business. Finally I closed the store part and now just live in the back of the building. Columbus is my home and always will be."

16

Catherine Louise Cyalthea Dunn

Miss Dunn moved to Ft. Davis, Texas, with her hus-band, Dr. I. J. Bush, in 1896. Dr. Bush served Villa as his Surgeon General. Miss Dunn had a career of teaching music in El Paso that spanned over sixty years.

"After two years at Ft. Davis we came to El Paso. Then we went back to Ft. Davis. There were many bears wandering around town. They had been made pets by the soldiers and then abandoned when the army left. The poor animals became regular pests.

"I remember that several hundred outlaws were camped not far from town. They would get supplies from Ft. Davis. They seemed to be all Mexicans, but their leader was an American. He claimed to be from a fine family in the United States. Anyhow, he came into town for food and medicine for his followers. He came to Dr. Bush and said that many of his men were sick and dying and some of them wounded. He asked Dr. Bush to help them. I went with the doctor, but I couldn't stay. The conditions were terrible. The doctor remained at the camp a week and did a lot of good work. We learned that this outlaw band was connected with Pancho Villa's and later joined him near Casas Grandes. I always thought that was when Villa heard about my husband."

"The first time that Villa sent for my husband and I accompanied him I was simply scared to death. Villa had heard that there was an American doctor at Doctor Arroyo. He sent a couple of his men after my husband. We went a long way, east of Casas Grandes. Finally we reached a stream. We had to cross it to reach Villa's camp. The only safe crossing was over a narrow ford. We got to one side and went down into quicksand. It was a very frightening sensation. Villa himself was waiting across the river. He jumped into the water with a couple of his men and got us out.

"We stayed at his camp till late that night and the doctor treated the sick and wounded. There were over three hundred guerrilla soldiers in camp. Pancho Villa begged us to stay longer, but we took our two men servants and left. I didn't draw a free breath till we were miles away.

"We traveled half the night and finally reached one of Colonel Greene's camps. We stayed over night. I remember there were two Chinese cooks. It was very luxurious compared to the camp we had just left."

A test of Miss Dunn's adaptability came on one of her excursions with her husband into the mountains of Mexico. It was to the south of Casas Grandes and over very rugged country. They traveled a route that only sure-footed mules could follow. Mostly they had to go single file along the narrow trail which was washed out in spots. Many places they could see far down on the jagged rocks below the bones of a horse or mule that had lost its footing.

After a night and two days on the trail they reached the crest of the mountain. Here they were amazed to see a rock and log house set back from the trail. There were shrubs, roses blooming, and other flowers in a real garden. They rode up to the door.

They were greeted by a *mozo* who said his master was away but he would want them made welcome. They needed no urging. Miss Dunn fell out of the saddle and was helped into a living room that looked to her like something remembered from dreams of civilization. Around the walls were shelves displaying Indian pottery and idols. The wide pine boards of the floor were covered by Mexican and Indian rugs. There was a bearskin rug in front of the fireplace and a mahogany piano.

After she had bathed leisurely, rested, and dined, Miss Dunn sat down at the piano. She played until she could no longer hold her head up. They stayed the night. After breakfast they were preparing to leave when their host arrived. Beaming his pleasure at their presence he approached his guests with outstretched hand.

Miss Dunn, the born and bred lady of the "Old South," stood rooted to the ground. The man whose hospitality they'd so enjoyed was a Negro. Furthermore she recognized him. He was Henry O. Flipper, well-known as the first Negro graduate of West Point. Flipper's presence at West Point had caused Miss Dunn's brother, Beverly, endless anguish while both were attending the school. After his graduation Flipper had been stationed at Ft. Davis. There he had become involved in some trouble with the military and had been discharged. It was rumored that he had then gone down into Mexico. Later it was reported that Flipper was working for Colonel William G. Greene as consultant for Greene's mining interests in Mexico.

Flipper continued to approach her, poised, smiling, hand extended.

Dr. Bush whispered to her to shake hands.

Almost fainting, praying that her brother would never know, Miss Dunn took a deep breath, held out her hand and managed a wavery smile.

"We heard rumors in the years to come," Miss Dunn says, "that Flipper was serving with Pancho Villa and his forces. However, in May 1916, Flipper wrote a firm denial of the story to a Washington, D.C. newspaper."

Soon after that episode Catherine went back to El Paso,

settling into the brick house on Myrtle Avenue. She was trying to bring classical music to honkey-tonk loving citizens when the Revolution got hot along the border. Dr. Bush established a clinic at Second and Campbell Streets. He often, while bullets bit into adobe walls around him, went across the international bridge to attend the casualties.

"My brother, C. P. Dunn, then owned a drugstore where the gas company now is," recalls Miss Dunn. "There was a dance hall upstairs. It was rather a rough place. My brother furnished the medicines for the doctor's clinic and Villa's outfit. However, my brother didn't like helping Villa or the Insurrectos and he quit the drugstore business.

"The doctor had his office in the Caples Building and it happened that on the fifth floor of the same building a junta of the revolutionists was established. Leaders of Mexico and citizens of the United States were just starting to take seriously the importance of the Madero revolt against President Diaz of Mexico. My husband was always very sympathetic to the underdog, and he found himself more and more interested in the plans of the so-called dreamers who dared to plot the overthrow of Díaz' long dictatorship. The doctor would come home quoting Abraham González who he'd known well in Mexico and who seemed to be the head of the activities in El Paso.

"I remember the occasion early in 1911 when González came to our home at daylight one morning in quite a state. He told us that he had just received an urgent message from Pascual Orozco, a leader of the gathering Insurrectos. Orozco was then at Samalayuca, twenty-five miles south of Juárez. There had been a battle with Federals near there a few days previously. Orozco needed a doctor to go to the camp and treat the wounded.

"Of course my husband was eager to go. He took another doctor with him and they hurried to the international border. Across the bridge they were taken to the office of Lieutenant

Colonel Tamborel of the Federals defending Juárez. Although Tamborel cursed the bandits, as he called the revolutionists, in both Spanish and English, he granted passports to the American doctors. However, he requested that they treat one of his wounded soldiers first.

"In Orozco's camp they had some dangerous experiences. It was too much for the tenderfoot doctor who accompanied my husband. He stood two days of it and then came back to El Paso. A train loaded with dynamite had been blown up, water was short, and there was almost no equipment for the doctors to work with. Wounded and dying were everywhere. My husband did manage to send me a note telling me to watch for an attack on Juárez just before daylight.

"However the battle took place instead at Bauche, a railroad station south of Juárez. The doctor told me later how he fastened the staff of a Red Cross flag to the top of a post in front of the section house he used as a dressing station. He also carried a Red Cross flag as he went between the lines but it didn't serve as much protection. He saw a bullet go through Orozco's canteen as Orozco directed the action. At the end of the day the doctor himself sported a bullet hole in the lapel of his overcoat. He often spoke of the many foolhardy El Paso citizens who drove down to Bauche to watch the fighting. They acted as though the bloody battle were only an exciting spectacle staged for their entertainment, while they themselves remained mysteriously immune to gunfire. Meantime supplies of water, food, and medicines were almost completely exhausted.

"Increasing numbers of desperate women, *soldaderas* and camp followers of the Federal defenders, gathered around the doctor's dressing station seeking help. Finally the doctor fastened a push car to a handcar with wire and topped the push car with a platform made of crossties. He loaded the poor *soldaderas* on this platform. Many of these women were accompanied by their children and some of them were wounded. The doctor took them all into Juárez where he left them with Federal authorities. Then he came home on the streetcar. He was exhausted and crawling with lice. I hoped he had had his fill of adventure for some time.

"I should have known better. The next morning President Madero, staying in the home of one of the members of the junta, sent for my husband. Of course he was eager to go. He came home and told me that Madero had offered him a commission as chief surgeon of his army with rank of Colonel. Naturally he accepted. His full rank was Coronel del Cuerpo Médico Militar del Ejercito Libertador. He was proud as a peacock.

"From then on I practically lost my husband to the cause of the Revolution. His hospital and clinic were always filled with wounded soldiers and civilians from Mexico.

"And then there was the famous incident of the McGinty cannon.

"This old brass, muzzle-loading gun was one used in the Civil War. Buried near Val Verde, New Mexico, by General Baylor of the Confederates, it and others had been dug up by Major Teel years later. The major brought two of the old cannons to El Paso. The McGinty Club came into possession of one which they proudly used on special occasions. When the McGinty Club ceased to exist, the Pioneer Club inherited the cannon and it was placed in City Hall Plaza.

"Anyhow, my husband—the adventurer—with other members of the junta, on a night in April, 1911, kidnapped that cannon from the very center of El Paso. With much secret plotting and several weeks' devious actions they actually managed to get the cannon and a ton of ammunition across the Río Grande and into the hands of the Insurrectos. At ten o'clock one evening our telephone rang. The doctor answered, I thought, with unusual speed. He smiled smugly as he replaced the receiver. When I asked him what the message was that gave him such satisfaction he grinned at me and said,

'The message was only that the baby is better.' Then he told me that that was code meaning that the cannon was safely delivered to the revolutionists in Mexico. I never knew the details of that exploit. I had a feeling it was better that I didn't know. I do know that the McGinty cannon served the Insurrectos well at Ojinaga. Afterward the gun was brought back to Juárez where it was placed on exhibition. Then with the whole Mexican garrison as guard of honor the cannon was triumphantly escorted across the international bridge and restored to its old post in the City Hall Plaza. My husband and the other members of the Junta who stole the cannon were proud members of the parade.

"The doctor knew most of the flamboyant company of adventurers, American soldiers of fortune, who joined the revolution. They were truly his kind, daredevils all. As a doctor he had to pass on the qualifications of many of them.

"I will never forget the horror and suffering in Juárez after that three-day battle of May, 1911. Dead, wounded and sick were everywhere. The Federals had brought typhus from southern Mexico and the disease spread. There was no sanitation then in Juárez. Wounded were dying from thirst and starvation as well as lack of care. The people of El Paso tried to help. I recall Mrs. Charles DeGroff and Mrs. Francisco Madero and many others furnishing quantities of food and medicine, blankets and bandages. We took carloads of needed supplies to the hospital. Two hotels in Juárez were commandeered to accommodate wounded and ill. Of course my husband worked day and night. He seemed to be everywhere at once—everywhere but at home. He and others like him truly did a wonderful work.

"During the years that followed my husband was often involved in the revolutionary battles in Mexico. He always had the adventurous spirit. I had a bit of that spirit also. I recall that some of my women friends and I were very curious about the cockfights that were then popular in El Paso and that the men found so fascinating. Though we begged to attend just once, witnessing the sport was always forbidden to us.

"However, one time several of us were determined to see a cockfight and we did. When we were refused admittance at the gate we turned away. However we made our way around to the back of the lot. There we managed to look under the high board fence and so satisfied our curiosity. I wasn't surprised to see my husband among the spectators. Right beside him was a swarthy Mexican who I recognized immediately as Pancho Villa. The guerrilla leader was at that time out of favor in Mexico and hiding out in El Paso. Villa placed a rooster in the ring, confronting another. Both cocks had blades fastened on their spurs. The roosters danced and struck at each other's throats. It was bloody and cruel beyond description. The men shouted and cheered on their favorites, so absorbed in the wicked sport that they never realized that we were also watching. We left in disgust. Believe me, one experience of that kind was enough for me and my friends. The doctor told me later that Villa's cock killed three others that day.

"Villa was a very forceful person, and a great contrast to my fair-skinned, brown-haired, six-foot five-inch, blue-eyed husband. The two men greatly respected each other and exchanged enthusiastic embrazos when meeting. Villa was always courteous to me. He paid me the great compliment of saying that I was *muy simpatica*. He loved music. One of his daughters was a beauty and a lady. She was taken up by New York society, we heard. A modest, retiring young woman, she refused to participate when invited to take part in a parade here. The only member of Villa's family that I knew even slightly was his brother, Hipólito. I once saw Juana, who was, I understood, his first wife. Pancho Villa was a strange, complex man, and the doctor and I often wondered what heights he might have attained had he been born into different circumstances."

Americans in El Paso watching Mexican Insurectos from across the Rio Grande

The swinging bridge over the Rio Grande from El Paso

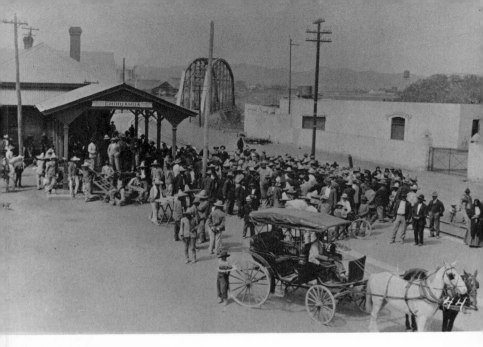

Chihuahua depot (Photo courtesy El Paso Public Library)

Villa in uniform (Photo courtesy Luz Corral de Villa)

Explosion at the Cumbre Tunnel, February 1914

General Francisco Castro and family leaving Ft. Bliss, May 3, 1914, after three months internment following the Ojinaga battle. Left to right: Mariano, Mrs. Herlinda De Castro, Jesus, General Castro, Francisco (Photo courtesy Mariano Castro)

Meeting between General Pershing and Villa at the Santa Fe Street International Bridge, El Paso, August 1914. (1) General Alvaro Obregon, (2) Villa, (3) General John J. Pershing, (4) First Lieutenant James L. Collins, aide to Pershing (Collins was the father of Colonel Michael Collins, the moon astronaut)

Soldadera with the rebels

Villa and wife Luz at the time
she was living in El Paso

One of Villa's troop trains

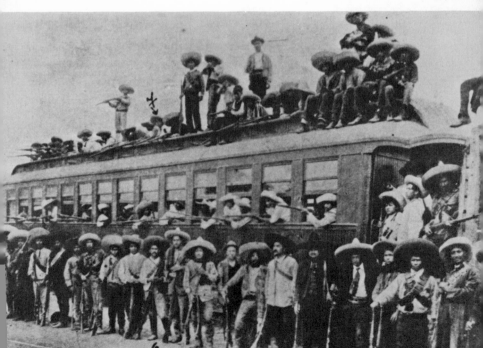

Villistas killed in Columbus raid

Arthur McKinney

Ruins of the two-story Commercial Hotel
in Columbus, New Mexico following the raid

Villa, his staff and others after the signing of the peace treaty in August 1920 at Tlahualilo. Miguel Trillo is to Villa's left

Soledad Séañez de Villa today painting a portait of Villa

olonel Selah (Tommy) Tomp-
ins, of the Seventh Cavalry
Photo courtesy M. G. Mc-
inney)

Villa en su Hacienda de Canutillo, Dgo. Junio 17-1921.

Foto "América"

Villa at his retirement ranch, June 1921

Villa's funeral procession in Parral, July 23, 1923

17

Dr. R. H. Ellis

Dr. Ellis, of El Paso, served simultaneously as medical chief-of-staff under Villa and personal observer for President Wilson during the years of the Mexican Revolution.

"Francisco Villa was held responsible for many of the widely publicized raids and incidents of violence against foreigners, especially United States citizens, when he was not to blame. Three such cases were the Benton killing, the Santa Ysabela massacre, and the Columbus raid.

"Untrained in diplomacy Francisco Villa was a natural target for undercover plots, especially those of Germany who was trying to cause trouble between Mexico and the United States in order to keep the United States too busy to enter the European War and to cover Germany's own secret plans to conquer North and South America, also to destroy the Monroe Doctrine which neither Germany nor Japan recognized.

"This account is concerned with exposing the widespread and accepted propaganda which made General Francisco Villa the scapegoat, the villain of the revolution, before the world. Pancho Villa was a specific person who could be pictured as a bogeyman, a treacherous savage for whose barbarous acts the Mexican government headed by Carranza would not be blamed. That the world largely accepted this image was the result of the Carranza-German propaganda campaign whose magnitude was never truly known by the American public.

"Prior to 1910 Venustiano Carranza, Governor of the State of Coahuila under the Díaz regime, was a protégé of the German Kaiser William II, and nurtured plans to himself become a dictator of Mexico. His insatiable interest in the affiliation of Germanized Carranzistas was increasingly noticeable from 1910 to 1920. He had voted in the Federal Congress, under Díaz, to adopt the 'international' German language for Mexico.

"Japan participated in the early plans. Before the downfall of President Madero, Carranza and Huerta entered into a compact with the German Imperial Minister Von Eckhardt in November, 1912, in which every island in the Pacific Ocean was to be given to Japan as submarine bases, and Japan was to have a naval base at Magdalena Bay, after the purpose of the Monroe Doctrine was defeated.

"Carranza was the owner of lands and mines worth appromately $35,000,000. As a senator from the State of Coahuila under Díaz, Carranza had the right to introduce reform bills in the Federal Congress, if he truly had the Mexican people's interests at heart. Instead he paid to the official newspaper's chief editor, German-Mexican Francisco Bulnes, $200 a month to avoid publishing anything about the reforms bills and only to eulogize him, Carranza.

"In Washington, D.C, Carranza's son-in-law, Elisio Arredondo, Mexican Ambassador-designate, zealously built up recognition for Carranza. He also paid newspapers to further the build-up. By 1914 Carranza became the sole mouthpiece of Mexico. He controlled the newspapers, mail, and cable offices. Only information he deemed beneficial to his cause was allowed to pass the censors and go out of the country. All news had to go through Bulnes' office in Mexico

City. American reporters had to get permission from Bulnes to send news back to the United States.

"The German propaganda machine in Mexico and the United States was extremely efficient, strongly anti-Villa and working to get President Wilson to recognize Carranza's de facto anarchy government. The plotters in their perfidy knew no bounds. True facts were hidden from metropolitan news offices. The world was kept in ignorance of the unspeakable horrors against foreigners in Mexico—Americans, Spanish, British, and French—and the persecution of religious orders committed by German-Mexican Carranzistas under orders given by Carranza and Obregón. These atrocities happened in the district controlled by Carranza and were blamed on Villistas who were not even in that region.

"Because of the total censorship of news coming out of Mexico, ably backed by the Bulnes brothers, there can be no authentic information for the historian. In Mexico the news was controlled and created by Carranza and by Dr. Herman Ridder, a professional propagandist. In Washington it came from the German Ambassador, Count Von Bernstorff, via the information service yellow sheet newspaper published by Dr. Bernhard Dernburg at the M. Bulnes Book Store, 810 Broadway, New York City, sold on the streets of New York and financed by Bernstorff. In 1916 Francisco Bulnes wrote a propaganda book, *"The Whole Truth About Mexico,"* subtitled, *"President Wilson's Responsibility."* This book was published by Mario Bulnes and later recalled from circulation.

"Two American journalists, John Reed, who appeared in the *Saturday Evening Post,* and Jim Roberts, both traitors to their country, working with Carranza, wrote slanted stories. Reed later went to Russia where he died. Roberts went to England to report on the damage Germany's Big Bertha's shells were doing there, was imprisoned and died in a British jail.

"The anti-Villa propaganda was extremely effective and artistically presented. Colorful stories picturing the guerrilla's barbarous deeds were tailored to affect the people to whom they were directed. It was said that some of the most lurid stories were taken by Herman Ridder directly from sixteenth century literature. Luis Guzmán, a Carranzista, also put out false stories about Villa. They had their desired result, as the world believed that Francisco Villa was one of the most heinous villains ever to give his country a bad name.

"As a fact, the Carranza administration, headed by Carranza and his brother, Jesús, was the most corrupt in the history of Mexico. It was necessary for foreign citizens seeking protection from looting and destruction of their property to hide under the bloody flag of Germany. General Calles, when he became disillusioned, stated, 'The only thing that Carranza has done is to excite and exploit for his own benefit, the patriotism of the Mexican generals, to use this force in his ruinous and selfish purpose, of maintaining himself in power at all cost, without regards to the international perils, to which he was exposing the nation.'

"The German involvement in Mexico and its threat to the United States were of a magnitude much greater than most Americans ever realized. Germany had publicly declared it did not recognize the Monroe Doctrine. It was Germany's plan to get the United States involved as an enemy with its neighbor, Mexico, so that the United States could not afford to go to war with Germany no matter how great the provocation. In New York the Mexico North Western Railway office was taken over by Carrancistas and became the headquarters for the German active agents.

"All these facts, obtained by close work with the Mexico revolutionary leaders and the British Naval Intelligence operating in Mexico, are substantiated by the records in a confidential file in Washington. The State Department removed this file exposing the treachery of another government,

Germany, for security reasons. It would now take an act of Congress to open its contents to the public.

"President Wilson, trying to get a true picture of the Mexican situation did send special envoys to Mexico, but his envoys were handicapped on account of never having been in that country and not speaking the language. They used interpreters instructed by Carranza. Wilson had no confidence in his vice-consuls and properly accredited Embassy. Many of those officials were recalled. In his correspondence there was no clue as to his motivation. He preferred obtaining information from his personal representative, Colonel Edward M. House, and me. However, President Wilson was not a confiding man, even to Colonel House who recorded his letters and day-by-day conversations with the president. These documents were also marked confidential by Congress.

"In Mexico City President Díaz had allowed Francisco Madero to publish his newspaper and make speeches against Díaz' continued rule of Mexico. However, in June 1910, Madero was jailed by Díaz' orders. Shortly afterward Madero was instructed to leave Mexico. That left Díaz still in office as President, supported by his same group of congressmen.

"Madero went to San Antonio, Texas. From there he issued his 'Plan of San Luis Potosi,' backdated to October 5, 1910 so that it would not be issued from the United States but from Mexico. Madero was named provisional president of Mexico, to serve until an election could be held.

"Among the Mexican leaders who consulted with him at Hotel Menger, San Antonio, where he stayed, was Venustiano Carranza who at that time asked to be appointed Secretary of War and Finance when Madero was elected president. Madero showed good judgment of character when he said flatly, 'I did not trust him.'

"Madero did trust Pancho Villa, when in March 1911, the guerrilla leader with his followers joined the gathering Madero forces. Villa joined in good faith, believing in Madero's proclamation to return the land to homesteaders, with full title, liberty, and opportunity for education and personal freedom for the Mexican people. Madero's trust was justified as Villa remained steadfastly loyal to Madero's ideals.

"As events proved, it was the wily Carranza who was treacherous, greedy, unscrupulous. A picture taken early in 1911 at Madero's headquarters across the river from El Paso shows a large group of revolutionary leaders, among them Carranza and Villa. Carranza even then was plotting Madero's downfall, using Huerta to further his plans.

"Even in November 1911, when Madero was officially elected President of Mexico, Carranza, with Huerta and Obregon, were setting in motion their plans for German-Mexican power in Mexico. By February 1913, Madero's doom was sealed. There followed in rapid succession the revolution, the bloody slaughter of the Ten Tragic Days, and Madero's forced resignation. On February 19, General Huerta was promptly proclaimed Provisional President. Madero and his vice-president, Pino Suárez, were brutally murdered on Februrary 22, 1913.

"On March 26, revolting against Huerta, Carranza named himself First Chief of the Constitutionalists and published the Plan of Guadalupe.

"When Villa, then working as a laborer at the smelter in El Paso, heard of Madero's assassination he returned to Mexico with nine men, leaving me, his doctor, to set up the port of entry and organize hospital aid. Working through the countryside he swiftly gathered an army of followers with the purpose of defeating Huerta. By late 1913 he had assumed command of his Division of the North, whose numbers increased steadily. General Francisco Villa then truly controlled the State of Chihuahua.

"In January, 1914, Carranza asked Villa to sign his Plan of Guadalupe, reminding him that Huerta, betrayer and murderer of President Madero, was their common enemy. He promised that there would be a general election to restore the Constitution of 1857, following which there would be the hoped for liberty and education, and the land returned to small landowners. The Plan was read to Villa. He signed his name in full trust.

"At the meeting with Carranza in Chihuahua City, Villa beat down his instinctive feeling about Carranza whom he had regarded as a 'reptile yellow belly.' He gave Carranza an enthusiastic *embrazo,* which was not returned. At that meeting Carranza constantly emphasized the differences between himself, a lawyer, governor, senator, and now First Chief, and Pancho Villa, the ignorant peon. However, believing it to be for the good of the people of Mexico, Villa swallowed his humiliation and dislike and addressed Carranza as 'My Chief.' Carranza, stroking his whiskers and shaking his finger, emphasized that he should be so addressed by all, including myself. Villa then introduced the members of his staff, among them Second Brigade Staff General Rosalía Hernández, guerrilla Yaqui, to Carranza.

"Carranza had signed a compact with the German Imperial Minister Von Eckhardt and Captain Franz Von Papen, Military Attaché from the Embassy of Count Von Bernstorff, Washington, D.C. Franz Von Papen was paymaster and supervisor of the army of active German agents in the United States, Canada, and South America, with 2,000 reservists and adherents, all of whom were to aid Carranza. They were to guard the Tampico oilfield for a pending German submarine supply base there. The whole purpose was the enlargement of the German empire. Carranza was determined to be Dictator of Mexico with the support of Germany and Japan.

"Carranza now presented the German, Maximilian Kloss, as field marshall over Villa. However Villa refused to allow his men to be commanded by anyone but his own staff.

"At that time I was Surgeon General with the Yaqui Independent Brigade headed by General Rosalía Hernández and was ordered by Carranza to go with him and to serve on his staff, in Communications. The country had been run solely on Carranza's reforms after Madero fell. There were no laws. Carranza disorganized all churches. Villa and I helped the nuns and priests to get out of the country as they were all exiled.

"The Plan of Guadalupe was a decree designed to further Carranza's campaign to become dictator of Mexico. It was Preconstitutional, without a cabinet, congressmen or court of laws. It stated that officials were not to obey any orders, only those given by First Chief Carranza. There were no laws, there were only Carranza reforms. One of the most far-reaching in its effects was the article of the Plan which gave Carranza the exclusive right to expel from the republic forthwith and without judicial process, any foreigner whose presence he might deem unwanted.

"From this article sprang the notorious 'Benton case' of February 1914, of which I witnessed. William S. Benton, known to his workers as 'the stormy Englishman,' had been for many years a rancher in Chihuahua. Under this article of the Plan of Guadalupe, Carranza moved to confiscate Benton's property. Benton, notoriously hot-headed, came to Villa's Juárez headquarters with his protest. Villa advised Benton to inform the British Vice-Consul. Villa had left his headquarters when Benton returned remarking that he was going to kill Villa. Instead Benton was killed under circumstances never satisfactorily publicized.

"The case had international repercussions, involving our State Department. Different versions of the Benton killing were given, but in line with the propaganda circulated, Villa emerged as the murderer. Carranza later rendered a report to the Washington British Embassy admitting that Villa was innocent of the act. But that report did not seem to reach the world which gasped in horror over the latest savage atrocity of Pancho Villa.

"Shortly after this episode Villa requested a meeting with General Hugh L. Scott, commanding officer of Ft. Bliss. Because he would be obliged to arrest Villa should he come over to the United States and government rules would not allow General Scott to cross the border, the two met one dark night in the middle of the international bridge. They sat in General Scott's car and talked for some two hours. General Scott was accompanied by his aide, Colonel Michie, and an orderly. Villa's guard waited at the end of the bridge. General Scott took the occasion to tell Villa that civilized people were horrified and repelled by the way Villa killed unarmed and wounded prisoners. General Villa was surprised that anyone would question his disposition of enemies.

"General Scott then gave him a publication written by the General Staff of the British Army dealing with the treatment of prisoners and conquered people, and explained what was regarded as the proper course of action. Villa took the paper, had it translated into Spanish, and passed it out to his troops. He seemed greatly impressed with the rules of civilized warfare, and from then on was guided by them, at least in part. At this meeting General Villa told General Scott about Carranza's pact with the Germans.

"When Carranza refused to call an election, promising to do so when his reforms were complete, Villa was disillusioned with him. Finally, when Carranza, long jealous of Villa's power, cut off supplies of coal and ammunition desperately needed by Villa's troops, Villa broke away and was in revolt against Carranza by September 1914.

"Nineteen fourteen was a year of increasing turbulence and growing threat of German agents working against the United States in our country itself and in Mexico. The incident of the United States Marines landing at Tampico in April, 1914, and the following trouble in Veracruz were actually the result of the Marines taking over a German submarine base, an innocent appearing fishing boat.

"Carranza was now openly friendly to and conniving with
the Germans. Besides Count Bernstorff of the German Em-
bassy and Captain Franz Von Papen, were Captain Kurt
Jahnke of the German Admiralty, Maximilian Kloss, Field
Marshall of the Constitutionalist Army, Baron Horst Von der
Goltz, sabateur Luther Witcke, whose code name was Luther
Wertz, organizer of raids, and Captain Franz Von Kleist
Rintelen of the German Navy Intelligence, organizer of United
States strikes and the I.W.W.

"In El Paso one of the German agents, Emma Goldman,
was arrested by the Justice Department while making a speech
in the downtown Plaza. She was deported, but John Reed and
Jim Roberts got away at that time. Billy Hayward, leader of
I.W.W.'s also escaped.

"One of the most audacious attempts at sabotage was
perpetrated in September, 1914, by German agents in the
United States. The incident was later fully described in a
magazine article by Horst Von der Goltz, alias Bridgeman
Taylor. It concerned the plotted dynamiting of the very important Welland Canal. This canal, twelve miles from Niagara
Falls, is one of Canada's greatest engineering projects and
forms a navigable waterway connecting Lake Erie and Lake
Ontario. It is a very important canal with large ships carrying
grain and other freight crossing it. It is regulated by locks
with one guard lock.

"According to Von der Goltz' statement on August 22,
1914, he, on six months' leave from his post as captain with
the Mexican Constitutionalist Army, was ordered to meet
Captain Von Papen, a jointly accredited Military Attaché of
the German Embassy in both Mexico and the United States at
the German agents' New York headquarters, the old Mexico
North Western Railway offices under control of German
military assistant director, Von Ezell. This narrator in capacity
of observer accompanied Von der Goltz and Luther Wertz,
and facilitated their entry into the United States at El Paso,
Texas.

"At this meeting was planned the sabotage that was known later as the Welland Canal Plot, a bold plan to blow up the locks of the canal, with the hoped for result that Canada would be forced to keep at home the large contingent of troops ready to sail for England, and also that the ships carrying grain and other foods to England would be destroyed.

"Horst Von der Goltz used a passport issued to him by the United States State Department, under the name of Bridgeman Henry Taylor. In New York Captain Von Papen gave him a check for $200 to pay the German sailors he had recruited to help carry out the mission. He bought explosives from Hans Tauscher, American representative of Krupps Arms, saying that it was to be used for mining in Mexico.

"In the middle of September, Von der Goltz and his four helpers took their explosives in suitcases to Buffalo where they registered at a hotel. As they prepared their sabotage work they were arrested and charged with plotting against the peace of the United States. Tauscher stated that he had no knowledge of the Welland Canal plot and had sold the dynamite in the belief that it was to be used for mining in Mexico. They were detained, with their arrest and trial kept secret.

"According to Von der Goltz, he was aware that he was shadowed by detectives and Secret Service agents from the time he arrived in New York at the headquarters in the appropriated Mexico Northern Western Railway offices, as it was well known that he was German. He claimed that he played the part of a noisy, bragging fool, loudly calling attention to himself because his maneuvers were only a blind, he acting the part of decoy to draw suspicion while the real plotters were Canadians never suspected of their pro-German activities.

"Horst Von der Goltz, on the way to Sweden, was taken off the boat at England, arrested, and imprisoned in England from November 1914 until January 30, 1916. The only charges that could be proved against him were those of being an alien enemy who had not registered as such, though Admiral

Hall and the British Intelligence department strongly suspected that he was a German spy. However, during that time Von der Goltz ran a successful bluff, claiming to be a Mexican officer, born in Guatemala of German parents, but not a German citizen, traveling on a false passport, as German names on passports were inconvenient.

"He steadfastly denied being a German spy taking pay from Germany and got away with it until in December 1915, President Wilson requested that the German government recall Captains Boy-Ed and Von Papen, its naval and military attachés in the United States. When the attachés' ship touched at Falmouth, England, Captain Von Papen's papers were seized. Among them was the check that Von Papen had made out to Horst Von der Goltz in the name of Bridgeman Taylor for $200 to pay the German sailors. The incriminating check was endorsed by Von der Goltz.

"With that indisputable evidence against him Von der Goltz had to confess that he was a German spy in the pay of the German government. In return for a promise that he would not be extradited or sent to any country where he was liable for punishment for political offenses, he signed a statement that admitted his connections with Captain Von Papen, and as little else as was possible implicating the German government. He was a witness at the Grand Jury proceedings in the United States in the following spring of 1917.

"The War Office was about to publish Von der Goltz' statement when the United States government asked that the whole story be kept secret pending the trial of two German consuls, one of whom was Krupp's agent in America, in which Von der Goltz was to be the principal witness. This was for fear that certain people implicated by the statement would take alarm and disappear before the trial. After the trial the statement was published in a White Paper by the American Government. This observer was subpoenaed as character witness at both trials, 1914 and 1917.

"Meanwhile in Mexico, German gold and German military science were backing Carranza in his campaign to become ruler of his country. The propaganda machine continually put out fresh atrocity stories about Pancho Villa, the savage bandit general whose activities were supposedly a constant series of thefts, rapes, and murders.

"In November, 1914, Villa met with Emiliano Zapata, the forceful Indian leader from the mountain state of Morelos. Zapata had one steadfast aim, to obtain the return of the land to the Indians. He and General Villa had much in common. Both remained constant to the ideals for which they fought so fiercely. I was present in Mexico City in December when Generals Zapata and Villa made a triumphant entry. As a joke only, Villa allowed himself to be photographed sitting in the presidential chair, flanked by General Zapata and General Urbina. When asked if he had ambitions to be president he replied that it would take a man of greater education and that he would stick to the military.

"By the end of 1914 the Mexican Revolution was causing danger and damage and great alarm among Americans on the border. At the border town of Naco, Sonora, hostilities were endangering citizens of Naco, Arizona. Villista General Maytorena had Generals Calles and Benjamin Hill backed up against the international line. On our side General Bliss was encamped with a force to protect American soil and citizens.

"The situation was crucial. Fifty-four Americans had been killed or wounded and Arizonans were talking of invading Mexico. At President Wilson's request, General Scott was sent to the border to 'drive those two armies away.' General Scott drew up an agreement calling for both armies to evacuate Naco, giving Calles the port of entry at Agua Prieta and Maytorena the port of Nogales. Calles and Hill gladly signed, but Maytorena balked. He claimed that more than 800 of his men had been killed and he wasn't going to ignore their sacrifice.

"Things were at a standstill when General Scott sent for Villa to meet him. Villa had said, earlier, 'There can never be another cause of friction on this border if you and I can get together, and I will come up from Mexico City any time you send for me.' Villa did not want to give the order to Maytorena to sign, and as General Scott says, 'We locked horns like two bull elk for two hours. Finally Villa gave in and agreed to make Maytorena sign.' In great relief, Scott shook hands with Villa, knowing, he says, 'as every man in that room knew, that Villa would carry out his promise once he had made it.'

"This friendly pact between General Villa and General Scott is recorded in a telegram (Congressional Records, House Document No. 1364, File No. 812,00/14176) as follows:

Special Agent Carothers to the Secretary of State.

El Paso, Jan. 9, 1915

I accompanied General Scott at conference with Villa this morning and acted as his interpreter. They arrived at amicable solution of Naco situation, Villa agreeing to order Maytorena to sign agreement which President approved. I anticipate no further trouble over this affair.

G. C. Carothers.

"In April 1915, at Celaya, Villa was dealt a massive defeat by Obregón. The German officer, Colonel Maximilian Kloss, put into use for the first time in Mexico, barbed wire, trenches and mine traps, and machine gun nests. Villa's customary method of battle, the furious charge, *el golpe,* was disastrous here. His troops, enmeshed in wire entanglements and stopped by trenches, were mowed down by machine gun fire. He was forced to retreat with heavy losses. At León in June there was a repetition of his defeat under the same circumstances. Now it was learned that many of his supposedly loyal troops were in truth Carrancistas who betrayed him, and many others then deserted to join the enemy.

"Even worse was to happen when Villa, desperately rallying his forces, attempted to take Agua Prieta, across the border from Douglas, Arizona, the first of November 1915. Carranza's Federal troops were permitted by our government to be transported upon American railroads across United States territory, from Eagle Pass, Texas, to Douglas, Arizona, across the international border from Agua Prieta. Carranza explained in applying for permission to use our railroads for that purpose that he could not reach the bandit-guerrilla any other way.

"The reason for our government's granting such a request went back to the Gadsden-Hidalgo treaty of 1854, when Mexico agreed to give up a desired railroad route to her west coast provided we permit the Mexican government to move troops across United States territory should it become necessary. Carranza's troops so transported caught Villa completely by surprise and he was badly defeated. This defeat was often regarded as the one which definitely marked his downfall, and was directly due to the United States letting his enemies use United States railways.

"President Wilson, knowing the proceedings, was obligated to recognize Carranza's anarchy de facto government for a period, as it was imperative to defeat Germany.

"General Scott stated, 'The recognition of Carranza had the effect of solidifying the power of the man who had rewarded us with kicks on every occasion and of making an outlaw of the man who had helped us. We permitted Carranza to send his troops through the United States by our rails to crush Villa. I did what I could to prevent this but I was not powerful enough. I had never been put in such a position in my life.'

"The Germans became more active in their campaign to cause the United States to intervene and become embroiled in trouble with Mexico, while they stepped up their sabotage in the United States itself. Colonel Edward M. House in the United States was contacted in 1916 by Admiral Hall, Director of Naval Intelligence of England, who headed the famous Room 40 Section. Admiral Hall believed it was necessary to discover everything possible about German activities in every part of the world, with special attention to Mexico.

"In my work in Mexico City I took part in obtaining the Germans' coded messages. We obtained all messages in their original form. These messages in their original form then were forwarded to the British Naval Intelligence who deciphered them. The messages then went on to their intended receivers who were never aware of the interception. Admiral Hall through the United States Embassy in England kept President Wilson informed.

"Thus, with the aid of the British Intelligence and their Room 40 code-breaking work, the United States was quite aware of the German plots and the movements of their spies. Some 257 telegrams and code cablegrams were intercepted and the copies sent on the regular route to the German Embassy.

"This was made possible by a valuable contact established in the Mexico City cable office. An Englishman in Mexico City owned a printing shop that had been used without the owner's knowledge to make forgeries of the "cartones" or paper money, widely used throughout Mexico at that time. The printer had been accused of doing the forging and was arrested and sentenced to be shot when I contacted the British Minister who interceded and obtained the man's release. This printer had a close friend who was working in the telegraph office, and to show their gratitude at my saving the printer's life, the friend from then on immediately purchased and passed on by courier all foreign messages to the British Naval Department.

"One of the messages handled in this manner was the famous Zimmerman telegram. This vitally important message was sent attached to another telegram to Count Bernstorff by way of the State Department in Washington. The American

Embassy was told only that the code message pertained to 'peace efforts.' When Admiral Hall had the message decoded he recognized its great importance, and through very delicate, roundabout maneuvers managed to convey its contents to President Wilson. The extreme care of this handling was to prevent the American government thinking the whole thing a hoax to cause the United States to declare war on Germany and join the allies. It was managed successfully, however, and had great influence on the United States' entry into World War I.

"This is the famous Zimmerman telegram which Admiral Hall had decoded on February 19, 1917, and passed on to Edward Bell of the American Embassy in London.

(To Count Bernstorff by way of State Dept., Wash.)
19.1.17

We intend to begin on the first of February unrestricted submarine warfare. We shall endeavor in spite of this to keep the U.S.A. neutral. In the event of this not succeeding we make Mexico a proposal of alliance on the following terms:—

Make peace together.
Make war together.

Generous financial support and an undertaking on our part that Mexico is to reconquer the lost settlement in Texas, New Mexico, and Arizona. The settlement in detail is left to you.

You will inform the President of the above most secretly as soon as the outbreak of war with U.S.A. is certain, and add the suggestion that he should on his own initiative invite Japan to immediate adherence and at the same time mediate between Japan and ourselves.

Please call the President's attention to the fact that the ruthless employment of our submarines now offers the prospect of compelling England in a few months to make peace.

Zimmermann.

"Dr. Arthur Zimmermann, German Foreign Secretary in Berlin, had kept up a flow of instructions to Imperial Minister Von Eckhardt and the Legation Kurt Jahnke and their army of active spies in Mexico. They were to constantly threaten the Americans and harass American colonies and border garrisons. These were to be border raids. As far back as 1914 strikes were planned against Columbus, New Mexico, and Nogales, Arizona. Such raids were to be given wide publicity and blamed on Villa, with evidence left to implicate him.

"The agent appointed to carry out these raids was Luther Wertz, known for his organizing ability. He directed raids from Brownsville to Nogales, was responsible for the raid on Glen Springs. These raiders, under Luther Wertz, were known from Brownsville to Nogales to the Mexican officials and the American officials. They had impunity and liberty of the north towns in Mexico who were receiving protection and encouragement with aid of Carranza's orders. During this period the United States had 150,000 soldiers along the border, stationed at Laredo, El Paso, and Nogales.

"In the meantime, on December 16, 1915, General Villa at a meeting with the vice consuls of Japan and Germany had refused to join them in a plot to strike Columbus and Nogales. One day, after the evacuation of Naco, while the two generals were driving around Juarez, Villa told Scott that a Japanese envoy had asked him what Mexico would do in case Japan, using the Pacific islands as bases, made war on the United States. Scott asked Villa what his reply was. Villa said, 'I told him that if Japan makes war on the United States you will find all the resources of Mexico against you.'

"On December 18, 1915, at Sabinas, Coahuila, Villa announced that he had ceased his revolt against Carranza and mustered out his army. He did not surrender. He made a farewell address and notified General Scott that he would remain in the State of Coahuila. He said that the majority of his generals were paid in German gold, were traitors to the cause, and were nothing more than Carrancistas under Obregón orders and were in it for loot. Villa remained in view of Sabinas.

Carranza and Obregón went to Juárez to take over the custom house. On Dec. 30, 1915, Obregón at a dinner at the Del Norte Hotel of El Paso invited American mining officials and owners to return to Mexico and reopen their mines, saying that they would be protected, the country now being safe under Carranza's rule.

"On January 9, 1916, believing Obregón and trusting Carranza's assurances of safety, a large party of American mining engineers left El Paso, headed for Cusihuiriáchi, Chihuahua, and their Cusi Mine there. Next day, near the station of Santa Ysabela, the train was stopped by a band of Villistas led by Pablo López and José Rodríguez.

"One of them got on at the front of the coach containing the engineers and their employees, seventeen Americans and one Canadian, and the other appeared at the rear of the coach. The bandits ordered the mining men to disrobe, led them out and shot them. One man, Tom Holmes, escaped. The others were left mutilated, stripped, and robbed. The brutal killing aroused such strong feeling along the border that it was necessary to put El Paso under martial law when the bodies were brought into town by train.

"Two months later, before daylight of March 9, 1916, a band of guerrillas attacked the little town of Columbus, New Mexico, taking the United States Cavalry there, commanded by Colonel Herbert J. Slocum, completely by surprise. Amid gunfire and shouts of 'Viva Villa!' buildings were burned and looted. Seventeen Americans were killed before the raiders retreated back across the international border.

"Both the Santa Ysabela massacre and the Columbus raid were blamed on the handy scapegoat, Francisco Villa. The incidents were prime examples of the vicious German-Carranza propaganda machine at work. Headlines all over the world pictured the terrible Pancho as a treacherous, savage murderer of American citizens.

"It was pointed out that Villa was extremely bitter over President Wilson's recognition of Carranza's de facto government and over the use of American railways to transport the federal troops that slaughtered his men at Agua Prieta. It was repeated that he had vowed to 'kill every gringo in Chihuahua.'

"However, both the Santa Ysabela massacre and the Columbus raid were directed by the German spy, Luther Wertz, who employed one of Villa's men, Pablo López, and José Rodríguez to carry out his orders under protection of Carranza. Wertz was following his own orders from Kurt Jahnke, director of agents for Germany, to raid American garrisons and colonies.

"The Carrancista authorities in Chihuahua, knowing about the pending massacre and raid made no effort to apprehend the group. Federal soldiers were withdrawn from the border. The raids were approved by Carranza, and were to be blamed on Villa. The raiders were known to the Mexican officials and the people. They did have impunity and liberty of the north towns in Mexico, were receiving protection and encouragement. I later learned from Ted Hutton of the Corralitos Ranch near Columbus that López' men had been seen camping near Columbus prior to the raid.

"An authoritative historian, Frank M. King, well-acquainted with Villa, states that the Columbus raid was staged by Carranza's agents in order to turn the United States completely against Villa. King says further that one of Carranza's men in El Paso later told him that a man resembling Villa in size and build was actually made up to look like Pancho. Then some Mexican soldiers who didn't know him were told that this was General Villa and that they were to follow him.

"In the darkness and confusion of the raid at Columbus, amid shouts of 'Viva Villa!' it is easy to understand how such a substitution would be successful. So one more outrage was laid at Pancho Villa's door, in fact splashed across the newspapers of the world.

"German agents attempted to get Villa back to the border to make sure he'd be blamed for the Columbus raid, but Villa wouldn't leave Sabinas where he'd gone December 18, 1915. His brother, Hipólito, was there at that time fulfilling a contract with the Chisos Mining Company at Castolon crossing to deliver cord wood for the furnace at their cinnabar quicksilver mine. This was part of the preparation for World War I. General Villa was still honoring the pact he'd made with General Scott to respect American property.

"General Scott stated that no man ever had as much right as Villa to turn against him, yet Villa maintained that General Scott was the only honest man north of Mexico, and never lost confidence in him. After the attack on Columbus General Scott refused to have anything to do with Villa until he had proof from two Americans that Villa had cleared himself of the attack. The two Americans that Scott waited word from were Major Considine at Castolón Ford and myself.

"During that crucial time of the Columbus raid, General Francisco Villa remained near Sabinas, Coahuila. I was with him. To clear himself on March 10, Villa sent an emissary who had connections with General Scott, Juan N. Medina, to General Scott in Washington. Villa sent word to Scott that on General Scott's orders he would report to the United States military officials in the United States, crossing at the Castolón Ford of the Rio Grande, Brewster County Terlingua District regular crossing.

"After the Columbus raid, Carranza soldiers were captured in uniform at Columbus by National guards. Placed in federal detention they made statements in writing pleading guilty, and admitting that they were Carrancistas under the direction of Obregón and the German agent, Luther Wertz, thus further absolving General Villa.

"Wertz was finally apprehended in Nogales, Arizona, and taken in custody to Ft. Sam Houston, Texas, January 31, 1918. Under death sentence Wertz exonerated Villa of all blame for the Santa Ysabela massacre and the Columbus raid. This was a written, recorded statement and is in the files at Washington, D. C. Wertz was hanged. However, as was the custom with German spies, at least one other agent took on Wertz' identity and for some years engaged in further espionage activities in the United States under the name of Luther Wertz.

"The United States Inspector General went to Columbus to investigate all the circumstances connected with the raid. As a result of the investigation Colonel Slocum, in command at Columbus, was exonerated of all blame. A garrison was not expected to be on guard constantly against a friendly neighbor.

"An extradition treaty with Mexico was in force at the time. Article IV states: 'Neither one of the contracting parties shall be obliged in this agreement, to hand over its own citizens, but the 'Executive' of either nation, shall be endowed with the faculty, of turning them over in his opinion it be deemed expedient.'

"In virtue of this treaty Carranza possessed the right to refuse to hand Villa and his followers over to the United States, but he was obliged to pursue, capture and punish them in conformity with the Mexican penal laws. The United States government had the right to set a time for Carranza to capture and punish the culprits, and if he failed to do so, for any reason whatsoever, the United States government had the right to declare war against Mexico in order to mete out justice with its own hand, or to decree some act of reprisal against the Mexican government.

"President Wilson acted with regard to the existing extradition treaty. No extradition was ordered. Knowing about the German agents on the border, the United States began by carrying out against Mexico the act of reprisal, to remove the menace. President Wilson's note to the de facto Carranza government concerning the attack upon Columbus, New Mexico, stated that the United States government was resolved to mete out justice, to pursue the raiders into Mexico, and exterminate the raiders. In a special message to the United States Congress for intervention in Mexico, President Wilson stated it was not for the purpose of interfering with their rights to govern themselves, but to serve notice on Mexico that we would protect our border and the lives of all foreigners in Mexico and the border, and to remove the German agents' menace. He added, 'That there will be no turning back, and this is to end the intolerable situation.'

"Carranza, manifesting a spirit of high cooperation with attention to the treaty as an ally constituted Mexico's military as a guide with the Punitive Expedition mission.

"In the official orders drafted by Secretary of War, Newton K. Baker, in consultation with General Scott, there was no mention of the capture of Villa himself, contrary to what was believed throughout the world.

"This is the telegram:

War Department Telegram
Official Business
Washington, March 10, 1916

Commanding General, Southern Department
Fort Sam Houston, Texas
Number 883.

You will promptly organize an adequate military force of troops from your department under the command of Brigadier-General John J. Pershing and will direct him to proceed promptly across the border in pursuit of the Mexican band which attacked the town of Columbus, New Mexico, and the troops there on the morning of the ninth instant. Those troops will be withdrawn to American territory as soon as the de facto government of Mexico is able to relieve them of this work. In any event the work of these troops will be regarded as finished as soon as Villa's band or bands are known to be broken up. In carrying out these instructions you are authorized to employ whatever guides and interpreters are necessary and you are given general authority to employ such transportation, including motor transportation, with necessary civilian personnel as may be required. The President desires his following instructions to be carefully adhered to and to be strictly confidential. You will instruct the commanders of your troops on the border opposite the state of Chihauhua and Sonora, or, roughly, within the field of possible operations by Villa and not under the control of the force of the de facto government, that they are authorized to use the same tactics of defense and pursuit in the event of similar raids across the border and into the United States by a band or bands such as attacked Columbus, New Mexico, yesterday. You are instructed to make all practicable use of the aeroplanes at San Antonio, Texas, for observation. Telegraph for whatever reinforcements or material you need. Notify this office as to force selected and expedite movement.

                                                        McCain.

"As General Pershing was in El Paso at the time General Scott recommended that he take charge of the Punitive Expedition. General Scott later stated that though Villa was not personally captured or killed since circumstances halted the expedition before it could do so, and as there was nothing in the actual order about capture of Villa himself, the expedition was a complete success. Pershing's troops captured and killed many of the raiders and brought some up for trial on the border in New Mexico. The raiding on American territory was stopped. The American army greatly benefited from the valuable experience in war training that was to serve them well in the coming European campaigns, where it was imperative to defeat Germany.

"Floyd Gibbons and R. Dunn were the only two news persons permitted to go with the Pershing Expedition. Villa was acquainted with Gibbons, one of the best journalists to cover the Revolution. I had many associations with Gibbons and know that he was level-headed and non-drinking.

"The Punitive Expedition returned to the United States, crossing the International boundary at Columbus, New Mexico, on February 5, 1917. I was with them as observer.

"There were many favorable things said about General Francisco Villa by people of good judgment who had close contact with him during those turbulent years of the Revolution. George Carothers of the State Department traveled in Villa's private train with him, and his influence over Villa was said to have softened the lot of many Americans in Mexico. Carothers stated that at no time was there a report made to him about Villa or his soldiers' wrong acts.

"Felix Summerfield, a former soldier of the German Army, with whom I worked, retained Villa's confidence and respect and returned it.

"A banker who handled Villa's money said that Villa had no fortune put away, that he used everything he could get to provide for his men. He also said that Villa was known not to drink hard liquor, and he would close all liquor stores when he took a town, in order to keep his soldiers under control.

"General Scott summed up his impressions of Villa by saying, 'He had the germs of greatness in him and the capability of higher things under happier circumstances.'

"There is no disputing that General Francisco Villa was much maligned. Whatever his crimes he remained true to his ideal of trying to help his oppressed countrymen. He was not allowed to live out his life as a peace-loving citizen. Even in the grave he was not allowed to rest in peace. Almost three years after his assassination and burial the tomb was opened and his body revealed, decapitated. The body gave evidence that the head had been severed shortly after death and stolen from the tomb in Parral. It was rumored that the tissue room of a hospital in the United States came into possession of the head which was recognized there, preserved in a jar.

"As time goes on and the facts are collected Francisco Villa will be proved to have been greatly misjudged. Documented proof of that is in the Luther Wertz signed exoneration of Villa in connection with the Santa Ysabela massacre and the Columbus raid; in Carranza's own statement that Villa was not responsible for Benton's killing; and the fact that when the German Ambassador, Count Von Bernstorff, was handed the persona non grata passport after our declaration of War on Germany, he admitted the truth about his intelligence and sabotage agents' arrests on the border, and exonerated Villa of blame.

"Though Villa rarely spoke of his home or family, he personally told me about the time the farm owner's son came into the family home and assaulted his sister. When Villa came home from hunting with a friend his mother told him what had happened. Villa asked the man what he intended to do about it. Villa's friend shot the man who later died. There have been many stories about that affair which caused the young boy to leave his home, but Villa told me this directly, and I believed him."

18

Jess Taylor

As a boy, Taylor lived in the Mormon settlement of Colonia Juárez near Chihuahua during the Revolution.

In the wildly unsettled conditions following Francisco Madero's revolution against the Díaz government, the Mormon colonies found themselves in a dangerous situation. By their thrift and industry they had accumulated large stores of supplies as well as work animals and, of course, that made them prey to the desperate bands of rebels and outlaws which were ravaging the country. Also the local thieves grew bold with the breakdown of authority.

Early in 1911 Jess was involved in a far-reaching incident which almost cost his life.

One night, tired of having his milk stolen, John Hatch, a fellow Mormon, hid in tall corn shucks and watched his barn. He saw a man sneak into the barn just before dawn. Silently John rose and went to the door. When the intruder started milking his cow John shouted "Alto" and raised his pistol. The thief scrambled up and ran. As he crawled under a fence, John shot him with a load of rock salt.

In the morning John and his brother, Ernest, followed the

thief's clear trail to the Toribio home nearby. With Jess' cousin, Alonzo Taylor, the sheriff, away and both the President of the colony, Thomas Cottam Romney, and Bishop Bentley in El Paso, the Hatch brothers were confronted by the problem of who had authority to issue a warrant for arrest.

Charles E. McClellan, Thomas C. Romney, and Guy Taylor (Alonzo's brother), discussed the matter and then called in other leading citizens for their opinions. They decided that Toribio must be arrested as a curb to the thefts the colony was suffering. They designated Amos Cox, with a written commission from the former *jefe,* as head of an arresting committee, with Guy Taylor and Ed Eyring assisting him. S. E. McClellan and Guy C. Wilson accompanied the arresting squad.

At the Toribio home the Mormons served their warrant and were allowed to search the house though Toribio was absent. A wounded man, presumably the thief with the rock salt injury, lay on a cot. Behind a tarp hung across the room as a partition they found a quantity of stolen goods—cured beef, wheat, bedding, clothes, food. The room was full of loot, most of which was recognized as belonging to the colonists.

The four men in the house at the time were arrested. As there was no jail in town they were locked in the tithing office. Since Sheriff Taylor was still absent, the Mormons prudently called in twelve Mexican citizens to help decide their course of action. Together, Mormons and Mexicans, they chose a former judge from Chihuahua City, Señor Jesus José Rodriguez, then employed by the Taylor Tanning and Manufacturing Company. Rodríguez agreed to assume temporary control of the case and immediately called a court session in the tithing office.

Immediately the trial was interrupted by a local native, Juan Sosa. Ignoring Rodríguez' order for silence Sosa shouted abuses and protests over the arrest of the prisoners. He was put out of the room by force, threatening, "I will kill every Mormon here and Señor Rodríguez along with them!"

Rodriguez ordered Sosa's arrest. Guy Taylor, with seven special deputies to assist, was commissioned to carry out the order. Deputized and armed with loaded rifles were Jess Taylor, John Telford, Leslie Coombs, Ed Taylor, Charlie Conover, Frank Lewis, and Ernest Hatch.

"We immediately went to Sosa's home," Taylor remembers. "Sosa, irrigating his corn, flew into a rage when we asked him about Toribio. He challenged our right to arrest him and dared us to take him.

"We moved forward, Frank Lewis in the lead. When Frank bent to pass through the wire fence Juan struck him a vicious blow with his shovel. As Frank fell Sosa struck him again. Juan had raised the shovel for the third blow when he fell before our shots. Then pandemonium broke loose. Juan's family rushed from the house, screaming and accusing us Mormons of murder. They were quickly joined by the neighbors, all cursing and weeping. Ed, Charlie and I helped Frank into a buckboard and drove away to find a doctor. We left Leslie, John, and Ernest on guard at the Sosa place. Guy went straight to Rodríguez to report what had happened."

To the Mormons' amazement, Rodríguez disarmed and placed them under arrest, explaining that it was necessary until there was a thorough investigation of the incident. If it were as they had reported, they would most likely be released. They were imprisoned in the tithing office with the four Mexicans already there. To make things worse Juan Sosa's body was brought in and laid out in the same room.

"We were stunned," says Taylor. "We had to take it until matters were straightened out, which we hoped would be quickly. Anything we could say or do in our own defense would only aggravate the dangerous state of affairs."

The next day the court session in the tithing room was attended by Lino Ponce, officious brother of Demétrio Ponce, self-appointed presiding officer of Casas Grandes, with three armed men. They announced that they were investigating the killing, as they called it, and congratulated Señor Rodríguez for arresting the Mormons for their unwarranted violence.

"Casas Grandes was sort of the county seat," Taylor explains, "and Colonia Juárez came under its jurisdiction. Well, the situation developed alarmingly. Lino Ponce seemed to have things all his way. It was decided that Leslie Coombs, John Telford, my cousin Guy Taylor, and I should remain as prisoners in the tithing office, still confined with the four Mexicans. They set four Mexicans, armed with our own guns, to guard us, and four Mormons were allowed to guard the Mexican prisoners. We were angry and disturbed, believe me, but we knew it only prudent to submit for the time being since feeling was so high that any action on our part could have brought on a riot."

Rodríguez prepared a report of the case which the Ponce officials didn't bother to read. They did confer with the guards and the Sosa family, then left for Casas Grandes in a buggy borrowed from Brig Stowell and promising in a threatening manner that court would be in session next morning.

In desperation the colonists turned to another American, Captain Oscar Creighton, a filibuster with the revolutionary forces in nearby Pearson. Guy C. Wilson, Thomas C. Romney, Miles A. Romney and E. L. Taylor, Jess' uncle, went to Pearson to see Creighton.

Still worried, feeling that Creighton himself was insecure, the Mormons returned to Colonia Juárez and placed a heavy guard around the tithing office and the road leading to Casas Grandes to prevent surprises during the night.

The next day things were worse. Toribio, openly flouting Rodríguez' authority, started spreading wildly distorted versions of the killing of Sosa. Rodríguez, hoping to prevent a riot, deputized Amos Cox with a mixed group of Mexicans and Mormons to assist him to arrest Toribio. When they approached Toribio he pointed to the rebel colors he had pinned to his shirt and defied them to take him.

When the arresting committee reported Toribio's action to Rodríguez he issued an order of arrest in the name of Francisco Madero.

Armed with this order, Cox brought Toribio in without any more difficulty. Rodríguez showed his control of the situation by handing Toribio a flag and by commanding him to wave it above his head and shout, "Viva Madero!" When Toribio obeyed he further commanded him to say, "Muerta Díaz!" which the prisoner also did. This show of force and authority had the desired effect of quieting the mob of hostile natives.

However, Ed Payne and his brother from Dublán arrived with the warning that a party of sixty men had gathered in Casas Grandes with the plan of raiding Colonia Juárez that night, releasing the Mexican prisoners and killing the Mormons. A heavy guard was set up around town and on its approaches. "We sure didn't get much sleep that night," recalls Taylor, "but everything remained quiet with no signs of attack, so I guess the raiders were scared off by our preparations."

The next day Taylor's uncle went back to Pearson to speak again to Creighton. He brought back the message, supported by Creighton's questionable authority, that the Mormons were to be released and the Mexican prisoners taken to Nuevo Casas Grandes the next morning. The Mormons were doubtful about taking their prisoners to Casas Grandes where they had no control over them.

Taylor's uncle explained that General Francisco Madero, on his way to attack Juárez with heavy troops, would be in Nuevo Casas Grandes that day, and this would provide the opportunity for the Mormons to explain the true state of affairs to him. A committee was delegated to take the prisoners to

Casas Grandes by way of Pearson. Another committee composed of Rodríguez, Guy C. Wilson, Hyrum Harris, and Thomas C. Romney, was to go directly to Nuevas Casas Grandes and see General Madero.

To forestall trouble it was decided that the Mormon prisoners would not be released until the party reached Pearson. Rodríguez commissioned Charles E. McClellan as acting *presidente* of Colonia Juárez in his absence, and told him to keep the town under strict guard, using academy students if necessary.

"Report to Captain Creighton," he told E. L. Taylor, "that the Mormon prisoners are being delivered to him for release, and leave town simultaneously with the team carrying the native prisoners. By the time you arrive in Nuevas Casas Grandes we will have delivered our prisoners, interviewed President Madero, and be waiting with instructions from him."

However, near Rancho San Diego, Taylor and his party received orders to take the Mormon prisoners on to Nuevas Casas Grandes. They did so. At Nuevas Casas Grandes they were caught in a mass of people, a jostling crowd of military recruits and spectators. There seemed to be no one to meet them. Suddenly the Mormons in their wagon were recognized by someone in the milling crowd.

"There are the ones who killed Juan Sosa!" a man shouted. "They killed a man because he shouted Viva Madero!"

The Mormons were pulled from their seats. Fists and guns were waved in their faces, and it looked like they were candidates for a lynch mob. They could see Hyrum Harris approaching on horseback, trying to reach them. They were still being roughly jerked around and abused when two men pushed through the crowd. With sharp authority they commanded the mob to fall back and were reluctantly obeyed.

The nick-in-time rescuers were Raúl Madero, brother of General Francisco Madero, and Pascual Orozco, at that time still a loyal follower of Madero. They helped the shaken Mormons into their wagon and sped them on their way through the still menacing throng.

Once clear the Mormons drove around the block and stopped at Dave Spilsbury's home. There they found Guy Wilson waiting for them. He told them that General Madero had approved their action and relieved them of their Mexican prisoners and that the colonists were to go back to their homes.

"We left immediately for Colonia Juárez," says Taylor, "with prayers of thanksgiving and gratitude on our lips and in our hearts, and sincere hopes for Francisco Madero's victorious campaign. We had just been through an experience at the hands of a hostile, unreasoning mob that we never wanted to repeat."

As soon as General Madero and his troops were safely away from the district, Demétrio Ponce resumed his persecution. He sent a squad of soldiers to the colony at night, hoping to surprise the Mormons and take Taylor and the others prisoner. Warned in time they escaped, but it became almost a game with soldiers slipping into town at odd times and the Mormons barely evading them.

They seemed to hunt especially for Taylor. Once Taylor was in his aunt's home when he was warned that he had been seen going in and the soldiers were coming. Hurriedly Jess donned his aunt's kimono and floppy sunbonnet. Then, walking sedately between two young girls, one of them his fiancée, he left the now surrounded house. The little group of "ladies" strolled across the street, went into a neighbor's home and out of the back door. There Jess mounted a horse waiting at the hitchrack and, modestly sitting side-saddle until he was safely out of sight, rode away.

When President Romney, marooned all this time in El Paso because of the destruction of the railroads, finally got back to Colonia Juárez, he sought the legal advice of Lawyer Edmund

Richardson, Jess' neighbor. Richardson advised putting the matter in court, and letting Leslie Coombs stand trial, because it could be proved that Coombs' gun had not been fired.

However, when Coombs appeared in court in Casas Grandes he was seized and thrown into jail in spite of all explanations. When Dr. Gay pointed out that Leslie was in a very weakened condition he was removed to an outer office which was more comfortable, and there he remained.

Again, indirectly, Pascual Orozco came to the rescue. Now turned against President Francisco Madero, who had successfully defeated Díaz Federals in Juárez and caused the overthrow of the old dictator, Orozco was back in Casas Grandes organizing his own revolution. He released all prisoners from the jails, and Leslie Coombs made his escape with the others and returned to Colonia Juárez, though half expecting to be shot in the back as he fled. In the turmoil of Orozco's Liberales or Red Flagger activities the Mormon case seemed to be forgotten.

"The first time I recall meeting Pancho Villa," says Taylor "was right after Madero had taken Juárez in 1911. Pancho came to the railroad camp called Kilometer 85 to contract for beef for the Madero troops. He okayed the deal with me for us to furnish the beef. We had no trouble about terms. Then, as always with us, he paid promptly and in gold."

On February 24, 1912, Jess Martin Taylor and Hazel Richardson were married in Colonia Juárez, by President Romney. In July they left with many of the members of the colonies, forced to flee to El Paso by threats and violence of Red Flaggers and hostile bands of rebels.

On the way to the train at Pearson the drunken bandit who held up George Redd and others of the departing colonists took a gold watch from Edmund Richardson, Hazel's father. This watch, later found concealed in the bandit's sock when he was arrested and searched, helped prove his guilt and led to his execution. Lino Ponce had three soldiers take the culprit to an old graveyard and shoot him. Next day Ernest Hatch, President Romney and Eli A. Clayson buried the man. Jess and Hazel never made their home in Colonia Juárez again, but went back for a number of visits.

"In 1913 we went back into Mexico to live," Taylor relates. "I went to work for the Corner Ranch, about forty miles south of Deming. I had quite a few encounters with Pancho Villa from then on.

"One time the Corner Ranch had some of its people kidnapped by Red Flaggers. I was sent to get assistance from Pancho Villa who was known to be friendly toward us."

Villa was camped below Casas Grandes and when he heard Taylor's story he sent General Talamente back with Jess. After three days of trailing the Red Flaggers General Talamente captured thirty-five of them and had them executed. Then he sent Jess with a letter to report to Pancho, which he did, and on the way met a large band of Villa's men going to reinforce General Talamente.

"There was an occasion when Villa wanted a saddle for a drummer who had joined his band. Villa was fond of music and took good care of his musicians. He sent me with this man to find a saddle for him, or, he suggested, I let the drummer take mine, which I didn't care to do. We went to a rancher I knew who lived about ten miles away and he sold a saddle to the drummer. Villa paid a good price for it in United States money.

"Another time Pancho offered to sell me eighteen mules, but I recognized them as American and was wary. Villa then offered me a bill of sale, but I still backed away from the deal. Most of these encounters took place during the two months I was at that railroad camp, Kilometer 85. Villa was camped there most of that time.

"I remember Pancho once asked me where Dick Dudley could be found. Dudley had two horses, one belonging to him and one to his wife, and Villa intended to take the horses. He did so, but returned Mrs. Dudley's horse. Then when he heard that Dudley had made the remark that he 'hoped Villa got killed.' Pancho went looking for him. The Dudley's, however, had wisely cleared out.

"Really, I guess we never had a better friend in those uncertain times than Pancho Villa. One time we went through Ascension in a spring wagon. Villa 'detained' us there overnight. We were very frightened, but he only visited with us and played with the baby, our first, daughter Jessie. In the morning he let us go on our way.

"A later time Pancho came to the Corner Ranch and wanted to buy sugar. Provisions were rather short, but we gave him some sugar. He never seemed to forget that little act for it was returned to us like 'bread upon the waters,' in Villa's protection and friendship throughout the next years. We always felt that the bandits that pillaged the country all around let us alone because of Villa's known friendship for us.

"Our people in Colonia Dublán and Colonia Juárez didn't fare so well. My uncle, E. L. Taylor, being one of the early settlers and a prosperous cattleman, was a constant target for all the bandits and renegade rebels. He was kidnapped and held for ransom many times. One time he was taken hostage in Chocolate Pass and the kidnappers took away his boots, feeling that would prevent his escape. He waited till his captors went to sleep, and then, barefoot he walked some thirty-five miles to Colonia Juárez over rocky brushy ground. He arrived home safely, exhausted and with badly bruised feet.

"Another time he had to hide in the attic of his daughter's home to evade capture. Once he hid behind the piano in the parlor and from there shot a Red Flagger's hand off. Finally Uncle gave up and went to South Dakota to live.

"Then there was Charlie Taylor who was captured by Villistas on the way to Colonia Juárez. They forced Charlie to thrash and grind wheat for the rebels."

Hazel Taylor's father had some rough experiences. One

time at Colonia Juárez, Richardson went to get his cattle and was driving them along when bandits captured him.

"They stood him up blindfolded and were going to shoot him because he had won a suit against their leader," recalls Taylor. "Just in time another group of outlaws rode up and asked who they were killing. They told him Lawyer Richardson, so this leader said, 'Don't kill him, he *won* a lawsuit for me.' They released Richardson, but kept his son, Ray, for ranson. They sent the father to the United States to get $700 ransom. When Richardson came to El Paso to get the money, the bandits, with Ray captive, started for the mill at Colonia Juárez. They met another bunch of bandits and turned back to Colonia Dublán and camped. They made Ray cook and wait on them. However he had left his horse bridled and when his captors went to sleep he escaped and got to Colonia Dublán. There he wired his father not to pay ransom as he was free.

"To tell the truth, the country was swarming with bandits on the prowl, small bands and regular troops of them. Some were just soldiers desperately in need of supplies, and some never were anything but thieves and murderers. Thinking of it now, I don't see how any of us got through those years and lived to tell of it."

After the attack on Columbus, New Mexico on March 9, 1916, a large band of angry and vengeful Villistas rode toward the helpless colonies of Juárez and Dublán. They passed within sight of the Corners Ranch where the Taylors still lived.

"I remember the uneasiness with which we watched them, a little distance away. Pancho Villa had always been friendly, but many of his followers hated us and coveted what we had. Besides, the feeling of many of them had changed from respect to distrust in the past year."

Word was sent to the colonies of the approaching troops. A priesthood meeting was held at the home of Gaskill Romney in Dublán and a committee appointed to go to Colonia Juárez to discuss the danger with President Joseph C. Bentley.

"Stories of the killing of rancher Ed Wright and the kidnapping of his wife, Maude, were fresh in our minds. Also there was the shocking murder of the three American cowboys whom we all knew, Arthur McKinney, Bill Corbett, and James O'Neil. They were working for the Palomas Land and Cattle Company and had been campfire friends of Villa and his bunch for years. But now, hunting strays, they'd run onto a Villa camp and had been killed on the spot. It sure seemed that Villa and his followers were really bent on destroying every foreigner they could, Mormons included. Rumors reached Colonia Dublán of the killing of the five Polanco brothers nearby because they worked for an American company.

"Believe me, the colonists awaited the approach of those Villistas that night with fear. However, by divine providence the attackers were diverted from their purpose.

"Columbus had really been devastated by the raid. Bodies were found on the desert around there for months after. Again, I guess we were protected by Villa's friendship for us as the raiders approaching Columbus passed the Corner Ranch, near enough to have been seen if anyone were out watching that night. I always thought that Villa knew about the raid, even if as many believe he did not personally lead it. I think it was a grudge business. Many of the leading men in Columbus had been having trouble with the American soldiers stationed there so the commander had ordered the guns locked up, though the camp cooks were armed. And of course, the raiders went in and killed the outposts before they knew what happened."

The Taylors went to live in Columbus after the raid.

The Pershing expedition marched down into Mexico and returned less than a year later, and there was speculation about what was accomplished. After the American forces left, the Americans still living in Mexico had a very precarious existence. Hostility and resentment were directed at them from all sides, both Federals and rebels, with even normally friendly natives feeling that the Americans had invaded their country.

Bands of rebels, many of them claiming to be Villistas, harassed the Mormon colonies. Pancho Villa, however, while terrorizing much of the countryside until the time of his retirement, personally continued his friendly attitude toward the Mormons.

19

Bishop E. L. Redd

A Mormon Bishop, Redd grew up in the Mormon settlement of Colonia Dublán. He was one of the hundreds of Mormons who fled Mexico in 1912.

"Villa was always friendly to our people. Even after President Wilson recognized Carranza's *de facto* government and Villa's former liking for Americans turned to bitter hatred and vengeance, he respected our colonies. Villa's personal regard and even protective attitude for us can perhaps be explained by the always peaceful teachings of our leaders and the other colonists. They seemed to impress him. Our real danger came from other leaders."

Though a very small child at the time of Francisco Madero's revolt against the Díaz government, Redd can still recall his parents' anxiety as the rapidly spreading Revolution threatened the colonists' peaceful existence. Nearby Casas Grandes suffered the first real battle. Early in March, 1911, Madero and his brothers, with Pascual Orozco and Guiseppi Garibaldi, attempted to take the town. A large relief force of Federals arrived in time to put the rebels to rout. They fled toward Juárez. There in May, Francisco Madero's troops defeated Díaz' Federals.

This resulted in unrest and outbreaks of violence and disregard for law and property throughout Mexico, especially in the State of Chihuahua. Mormon Church leaders in Salt Lake City, aware of the threat to the colonists, sent A. W. Ivins, a member of the Council of Twelve, to advise them.

Ivins recommended that the Mormon community remain perfectly neutral and judiciously solicit the protection of whatever faction was in power.

The Mormons were able to maintain strict neutrality.

More than one miracle was experienced and witnessed by the colonists during the next years. Redd has his own childhood memories of these experiences that were reinforced as he grew up by the frequent recounting by his people.

Early in 1912 Pascual Orozco broke away from the Madero government and organized his own revolution. Forced out of the southern part of the State of Chihuahua, he made his headquarters at Casas Grandes. For several months he respected the neutrality of the Mormon colonies. However when federal forces from the State of Sonora approached, Orozco's troops under General Inez Salazar were strongly in need of arms and ammunition in order to stop them. On July 24, Salazar demanded supplies from the Mormons, saying that all former promises to foreigners were now void.

On July 25, President Junius Romney, Hyrum Harris, Guy C. Wilson and Henry E. Bowman met with Salazar at Casas Grandes to discuss the situation. Salazar demanded that Romney order the colonists to surrender all arms and ammunition. He refused, saying that the arms were personal property. Salazar then said that Romney and Bowman would be held prisoners until the order was carried out.

Salazar then ordered Lino Ponce, one of his followers, to take fifty men and search every house in Colonia Dublán for guns and ammunition. To prevent this happening, Romney agreed to name a central place to which arms would be brought by the townspeople. In the meantime the rebels had trained six cannons on the town.

With his people "under the gun" and with Salazar's assurance that if the colonists brought all their guns and ammunition to the designated place their homes would not be searched, Romney reluctantly gave the necessary order. He then went to Colonia Juárez and informed the citizens there of what had happened. As there were then some 2,000 well-armed rebels in the territory and the Mormons of Dublán were disarmed, it was decided that it was unsafe for their women and children to remain in Mexico. It was unanimously voted to move the families out at once.

On Sunday, July 26, 1912, the evacuation began. The regular train left Pearson at noon, and by mid-morning a long train of wagons loaded with all they could carry headed down the road for the town. Women and children rode on top of the bedding, trunks and boxes. The next evening the remaining women and children of Colonia Juárez left on the six o'clock train from Pearson.

The Redd family was among those that left on Sunday.

The smoothness of the evacuation was upset when a drunken bandit stopped the lead wagon and at gunpoint demanded money. The thief in turn held up the wagons of Grandfather McClellan, Bishop Bentley, Byron MacDonald, and the Redd family. George Redd was forced to give up twenty dollars.

The train trip to El Paso was crowded, hot and very uncomfortable. Within the next few days some 2,300 Mormon refugees from the colonies of Juárez, Dublán, Díaz, García, Pacheco, and Chuichupa arrived in the border city. All the railroads running into El Paso had a special transportation rate of one cent for Mormon colonists in order to help them flee Mexico.

Mayor C. E. Kelly of El Paso and the townspeople furnished what aid they could to the refugees, but suffering in the blazing midsummer heat was intense and most of the shelter available was tin-roofed, unfloored sheds in a lumber-yard. El Pasoans recall seeing Mormon women with their clothing packed into five-gallon milk pails. The *Herald* of August 3, 1912, speaks of large quantities of magazines and toys brought by citizens to the newspaper office for the refugees.

On January 31, 1913, sixty-five of the colonists, among them the Redd family, started the return trip home. The next day they made the last stage of their journey by wagon from Columbus. They arrived in Colonia Juárez to find their Church occupied by a garrison of drunken Red Flaggers.

In spite of such a discouraging homecoming the Mormon people held to their neutrality. Throughout the next seven years, the colonies suffered raids, thefts and threats from Red Flaggers and independent bands of bandits that harassed the country.

"On February 9, 1914, my father, George Redd, was killed. A group of rebels were robbing Father's property. He went across the street to see the Mexican policeman and asked him to go with him to stop the thievery. As the two men reached our house the robbers opened fire and shot them both. The policeman was killed instantly. The man who shot him was his own son, who mistakenly took his father for my mother's uncle. My father had his knee shattered and died several hours later from shock and loss of blood.

"I was five years old at the time, with a brother and a sister older than myself, and a brother and a sister younger. Seven months after my father's death my mother gave birth to another boy. But we continued to live in our home in Colonia Juárez."

During these times Villa tried to protect the colonists. At Casas Grandes on one occasion he captured and executed a number of Orozco's leaders and followers. Though he was rumored to lead many murderous raids on ranches and even settlements of foreigners, especially attacking Americans in later years, he seemed to deliberately bypass the Mormon colonies.

Colonia Dublán, about eighteen miles from Colonia

Juárez, actually suffered more looting and destruction during the period when many of its citizens were forced to be absent than had Colonia Juárez. It was estimated that a good $100,000 worth of merchandise was stolen there. Families returned to find their homes despoiled, furniture gone, carpeting, curtains, and shades torn, even portraits ruined by smashed bottles of blackberries.

"Still both the colonies were beautiful places," says Redd now. "The fertile soil continued to produce wonderful crops. Ears of corn grew almost two feet long. Fruits were fine and plentiful. The mills and shops were very busy.

"I remember when Villa and two or three hundred of his men stopped in Colonia Juárez, we children were allowed to sell them fruit and garden produce. The Villistas would camp along the river with the permission of our Stake leaders. It was said that Villa stole and slaughtered cattle while on the march, but he bought lots of beef from us, never haggling about the price. He always paid for everything promptly and in gold. He and his men seemed friendly and joked with us children. We liked to go to their camp."

It was not Villistas but a band of Red Flaggers under Tomás Pérez who confronted Anson B. Call, Bishop of Dublan on November 14, 1914. Call was working at his job of bookkeeper for the Romney and Farnsworth Mercantile Company. They "arrested" the Bishop for giving information, they said, that led to the arrest and execution by Villa of José Para, one of the Red Flaggers. They acted, they claimed, under orders of General Castillo, a former Villista.

Call denied their charge. Pérez would not listen to Call's protests of innocence. He said that he had orders from General Castillo to bring him in. Call kissed his wife and family good-bye and then was taken away.

At the rebel camp Bishop Call found his friend, William Young, who had also been kidnapped. Pérez offered to release Young on the condition that he go home and get a gun which he had refused to surrender. Call insisted on Young's leaving, thinking of Young's family.

Young made the trip in record time and was back in camp with the gun within a few hours. He brought Morley Black with him. Both men pleaded with the Red Flaggers to let Call go back to Dublán with them. Pérez agreed to release Bishop Call if Young and Black would raise 10,000 pesos as ransom. When they said that was impossible Pérez reduced his demand to 5,000 pesos, but that was still beyond the reach of the colonists. Finally Young and Black reluctantly left the camp to see what they could do to help Call.

The Red Flaggers then took their prisoner to Rancho San Diego, six miles below Colonia Juárez. This was one of the properties which had been confiscated from Luis Terrazas by the revolutionists. At the ranch they informed Call that if the Mormon people could not raise 1,000 pesos ransom they would execute him at three the following morning. With crops destroyed and stores continually looted, with clothing and food constantly stolen from them, the colonists had no hope of raising even that small sum to save Call's life.

So, at the darkest part of the night, Call was led out and placed with his back against the trunk of a large cottonwood tree. The six-man firing squad stepped back four paces and cocked their guns. Call prayed.

Bishop Call straightened his shoulders and looked at the lieutenant in charge of the firing squad. *"Uno,"* the officer snapped. And then, *"Dos."* Call stood still.

The Mexican officer opened his lips. Call froze. The officer hesitated. Then, instead of uttering the count of *"Tres"* that would have ended the bishop's life, the lieutenant asked what Call was willing to do to save his life.

Call let out a sigh. Hardly knowing where the words came from he answered that he would go to Colonia Juárez and try to raise two hundred pesos. Surprisingly the officer agreed to present the offer to Pérez in the morning, though he didn't think Pérez would accept. More likely Call would be executed at sunrise. After suffering hours in agonized suspense, still holding fast to his faith, he was taken to Pérez just as the sun rose. Amazingly, Pérez agreed to the proposition.

Under guard, Call was sent to Colonia Juárez, the colony nearest the bandit camp. There he went to see President Joseph C. Bentley and explained the situation. A committee was promptly formed which canvassed the community house-to-house and raised the two hundred pesos. That afternoon Bishop Call returned to Colonia Dublán and his family.

"There was great rejoicing in our colony," Redd says now. "Bishop Call told us how he felt as he stood under the cotton-wood, waiting the order that meant certain death. Then, as he prayed, he witnessed the power that stayed the Red Flagger's final command. Even the very young children, such as I, realized that a miracle had taken place that dark night."

A second episode involving Colonia Dublán took place less than two years later. The colonists had just heard of the attack on Columbus. On January 14 the *El Paso Herald* reported rumors from south of Columbus that Villista forces had ordered to burn at the stake all Americans refusing to pay ransom to Villa for their safety.

Even then the Mormons could not believe that their former friend would turn against them. However, many of Villa's leaders, rebellious and hostile, were known not to share his feelings. Such was the situation on March 10 when a rider came in one afternoon with the report that a large band of Villistas was approaching and would probably reach Colonia Dublán during the night.

"As is the custom when a problem faces us, a meeting was held. Our family was called with others from Colonia Juárez to meet at the church in Colonia Dublán," Redd recalls. "For a long time the men of the colony discussed what might happen and how they would meet the danger. The Mormons, always a peaceful people, were averse to fighting and had no real defense to offer."

Bishop Call spoke quietly to the assembly. "We must either fight or put ourselves in God's hands," he said. "As an adversary against trained, well-equipped troops we would be weak indeed. But we do know that God is greater than any evil that may confront us. I say, go home men, gather your loved ones around you, kneel down and pray. Put out every light in the town. Do not let even the light of a candle show the enemy where to find us. Remain absolutely quiet. Keep the children quiet and try to make them understand that God can and will protect us. How he is to do this, we leave in his hands."

"I know that my mother tried to appear unafraid," Redd says. "She and a neighbor took us children to a large house in the center of town. They spread pallets on the floor of two of the upstairs rooms and put us to bed, bidding us to be very still and to remember to say our prayers. The grown-ups remained downstairs in the dark. By ten o'clock not a candle glimmered anywhere in Colonia Dublán. In spite of our excitement we children fell asleep.

"We woke in the morning to find everything peaceful. Everyone was going about his usual activities. Not a sign of a Villista was to be seen. Colonia Dublán had been spared."

In 1943, twenty-seven years later, Redd learned why the vengeance-bound Villistas, led by Colonel Fierro, known as "The Butcher," did not attack Colonia Dublán that night. Redd was at that time working at a large smelter in Chihuahua. He had a number of Mexicans working for him who had been in Villa's army, and as they ate their lunch they told many tales of their adventures.

Several of the ex-revolutionists had ears missing. They explained that Villa had their ears cut off when they deserted him and joined the Federal troops. Two of the men were minus both ears, which meant two desertions. Now they laughed at what most people would consider an inhuman punishment. Redd was always astonished that they seemed to bear no grudge against their former leader. One of them told Redd that Villa had cut off so many ears that they filled a flour sack.

With barbaric humor he sent this sack of ears to a Federal captain not far from Villa's camp.

One day one of the men, Felipe Garza, spoke of having ridden with Colonel Fierro. Naturally curious, Redd asked, "Why didn't Fierro attack Dublán that night right after the Columbus raid, when he was known to be riding on that colony?"

"That, señor, is a night I will never forget," Felipe said. "It was a most mysterious happening. Pancho Villa, you know, was very angry with the American President because he had proved a traitor to Villa's friendship—so Villa issued orders to all his bands that every American along our path should be killed. Colonel Fierro who was riding south from the border told us that we were going to raid and murder every man, woman and child in Colonia Juárez and Colonia Dublán.

"That was not good news to many of us. We liked the Mormons. They had been kind to us and shared food with us many times. It made us sad to think that we were going to have to turn on our friends. However, we were first of all soldiers and Colonel Fierro was a hard, cruel leader. He deserved his title of 'Butcher.' He would kill a man just to watch him die. We knew we would have to obey his command.

"We traveled all that day, seeing few people along the way. It was late that night, about midnight, when we reached the outskirts of Colonia Dublán. And there, señor, we got the surprise of our lives. The long, straight streets of the town were ablaze with lights from huge campfires burning at every intersection. Not only that but great numbers of soldiers were there, plainly seen in the light of the fires. Huge piles of guns were stacked at hand, ready for business. Ready for us.

"Colonel Fierro was very angry. He said that we were to go around town and come in from the east.

"So we rode to the east only to find the same bright campfires, the same army of soldiers ready to defend the town. Colonel Fierro was a fighter, a brave though bloody one, but even he could see that we were greatly outnumbered. The soldiers could shoot us down before we hardly started to attack. Fierro turned away from the town and cursed. We rode around town, taking care not to come within gunshot distance to any of those soldiers guarding Colonia Dublán.

"We went to the northern arm of the lake near Colonia Dublán and the company turned west to get around it, hoping the soldiers wouldn't follow.

"We all knew the treachery of that lake. We knew, as did Colonel Fierro of the bad quicksand, powerful enough to pull anything under. Fierro was so angry at not being able to attack Dublán that he was not thinking straight. While we watched from the banks Fierro plunged his big horse into the water. The moon had come out and we could see everything clearly. The horse started swimming and then suddenly it went down. Horse and rider disappeared right before our eyes. I tell you it truly seemed like a devil dragged them under. Colonel Fierro was a very large man, weighing maybe two hundred and fifty pounds, and he always wore heavy bandoleros with ammunition, around his body. Some say his saddlebags were loaded with gold that night. He never had a chance. A couple of the men started into the water, but they stepped back, afraid of the quicksand.

"We waited there a little while and then we rode around the long arm of water and away. I heard that Fierro's body was later found. Many of us who were friends of the Mormons thought the great Dios had taken Fierro's life to spare them."

"Felipe," Redd said, "what would you say if I told you that there was not even one soldier in Colonia Dublán that night of March, 1916, nor was there even so much as a candle burning in town? It was absolutely blacked out."

"Madre de Dios," Felipe whispered. "Madre de Dios." And he made the sign of the cross.

20

Isaac (Ike) Aldarete

*Aldarete's father owned a prosperous gambling house
in Juárez that was confiscated by Villa.*

"Before the revolution and the take-over of Juarez by
Madero's forces in 1911, Pancho Villa was not well known in
El Paso. My father, Ike Senior, was one of those who befriended Pancho during the times he was on the run from
Mexican Federals and hiding out in 'Little Chihuahua,' south
of the business district of El Paso. For a period Villa used to
call around for a weekly handout at the Courthouse where
my father was District Clerk for eighteen years. My father
helped many of the refugees from Mexico temporarily down
on their luck.

"A little later, after Madero defeated General Navarro's
Federal troops at Juárez, Villa became one of the best known
leaders under him. My father continued being friendly with
him. He would send his car over to Juárez with his driver,
Barnardo, to take Villa wherever he wanted to go. I often
went along. I was a little afraid of Pancho in those days, but
I was fascinated by him, too. I remember we came to a deep
rain puddle in the road one day and Barnardo started to drive

around it. Pancho said, 'Go on! Go on through!' We went ahead, the Winton splashing and floundering and Pancho laughing very loud.

"By November in 1913 the days of helping Pancho were over. Villa was becoming a famous military leader and had plenty of his own cars to command. He was the high-riding ruler of the State of Chihuahua and no one on either side of the border doubted it. I was still very young and my close friend, Alex Gonzales, was even younger when we crossed the Rio Grande, not caring what would happen, to call on Villa just after his sneak attack and overthrow of the Federals in Juárez.

"We went straight to his headquarters, the Cuartel, not far from the bull ring. There were horses picketed in the yard and Alex reminded me that Villa was said to always keep a fast, saddled mount close at hand. A lot of fierce looking soldiers were going in and out of the building and standing around. Alex and I walked right through the door and told one of them that we wanted to see Villa. The soldier just looked at us and I said that he should tell the General that I was Ike Aldarete's son from El Paso. I'd always heard that Villa never forgot a friend or a kindness and knowing all that my father had done for him I was sure he would see us.

"The soldier went into an adjoining room and came back and beckoned us to come inside. There was Villa sitting behind a big desk. He got up and came around to shake hands with us, squeezing our fingers in a bone crushing grip.

"Villa didn't look much different from when Barnardo and I had chauffeured him around not so long ago. He needed a shave and his moustache needed trimming. His dark eyes, well, his eyes looked right *into* you as though he could see at one glance everything he wanted to know. I'd say the overall effect was one of power and authority. Villa's clothes didn't matter. They didn't matter to him and they didn't matter to anyone else. Villa left no doubt that here was a real man.

When he called us *amigos,* Alex and I felt ten feet tall. We sneaked glances around to see if the soldiers watching were impressed. They seemed to be.

"We congratulated Villa on his big victory and invited him to come around to the keno halls where we now worked for my father. We acted pretty cocky. Villa nodded and we left, feeling very smug and proud of ourselves.

"My father at that time was one of the owners of the very prosperous Keno Hall and Crystal and Diamond Palaces in Juárez. Because of his political position in El Paso he was a silent partner. Alex and I worked part time in the gambling places, doing the 'calling' for the games. As we were bilingual we did the calling in both Spanish and English. Alex was especially popular with the Keno players.

"Gambling was very big in Juárez during those years. General Juan Navarro, who was commander of the city garrison at Ft. Hidalgo until Madero defeated him in 1911, was a nightly customer of the keno halls. Everyone from El Paso would come over the Río Grande to patronize the games and often reported seeing Pancho Villa sitting in the Tivoli drinking pink lemonade and watching the games. Villa kept away from the games. He also avoided hard liquor and smoked very rarely.

"The evening before Villa's famous sneak attack and capture of Juárez [November 15, 1913] there was a rather unnatural atmosphere around the clubs. Alex and I noticed an unusual number of strangers of the guerrilla type mingling with the crowds. We learned later that those were Villistas. We boys were fortunately back across the river and safely home when not long past midnight Villa and his men swarmed into town, taking the Federal garrison completely by surprise. Villa was established in complete control by morning. Dead men lay like rats in the streets, especially around the red-light district of Calle Diablo.

"My father and his partners could not have been warned

of what was going to happen but from living on the border
their instincts made them act quickly. Father's driver,
Barnardo, had the Winton Six at the back doors of the
gambling halls with the money bags hidden next to the motor
of the car before the city of Juárez realized it had been
captured. Barnardo drove across the bridge and into El Paso
with the money, with no one the wiser.

"For a couple of weeks after Alex and I visited Villa our
business affairs seemed to go on as always. We understood
that Villa received his usual percentage of the 'take' of the
gambling proceeds, but that was expected. Villa himself
dropped in to watch and occasionally play a bit. When he
played he didn't want to be bothered. One evening an officer
came in with the information that a Federal soldier who had
been hiding in a barn had been captured. The officer wanted
to know what to do with the prisoner. Pancho was in a surly
humor. He said, 'Shoot him!' No one dared to say anything.
The poor prisoner was taken out and 'dobe-walled' without
any more discussion or delay.

"Shortly after that incident Villa's attitude cooled toward
us. We figured he must have found out about Barnardo's
sneaking the money away from our gambling halls and across
the river on the night of the attack. That money was quite a
bit of loot that Pancho had lost. Villa had his ways of finding
out things, that we knew very well. Anyway, the word got
out that it wouldn't be safe for my father to be seen around
Juárez. So he stayed on the United States side of the border.
However he still sent the Winton Six with me sitting beside
Barnardo to make daily collections from the halls. I felt
daring, but we were left alone.

"One day Barnardo and I happened to have the car
parked near the Cuartel which always fascinated me. All of a
sudden one of Villa's lieutenants and three soldiers came
hurrying out the door. The officer looked around and saw us.
Barnardo had already started the motor and was putting the

car into gear when the officer raised a hand and stopped him.
He ordered Barnardo to drive to the wholesale grocery opposite the little plaza. Then the soldiers climbed into the car
and one of them got in front beside me.

"Barnardo drove where he was ordered. When we stopped
all the soldiers piled out of the car and went into the grocery
store. We watched them through the windows. There wasn't
any question about what they were doing. They were ransacking the place. I whispered to Barnardo that we'd better
go. He eased the car out of gear and luckily for us it was
downhill enough so that the Winton rolled away without
making a sound. As soon as he could Barnardo started the
motor and we headed for the bridge and over without looking
back. At home my father said we'd done right. We decided
that Barnardo and I had better steer clear of Juárez from
then on.

"Right after that Villa took over our gambling halls, lock,
stock, and barrel. My father went over to see about it and
was arrested and put in jail. The American Consul, Mr.
Edwards, got him out. So it seemed that General Villa had no
more friendly feeling for the Aldaretes no matter how my
father had helped him in the past.

"Villa did have gratitude for his friend Theodore Kyriacopulous, owner of the Mexican Club in Little Chihuahua. Villa
showed his appreciation by turning over our gambling halls
to Kyriacopulous and to Villa's brother, Hipólito, who had
always wanted it. At the same time he awarded the lottery
concession to Carlitos Jáuregui, the clerk who had helped him
escape the Mexico City prison and who had stayed with him
ever since. Those three made fortunes out of our businesses.

"Anyhow, my father refused to stand still for such high-
handed treatment. He and his partners belonged to a corpora-
tion called Sociedad Anónima. At a meeting someone suggested that my father and Alex Gonzales—my friend's father
—being American citizens, should go the American Consul

and claim the gambling halls as American owned property. The Gonzales family like mine had for generations been well-known and respected in both El Paso and Juárez, helping in civic projects in both cities.

"Consul Edwards, a fine man, agreed to go with my father and Mr. Gonzales and drove with them to Villa's head-quarters, still the Cuartel. The building was always well guarded, with Villistas armed to the teeth and being very careful who they let inside. Out of respect to the Consul they admitted the Americans. My father often described the meet-ing to us. Villa received them sitting behind his desk. All three greeted General Villa. He ignored my father and Mr. Gon-zales and spoke directly to Consul Edwards. He said, 'What do you want to bring that trash in here for?'

"My father said Alex turned to him and said, 'We're in a hell of a fix. We might as well go.' They turned and left and they were sure glad that Consul Edwards was with them. We never got our property back as long as Villa was in power.

"One of Villa's dreams was of a free bridge between Mexico and the United States. He picked a spot in the Lower Valley and had plans drawn up for such a bridge. My friend, W. B. Glardon, tells about seeing Pancho come into his father's electrical shop to order lamps for his planned bridge. Darbey-shire-Harvey Iron Works molded a three-light standard follow-ing Glardon's design. Villa liked the lamp. It was made of solid cast iron in the shape of a T about nine feet tall and weighed a good 500 pounds. Pancho ordered eleven more of the lamps and paid for them in advance from a big money roll he pulled out of his pocket. Right after that Villa went somewhere else. His power declined and all friendship between him and our country was gone. He was never able to build his bridge or to get his lamps.

"Today, there's only one of the twelve iron lamps that I know of. It stands in front of the Jacobs home in El Paso's Lower Valley. It is lit every evening and really is distinctive, looking like it would last forever. It's funny but in 1929 my friend Alex Gonzales did build the bridge where Villa planned it at Zaragosa. It wasn't entirely free but people seemed glad to pay the twenty-five cent round trip toll. Later the U.S. government bought the bridge from Alex."

21

Nina Kyriacopulos

Mrs. Kyriacopulos and her husband, Theodore, were close friends of Villa from 1913 until his death. Mr. Kyriacopulos ran the gambling halls in Juárez during Villa's occupation of the city.

"My husband, Theodore, had come to Mexico from New York. He had a partnership in a soft drink factory in Jiménez. His eyes bothered him and he came to El Paso for treatment. He was staying at the St. Charles Hotel when he met an old friend, another Greek. This man had known my family ever since I was a small child. He brought Mr. Kyriacopulos to our home, The Roma Hotel, which was owned by my father, Carlos Triolo. We are of Italian descent. Mr. Kyriacopulos took a room at our hotel.

"I was a young girl at that time and full of romantic notions. I thought Mr. Kyriacopulos was very exciting. A reporter once said my husband had *savoir faire,* and I always thought that was a good description. He was attracted to me, too, and said that when he got his eye troubles straightened out he was going to marry me. Sometime later he had a successful eye operation in Mexico City. He wired me that his sight was saved and that he was now going to marry me.

"We settled down here in El Paso. My husband was a very

good businessman. He spoke Spanish better than Greek. He was well liked by the Mexican citizens here as well as the exiles from Mexico. He owned the Emporium, a bar and club at the corner of El Paso and Second Street. The place, which was very popular, came to be known as the Mexican Club as it was in that part of town called Little Chihuahua.

"When Pancho Villa came to El Paso early in 1913, he took a room in my father's hotel. He became a regular visitor at the Emporium. Pancho had an unstable temper, but he and my husband got along very well. The club was a meeting place for revolutionary leaders, reporters, spies and others looking for information about what was going on in Mexico. My husband told me that every day they heard new rumors of revolts and uprisings. They even heard about the activities of Pascual Orozco and his Red Flaggers, and of Zapata, the Indian leader, clear down in the State of Morelos.

"We knew of course that Pancho Villa had just escaped from prison in Mexico City and had come across the international line and to El Paso for safety. No one knew that he was actually here until a reporter recognized him and found that he was actually registered at my father's hotel under his real name, Doroteo Arango. An article appeaerd in the *El Paso Herald* saying that Colonel Francisco Villa was here and planning to stay in the United States.

"Carlos Jáuregui, who helped Villa escape from prison in Mexico City, was with him. Villa had money to live on. Some said it came secretly from Raul Madero. Also it was said that Governor González of Chihuahua had given Villa a lot of money and told him that it was better for everyone if Villa stayed in the United States, at least for a time.

"Right after Villa came to El Paso he got word to Governor Maytorena of Sonora telling him to warn President Madero of plots against him. Villa had heard of them while in prison at Mexico City. His warnings seemed to be ignored and Villa got very restless.

"But Pancho settled into the life here. He liked ice cream and got it almost every day at the Elite Confectionery. He was also very fond of peanut brittle and always carried a supply in his pocket. Though he was always eating candy, Pancho said he had a very delicate stomach and had to almost live on squab. He kept a box of live pigeons in his room at my father's hotel. That was accepted as one of his little personal oddities and no one thought much about it. As my husband used to say, in the state of nervousness that Pancho lived in at that time it was no wonder he had to pamper his stomach. Later we found out that the pigeons were really homing pigeons and that Villa was sending messages down to friends in the ranch country of Chihuahua.

"My father told me that one day an agent from Huerta came to see Villa in his room at the hotel. The agent tried to get Villa to go back to Mexico, telling him that Huerta needed him and promised all kinds of promotions and rewards. Villa grabbed the man and threw him down the stairs and Huerta's spies didn't approach him again. At least not there.

"My husband knew more of what was going on than most anyone in either Juárez or El Paso. He told me about the time a German officer, General Maximilian Kloss, made a proposition to Villa in the Emporium. Villa was sitting by himself, drinking strawberry pop which he liked—you know he didn't drink hard liquor—when this German officer came up and sat down at Villa's table. The German talked to Villa and then seemed to be arguing. At first Pancho didn't say much, just listened. Then he stood up and leaned toward Kloss. My husband was called away then and when he returned Pancho was drinking his soda alone. He called my husband over. He told him that the German officer had wanted Pancho to sign a treaty assuring Germany of his help in getting some submarine bases and refueling stations off the coast of Mexico. Villa refused in no uncertain terms.

"Madero's assassination hit Villa very hard. He cried and

vowed revenge. Within a few days Villa slipped out of El Paso
and crossed the Río Grande into Mexico at night with only
seven or eight men. Before he left he turned his pigeons loose,
each carrying a note down to Chihuahua."

Villa quickly raised a large, enthusiastic army in northern
Mexico. By November of that year, 1913, Villa was a major
power in Chihuahua. His sneak attack on Juárez and his complete takeover of the city from Huerta's forces, came to be
regarded as one of the most brilliant actions of the Revolution.

"What is not generally known," says Mrs. Kyriacopulos,
"is that a train of refugees from Chihuahua beat Villa into
Juárez by only a few hours. It was said that those fleeing
from Mexico on that train carried a good million dollars in
gold and silver and other valuables. The passengers had received word somewhere along the line from Chihuahua that
Villa was on the march to Juárez. They chipped in and paid
the engineer and fireman a large sum to hurry the train into
Juárez and to the safety of the border ahead of Villa."

On November 23, the forces of Villa—now General Villa
—drove off the Federals in a bloody engagement south of
Juárez, near the small railroad station of Bauche, Mrs. Kyriacopulos recalls the terrible suffering of the wounded and ill
in Juárez following that event.

"Pancho's wife, Luz Corral, was here then and we, with
the help of many of the citizens and merchants of El Paso,
helped as best we could. I remember that the Popular Store
and the City of Mexico Store here furnished blankets and
clothing. A local bakery helped with food donations. My husband and his friends contributed also.

"Mrs. Del Campo with the Red Cross volunteered her services as did many women of El Paso. Some Juárez homes
were converted into hospitals. Doctors and nurses from El Paso
gave their help. Dr. Bush treated and cared for many of the
wounded in his hospital at Second and Campbell Streets.
Dr. G. B. Calnan, Dr. Miller and Dr. R. H. Ellis were among

the El Paso doctors I remember as working tirelessly to help the suffering."

El Paso was truly concerned about the misery in her neighbor city. The *Herald* of December 6, 1913, carried an item about money being donated for relief and noted that D. M. Berry sent $1 toward the fund. The money was turned over to Dr. E. F. Miller. The *Herald* of December 7 reported that the Tivoli Hotel in Juárez had been turned into a hospital and plans were made to use the big tin covered gambling hotel for the overflow. On December 11, five wounded rebel soldiers were brought from Juárez to Hotel Dieu by the Red Cross.

By this time General Villa was undisputed military ruler of the State of Chihuahua. He made his headquarters in Juárez. He brought with him a carload of silver and gold bullion which he exchanged for $750,000 American money. With this huge sum he bought war material and supplies from the United States, as well as automobiles from local dealers, paying cash for everything. Villa at this period meant big business for El Paso, though Theodore Kyriacopulos was never, as rumored, Villa's purchasing agent, his wife states.

"Villa rented a house at 1610 North Oregon for Luz," says Mrs. Kyriacopulos. "This was the period when Luz and I became really close friends. There were three one story houses there, high on the hill, looking west. Ours was the middle house, and the Villas lived next door. Villa chose this location so that he could cross the Rio Grande and go up the hill to Luz's house without having to go through town. He would cross the river close to the Smelter.

"Villa affectionately called Luz *La Guerra,* meaning the blonde, though she really was a brunette. That Christmas of 1913 my husband suggested to Pancho and Carlos Jáugueri, who was still with Villa, that maybe we could help choose a gift for Luz. Villa thought that was a good idea. I went with the men to a little jewelry store on Mesa and Villa picked out a dinner ring. It was very pretty, set with two rows of small diamonds. Luz was surprised and very proud of her gift. She still wears it as I noticed when she last visited me.

"I especially remember an occasion when Luz was our neighbor on Oregon Street. A Mrs. Brown, prominent in El Paso society, gave an afternoon tea honoring Luz. Pancho gave Luz a handful of gold coins and told her to buy the prettiest dress she could find. Luz bought a close-fitting black silk with the bodice covered with spangles. She looked lovely and received many compliments. She was pleased and so was her husband. Luz was then a very shy young woman. Villa was at that time very much in favor with the military and civic leaders here and was entertained at Ft. Bliss and in town.

"Of course everyone knows that Villa was quite a lady's man. He had several marriages and many love affairs. However I always felt that he loved Luz the best and was faithful to her in his way. He always seemed happy to be back with his 'little blonde' when one of his affairs came to an end.

"Even though he was then so important and powerful, I remember that Villa was still cautious. When he was out around the country in Mexico, on battle trails, or just moving around, he never slept twice in the same place. Also he would eat around at different campfires with his men, no one ever knowing just when he would show up. He was very wary of being poisoned. During this period he confiscated practically all the cattle belonging to the big ranches in Chihuahua. He sold the cattle, much of it here in El Paso, to raise money to continue his fight against Huerta.

"I want to say something about Villa's honesty here. Pancho Villa was truly a man of his word. There was the time he and three of his men 'borrowed' some horses from the Longwell Stables on San Francisco Street. Pancho said he wanted to try out some horses, so the stable workers saddled two fine looking mounts. Villa had a couple of his men ride them around for a short time. The men came back and the horses were all right. Villa then asked for two more good horses to be saddled and brought out. He and his three men then rode away, presumably for another short trial. However they went clear out of town. When my husband later took Pancho to task about this episode, Pancho laughed at the 'joke' he considered he'd played on Longwell. Several weeks later Villa stopped by the stables and paid for the horses and saddles. In fact he gave Longwell a bonus for having played the trick on him."

Mrs. Kyriacopulos recalls the time that Villa turned over the keno halls in Juárez to her husband as an expression of gratitude for his friendship and help. "Yes, it is true," she says, "that my husband ran the gambling hall during Villa's occupation after he captured Juarez in 1913. Of course he turned back a percentage of the profits to Villa; that was the way those concessions were operated. My husband also kept his own business here in El Paso, because with the Revolution going first one way and then another, things in Mexico were always uncertain. However, we did take a trip to Greece on the money that we made from the Juárez Keno halls.

"The last time I saw Pancho Villa was not very long before the Columbus Raid in 1916. He visited us here very briefly. I don't believe that Villa himself was actually in Columbus at the time of the raid. He really wanted to take his troops through El Paso to Baja California but was refused permission to do so. His men pulled the Columbus raid. They were desperate, low on food and ammunition, everything.

"Everyone read and heard about the time Pancho Villa was wounded in the leg when General Pershing's expeditionary forces were trying to catch up with him in Mexico. There were many stories about that, but we knew what really happened then. We know because Villa sent for my brother, Dr. Jerome Triolo, to attend his injury. He trusted my brother and knew that he would come as quickly as possible. Villa's wound was not received in battle, but was caused by the carelessness of a young soldier who was cleaning his gun which he thought was

unloaded and which went off, hitting Villa. There was no doctor in camp and when the leg began to give a lot of pain,
Pancho sent for my brother. Pancho was hiding at this time
in a cave where he could watch Pershing's troops riding the
trail below, quite a distance away. My brother stayed a week
in the cave hideout while the wound healed. Jerome, always
a prankster, took a picture of Villa taking a bath in a wash-
tub. He had a lot of fun with Pancho about that picture, telling him he was going to hold it for a bribe in the future.

"My husband just missed being in Parral when Villa was
assassinated. My brother had sent tickets for us to attend a
big Fourth of July celebration in Madera. My husband said he
would go to Madera, but after the celebration he would have
to go to Parral for two or three days. Villa had sent word
from Canutillo that he wanted to see my husband in Parral.
It was something to do with a loan of $5000 that my husband
had made to Villa. In fact my husband had filed suit to collect the money, which had been advanced to the Agencia Commercial and which had not been repaid. We always felt that
Villa intended to settle that debt when he sent for my husband,
as he always had fulfilled his obligations. However, he was
killed before my husband could see him.

"Luz Corral and I have remained friends throughout the
years. Whenever she came from Canutillo or her home, La
Quinta, which Villa had built for her in Chihuahua City, she
always stayed with us. I remember one time she came from
Canutillo in 1920. She brought with her two of Villa's children, Micaela who was nine and Agustín who was eight. Luz
always regarded all of Villa's children as her own and was a
loving mother to them. When she and the children returned
to Canutillo they were escorted by Alfonso Gómez, one of
Villa's former officers. Pancho took good care of his family.
Luz still visits me when she comes to El Paso and we talk of
those old times."

22

Mabel Silva

Mabel Silva was married to Villa's brother, Hipólito. At the time she met Hipólito—November, 1914— Mabel was going to school and working part time as a cashier at the Hidalgo Theater in El Paso.

"Pancho was kind and sympathetic to me. He loved Hipólito very much, but he always knew Hipólito had no right to take our children and keep them away from me.

"Hipólito was a very different kind of person than his brother. Hipólito liked to have a good time. He loved to spend money and always seemed to have plenty. He was very handsome. He would always drive up to the picture house in a beautiful Cadillac."

Mabel was at first hesitant about accepting Hipólito's attentions. Her mother was very strict about proprieties and Mabel knew that she would consider that even though Hipólito was a very prominent person in El Paso, her daughter should not go out with him unless properly introduced. Then Mr. and Mrs. Roy Martin, owners of the Linden Hotel, invited Mabel to spend a social evening with them. Hipólito was included in the party, and after that the courtship moved fast.

They were married first by a Justice of the Peace and then later, on February 28, 1915, in a church in Juárez.

Life with Hipólito was exciting though Mabel knew almost nothing about his business affairs. She did know that Pancho had a fierce sort of protective love for his younger brother, especially since their other brother, Antonio, had been killed in a duel in Chihuahua City. It seemed that Pancho could deny Hipólito nothing. He gave him the very profitable Juárez roulette and poker casinos to run and kept him supplied with fine cars. And Hipólito was not stingy with his bride, often buying diamonds for her.

Hipólito at times served as buffer between his brother and American associates who never knew just what to expect from Villa. Bud Rutherford, a reporter from El Paso, tells about securing an interview with Villa in Juárez through the help of Roy Martin. Rutherford says, "I didn't know then that Martin sent me into that interview with the powerful and unpredictable Pancho with a strong hand. In the next room all the time was Hipólito Villa, brother of the general, the one man who could control his wildest rages." Martin was said to have provided most of the arms for Villa. Martin was a very important friend to have, as Mabel Silva had learned.

Hipólito had been appointed Pancho's Superintendent of Military Freight, which meant that he had the responsibility of ordering and clearing the very large shipments of arms and supplies that poured across the international border from the United States into Mexico. As Villa's financial agent in El Paso, Hipólito with his dress uniform cut a fine figure. He made many friends with his free spending and important connections. He even went to New York to buy military supplies for his brother.

Mabel was very happy when their baby daughter, Mary Louise, was born.

However, while Mabel had been occupied with having her first child and her husband was busy with his own affairs, the war had turned against Villa. Villa was becoming hard pressed for money. He sent increasingly urgent requests to Hipólito in

Juarez for ammunition. In October there were rumors along the border that through Hipólito, acting as Villa's agent in Juárez, the brothers were selling stolen supplies and goods of all kinds in the United States in a desperate effort to raise funds.

On October 16, 1915, Zachary N. Cobb, Collector of Customs at El Paso, wired the State Department at Washington: "The port here should be closed outright . . . We must break up the band of commercial thieves operating here who are now at the root of the Villa menace . . . and who if not broken up will be conspirators, ammunitions smugglers, and managers of new revolts."

"I do not really remember about many of the things that happened then," Mabel Silva says now. "I was so young, still in my teens, and was completely and happily occupied with my tiny baby. I knew things were bad with my husband and his brother, that is all. Then one day someone called from Juárez and told Hipólito to get all of our money and jewelry and other things of value out of the house right away, as we were going to be investigated.

"My aunt, Mrs. George Benton, had a safe in her home, and we hurried and put our valuables there, most of my rings and everything. But the customs officials went there and took them, even my personal jewelry, including my four-carat diamond. I never got them again, even though Roy Martin got us very good lawyers, Tom Lea and Paul Thomas, to protect our rights."

The *El Paso Herald* of November 10, 1915, carried the story with big headlines:

$500,000 FOUND IN VILLA SAFE—Customs Officials Say Saw Piles of U.S. Currency and Gold; Not Taken
Villa and his brother, Hipólito, have $500,000 laid away for a rainy day, U. S. Customs officials declare. When they seized $30,000 worth of jewelry belonging to

the two Villas Tuesday morning at the home of George Benton, 329 Leon St., the customs officials declare that there was at least $500,000 American currency and gold in the safe in which the jewelry was found. The money was stacked in piles of bills, with the small drawers filled with gold coins, the customs men declare, and they say it was not less than $500,000 worth.

None of this money was taken, as it was the property of the Villas and only the jewelry, which they claim was smuggled, was seized. This jewelry is being held at the custom house pending the settlement of ownership and it will probably result in a case in federal court in an effort by Villa and his brother to claim the jewelry.

To the customs officials, Hipólito Villa stated that the jewlery was not smuggled, but that it was the personal property of himself, his brother, and their wives. He says much of the jewelry had been presented to them by American business men and was of American manufacture. The customs officials declare, however, that none of the rings which were seized fitted the fingers of any of the Villa family.

A story in the *El Paso Herald* of November 22, 1915, tells of some of the efforts made by Hipólito to regain the seized valuables:

Atty. O. L. Bowen, acting for Colonel Hipólito Villa appeared with witnesses from the El Paso jewelry firms of W. W. Hixson and Silberberg Brothers before U. S. Treasury department agents, here, stating he wanted to have a look at the $35,000 worth of diamonds and jewelry recently seized by customs authorities as smuggled articles belonging to General Francisco Villa's brother and sister-in-law. Collector of Customs Z. L. Cobb refused them permission to see the gems, declaring that claim would have to be made without seeing them.

There were now many rumors about Pancho and Hipólito, and even their wives, being seen on the American side of the Río Grande, carrying large sums of money and satchels supposedly carrying jewelry. They were said to be searching for safe places to cache their valuables.

The *Herald* of December 28, 1915, says:

$25,000 of Villa jewelry confiscated by U. S. Customs officers included a medal given to Hipólito Villa for personal valor, diamond screw sets, rings, pins, and a diamond necklace. Hipólito Villa will make an effort to claim the jewelry at the next term of court.

"That is all true," Mabel states. "They were my personal earrings and my husband's medal. We were very frightened and didn't know what might happen next."

However, before that item appeared in the paper the Villa families were leaving El Paso, as is shown in this story in the *Herald* of December 22, 1915.

The objective of the Villa families is the Argentine republic in South America, according to advices received by government officials. The households of Hipólito and Francisco Villa bought through tickets over the Southern Pacific Railroad and by way of the United Fruit Company's steamer, sailing Saturday for Havana. Three of the family left on the 10:30 train Tuesday night for New Orleans where Mrs. Luz Villa and Mrs. Hipólito Villa and households are waiting for the Saturday steamer. Three of the last to go of the Villa families are scheduled to leave tonight and tomorrow. Reports to the federal authorities here are to the effect that arrangements have been made for taking a steamer from Cuba to Buenos Ayres, Argentine, and that negotiations have already been concluded for the Villas to go into the cattle raising industry on big ranch property in the South American republic.

The *El Paso Herald,* December 30, 1915, reports:

> Francisco Villa's family and his brother, Hipólito Villa, arrived in Havana, Cuba, today on board the steamer Atenas, from New Orleans.

"Many of the family were along on that trip," Mabel recalls. "Hipólito's sister, Martinita Flores, and a Mrs. Rodríguez were there, as well as Luz Corral. All were sent by Pancho because trouble was stirring. We were only in Cuba for about two months when Hipólito was arrested and put in jail. He was there for three months. We always thought it was on a trumped up charge, to get back at his brother, Pancho, some way."

The *El Paso Herald* of April 7, 1916, has this story about it:

> Havana, Cuba: Colonel Hipólito Villa, brother of Francisco Villa, who was arrested here on February 7th at the request of the American minister and has been held pending extradition proceedings, has been released. He is . under indictment in Texas on a charge of complicity in cutting a railway line near El Paso last December in an attempt to hamper the movement of Carranza forces through American territory to attack the Villa forces in Mexico, but the Cuban Secretary of State announced that the U. S. has failed to produce evidence warranting his extradition.

"I remember," says Mabel now, "that during those months that Hipólito was in prison I would take my baby girl, Mary Louise, with me and we would take lunch to Hipólito and visit with him.

"It was our friend, George Holmes, a nice old man from Ysleta, and a good friend of both Hipólito and Pancho, who made bond and so got my husband out of prison. Mr. Holmes came all the way from El Paso to help us. There was another man in prison with Hipólito and Mr. Holmes got them both out."

Holmes, one of the American soldiers of fortune involved in the Mexican Revolution, was a loyal friend of the Villas. And in return Pancho showed his gratitude. When Holmes was convicted of violating the neutrality laws, he went to Mexico and joined the guerrilla general. He was given the position of a commercial agent, and it was said that Villa always took care of him after that, saying that Holmes had originally got into trouble helping him and he would never desert Holmes.

Though difficult, Holmes did manage to help Hipólito get out of Cuba and to San Antonio. He sent for Mabel and met her in Corpus Christi. They stayed there for three weeks, till after her second child, a son whom they named Frank, was born. Then they went back to San Antonio, where hipólito had to report regularly to the authorities.

"At that time," Mabel says, "my husband pawned the rest of my diamonds to raise money for the revolution in Mexico. I never saw any of my jewelry again. Forty days after our son was born Hipólito went back into Mexico to join Pancho. He left me with nothing. I had to work as a maid to take care of myself and my babies. His sister, Martinita, was always good to me, especially then when I needed help so badly.

"Finally my mother came to San Antonio and took me and the children back to El Paso. I went to work for Mr. Schuster again, at the Estrella Theater. Then he built the Colón Theater and I worked there for a while. Those were very hard years for me. For a time I worked as a maid for A. B. Fall in his beautiful home on Arizona Street. Mr. Fall was a man of great influence in Texas and Washington. The Falls were really fine people and I always enjoyed working in their home.

"Hipólito never came back to me as my husband, though he was in Juarez often and I heard of him at times. When little Frank was three and Mary Louise five. Hipólito sent word that he wanted to see them. He asked that I bring the children to him in Juárez. The children were eager to see their father and I thought it would be all right to take them over there. So my aunt and I took Mary Louise and Frank to see Hipólito. That was a big mistake. When it came time to go back home to El Paso, Hipólito would not let the children go with me. I became angry, then frightened, and cried and begged him, but he refused and my aunt and I had to return alone. I didn't know what to do, but I thought surely that the next day at least he would bring or send my babies back to me."

"It was two years, two long years of terrible anxiety before I had my children again. Soon I learned that Hipólito had taken them to Canutillo where his brother was now retired. I heard all kinds of rumors. One time we heard that Mary Louise was in Torreón, that she was sick, even that she died."

An item in the *El Paso Herald* of November 8, 1922, confirms her story:

VILLA'S EX-WIFE WANTS
PROBE OF CHILD'S DEATH

Mrs. Mabel Silva, 2104 East Yandell Blvd., former wife of Hipólito Villa, has appealed to the Mexican consuls in Chihuahua City and Torreón to investigate the reported death of her six-year-old daughter, Maria Louisa, who was recently in the custody of Hipólito Villa at Torreón. Mrs. Silva has also requested the American government to effect the return of her five-year-old son, Abdón, for whose abduction Villa is under bond in Peace Justice Rawlins' court, more than a year ago. Villa is expected in Juárez soon. His agents say Maria Louisa is alive at Torreón.

"The paper here, the *Herald,* did what they could to help me," Mabel says. "I finally went down to Boquilla. I was

afraid to go clear to Canutillo. Pancho met me at Boquilla.
When the Mexican newspaper reporters wouldn't leave me
alone there, Pancho chased them away. He was always kind
and good to me. He promised to get my children returned to
me and I knew then that I would get them back all right."
Villa kept his word. Mabel Silva returned to Juárez and
Hipólito soon brought the children to her. She brought them
back across the border and to El Paso, and there settled down
to work and care for her family.

"Of course I later heard many stories of the children's experiences, especially in Canutillo," she recalls. "One time at
Canutillo little Frank was sitting beside Pancho at dinner. He
wanted the sugar and when he kept asking for it, Pancho, busy
talking, told Frank to be quiet. Little Frank got mad and said,
loud as he could, 'When I be a big man I'll bring the American army down to kill you!' That got attention. Pancho broke
off talking, looked at Frank and roared with laughter. He was
very pleased with my little son's spunk and said that Frank
was just like him. He was very good to the children while they
were at Canutillo. He even bought Frank a pony to ride. Mary
Louise told me that one time there she saw her uncle, Pancho,
pull out a tub, and in the tub was lots and lots of money, bills,
and silver and gold.

"It was not so long after the return of my children that
Pancho was killed in Parral. It was a terrible thing. But even
while I felt sorry for Pancho I was greatly relieved that my
babies were safely away from Canutillo and home with me.
I read in the paper about Hipólito going down to the ranch
after it happened."

The *El Paso Times* of July 22, 1923, carried the story.

HIPÓLITO TAKES CHARGE

Hipólito Villa, brother of the slain leader, arrived in
Parral yesterday afternoon to take charge of Villa's body.
He has been his brother's business partner for the last two

years, and managed Villa's summer home ranch, on the outskirts of Chihuahua City. It is known as Fresno Ranch. During his campaign a number of years ago General Villa appointed his brother as financial agent. Hipólito was stationed at Juarez.

"My son grew up in El Paso," Mabel Silva says. "He served in World War Two. But my beautiful daughter, Mary Louise, died when she was nineteen. My children were always good, smart children. I will always be proud of them."

Hipólito Villa continued to be in the news during the next years. Some months after the assassination of Pancho it was rumored that Hipólito and a Manuel Cháo had sought to incite a war of revenge. Governor Enríquez of Chihuahua ordered federal troops to take over Canutillo and to take Hipólito prisoner. Hipólito was jailed for a time in Durango while things cooled down. The authorities were taking no chances of a revival of the revolution through Villa sympathizers.

Hipólito however continued to get into trouble and to make trouble. The *El Paso Times* of February 9, 1924, ran this item:

> Hipolito Villa is demanding $200,000 gold for the release of T. J. Mackenzie, general manager of the Boquillas Power Company.

The *Times* of April 20, 1926, reported:

> Despite efforts to keep the fact secret it was learned last night that Hipólito Villa, brother of the late Francisco Villa, was arrested by a special police officer and lodged in the Juárez jail yesterday while orders were issued to arrest two well known revolutionists . . .

And the *Times* of July 25, 1926, said:

Torreón, Coahuila, Mexico—Released from the Durango penitentiary under 4,000 pesos bond. Hipólito Villa, indicted as a bandit by the Calles government, has returned quietly to his ranch in the State of Chihuahua.

"Hipólito married another woman late in his life without getting a divorce from me," says Mabel. "I did get a divorce."

Hipólito continued to live on and operate the ranch at Fresno. The *El Paso Herald-Post* of November 18, 1957, carried a story of General Hipólito Villa's meeting and interview in El Paso with authors William V. Morrison and Dr. C. L. Sonnichsen.

"Yes, I read the story," Mabel says. "At one time during those years, Hipólito wanted me to return to him, but I didn't consider doing so, though I hold no ill will toward him."

"I remember those old times very well. I was so young that I didn't really know what was going on, though. All I thought of was my family.

"Luz Corral telephoned me when Hipólito died. He had been alone on his ranch at Fresno for three days, and was so discovered, dead, by a workman. It saddened me to think of it."

23

Daniel J. (Buck) Chadborn

Chadborn was living in Columbus, New Mexico at the time of the raid on the town. He was a cattle inspector with the Panhandle Cattle Association and was also a deputy sheriff of the town.

"The officers on this side of the line had lots of help from Villa. I remember one time when some of Orozco's Red Flaggers stole twenty-eight saddle horses from me. My special pet, Nigger Baby, escaped the thieves and came home. I immediately reported the theft to Villa's men at the office in the Commercial Hotel and they promised to do what they could. Soon after that all my horses were returned to me.

"As cattle inspector I had frequently an occasion to cross back and forth along the international boundary. To show how co-operative Villa was he gave me a safe conduct pass for my protection though I didn't ask for it. It was presented to me in Villa's Columbus office by two of his right-hand men, Leoncio J. Figueroa and Antonio Moreno.

"Yes, Villa was still riding high in Chihuahua and feeling very friendly toward Americans the year he kept his office in Columbus. You might say that Columbus was then about at its zenith, too."

In 1915 Columbus was a thriving town of several hundred citizens, plus the encampment of the 13th Cavalry soldiers at Camp Furlong. It looked forward to an expanding future. The weekly paper, *The Columbus Courier,* strongly promoted a real estate boom. The paper pointed out that Columbus was strategically situated, being the only gateway from Mexico into New Mexico, and the only port of entry on the long stretch of border between El Paso, Texas, and Douglas, Arizona. The Palomas Lakes, a few miles away, expected to become a summer resort. Columbus was the shipping point for thousands of cattle sent into the United States from Mexico and those sent east from the ranches of the Mimbres Valley, New Mexico.

The Florida Mountains nearby with their history of Indian battles not too far in the past were attracting visitors. The picturesque Tres Hermanas peaks at the eastern end of the range showed an abundance of agate and crystal formations that made the area a rock-hunting paradise.

Columbus in the fall of 1915 was peaceful, prosperous, friendly, and pleasantly drowsy.

Then in the pre-dawn hours of March 9, 1916, Columbus was invaded by a band of marauders composed of hundreds of hostile Villistas, remnants of the once powerful guerrilla leader's army. Columbus became an historic battlefield, site of the last invasion of United States soil by foreign troops. Newspapers headlined the news of the Columbus raid across the country.

"I was awakened about 4 A.M. on that morning by the sound of shots. My ranch home was on the eastern outskirts of town. Jack Thomas, another deputy sheriff, was working for me on my ranch and staying at the house. We both jumped up, grabbing our clothes and our guns. At first we thought the commotion was just some cowboys celebrating. By the time we were dressed we knew it was more serious than cowboys shooting into the air to let off steam. There were more shots and quite a bit of yelling going on right in the center of town.

"Jack and I took my wife and the three children to a sort of storm cellar near the house. Our neighbors, the John Moores and their two children got to the cellar about that time. The women and kids were plenty scared, but we figured that with the entrance to the dugout hidden by brush they'd be safe down there.

"By the time we got into town there were several buildings burning. Bullets were flying everywhere. In the light from the fires we could see a milling mob of Mexicans wearing the big sombreros and crossed gunbelts of Pancho Villa's followers. There were bands of them, shooting and yelling 'Viva Villa!' and 'Viva Mexico!' The Commercial Hotel was blazing. I remember a couple of Customs men, Jolly Garner, nephew of John Nance Garner, and Ben Aguirre, saving a woman from the second floor of the hotel. They got her out and down to the ground by lowering her with sheets tied together. The hotel burned clear to the ground.

"The raiders were plundering and looting the burning stores of everything they could carry out. Many of them were just kids. I found one dead boy about fourteen holding a pair of woman's black patent slippers. Another dead boy had his hands fully of candy. I saw Steve Birchfield, a rancher, who'd escaped from the hotel. He was still shaking from his experience. The bandits had caught him in his hotel room and demanded his money. In desperation Steve gave them his checkbook. Then, while they were fighting over it, he slipped out and ran. It was a plain miracle that he wasn't killed, because several men in the hotel were shot down. At daylight, all of a sudden it seemed, things got quiet. The Villistas pulled out and hit south for the border."

A group of citizen police, led by Chadborn and including Jack Thomas and Dick Rodríguez, Chadborn's friend who had worked in Villa's office, went after the retreating Villistas. They followed the raiders some thirty miles south of the international line, into the rough mountain country of Chihuahua. There, because of the danger of riding into a trap in the rugged country that was familiar to Villa and his followers, the pursuers turned back to Columbus.

"Of course I knew the townspeople who were killed and some of the soldiers, too. It was a tragic list."

The dead were identified as: C. C. Miller, Charles DeWitt Miller, J. J. Moore, William T. Ritchie, John Walton Walker, Dr. H. M. Hart, Mrs. Milton James, W. A. Davidson, Harry Davis, John Nievergelt, Harry Wiswell, Frank T. Kindvall, Fred Griffin, Mark A. Dobbs, Paul Simon, James Dean, Jesse P. Taylor, and Thomas Butler.

Chadborn went out to his ranch home and brought his family into town. Mrs. Chadborn said later that the time spent in the dugout was the longest she lived through in her whole life. The next day many of the women and children were taken to Deming to stay with friends or relatives. The Chadborn family stayed at Sheriff Simpson's home.

"When we caught our breath we figured out something of what had happened. Everyone generally agreed on the main facts. The Villista guerrillas had surprised and killed the guard at the gate at Palomas. Then they sneaked into town, using the cover of that drainage ditch you see running north and south, it being deep enough to hide them. They swarmed through the streets yelling and shooting at anything that moved. The first killed was an army sentry, Private Fred Griffin, who challenged them. Before he died he killed three of the Mexicans. The soldiers had some trouble getting to their arms, and they surely were outnumbered, but they fought hard to repell the Villistas. This was borne out by the number of dead they left.

"Now, as to why the attack was made on Columbus has been explained and argued and never really made clear. Of course a lot of it was for the purpose of looting. Those Villistas were hungry and ragged, desperate for everything. They didn't need much excuse for striking and grabbing what they could.

Then, too, it could have been purely for retaliation. Toward the last of October, before the raid of course, Jack Thomas and I watched more than 1,000 Carranza federals go through Columbus on a train headed for Douglas, Arizona. Now, that was an American train going over American territory, carrying *de facto* Mexican government troops on their way to fight Villa at Agua Prieta, across the border from Douglas. What happened there is history. The Carrancistas caught Villa's troops by surprise and almost annihilated them. No wonder Villa was hostile toward the United States.

"Then there's the question coming up again and again of whether Villa personally led the raid. I never thought he did. But it was sure led by two of his men. Pablo and Martín López. Villa might have been waiting outside of Palomas. Or it might have been someone else who was taken for Villa. I wouldn't know.

"Another thing that has caused endless argument was why the commanding officer of the army camp at Columbus, Colonel Herbert Slocum, seemed to be caught napping. There was a lot of hard feeling and criticism at the time, but likely most of it was unjustified. Colonel Slocum was receiving conflicting reports about Villa's whereabouts every day. Villa was said to have been seen at the time at a dozen points along the border and in the interior. Regulations didn't allow the colonel to send anyone down into Mexico to report to him. He had to rely on what he could learn mostly from Mexican nationals going back and forth. I'm one of those who could never figure out why he didn't pay more attention to Juan Favela and his warnings. Favela was well known in the community as an honest man and a good citizen.

"Anyhow, when those Villistas finally hightailed it south they left close to two hundred of their own dead in and around town. We gathered them up and hauled them into the desert. There we soaked the bodies with gasoline, stacked and burned them. It was horrible. The stench seemed to hang in the air for weeks.

"It will never be the same again as before the raid, no matter how high the mesquite grows up to hide the ruins. My friend, Arthur McKinney, who thought he was Villa's friend until Villa murdered him, lies buried at Columbus, as do many other victims. Villa certainly wasn't a good man, but I wonder sometimes if Columbus might have escaped her doom if Pancho Villa hadn't believed that he was double-crossed by his one-time friends in Washington. Who knows?"

24

Pearl McKinney Wallace

Mrs. Wallace was six years old when her mother died and was taken from El Paso to Mexico to live with her oldest brother, Arthur. Arthur McKinney was the foreman of the Polomas Land and Cattle Company located near the Mormon colony of Dublán in Chihuahua.

"Pancho Villa murdered my brother Arthur just two days before the Columbus Raid. As a little girl I was always terrified of Villa, and his later actions bore out my feelings.

"It was at my brother Arthur's ranch home near Dublán that I first remember seeing Pancho Villa. Villa was at that time friendly to all Americans, especially the Mormons. He turned against them later when President Wilson recognized Carranza instead of him. Many people agreed with Villa that he had been double crossed, but no one realized how savagely he would turn on those who had considered him a friend.

"Villa would often come and visit with the family of Mexicans who worked for my brother and his wife. When I'd see him coming I'd try to get into the house. If I was still out in the yard playing, Villa would always come over and stroke my red hair. To me he was repulsive, big and burly and dirty looking. I didn't want him to touch me. I learned later that it is an Indian superstition that anyone having red hair is related to the sun god, and to touch such hair brings good luck. Well, my hair was certainly red enough to attract even Pancho

Villa! It was so long that when I was a little older I could sit on it. It was also said that Indians never scalped red-haired people. Anyhow, I always resented being singled out for Pancho Villa's attentions.

"Many a time I saw Villa come into the big ranch kitchen for coffee. He especially liked the cookies that the Negro cook, Old Buck, would have in his 'sweet jar' as he called the lard can he used for storage.

"The big company ranch house where Arthur and his family and I lived had been built over ancient Indian ruins, believed to be of the Montezumas. The underground ruins were discovered when the well was dug. Some of the rooms extended under the ranchhouse and could actually be used for storerooms.

"They were put to very good use when Arthur and his family, with the Mormon colonists and other foreigners, suddenly had to leave their homes. The revolutionary battles between federals and rebels had grown so violent that the lives of the people around Dublán were not safe and they couldn't stay there. They were given two hours to get ready to leave, and each was allowed to take only one piece of luggage. They had to ford the Agua Caliente River to reach the railroad. In the little time they had before leaving, Arthur and his wife put their most precious belongings down in one of the old Indian storerooms. They hid all their valuables and antiques there, among them a sewing-machine that had been my mother's and was now mine. I wasn't there at the ranch when this happened—I was going to school in Del Rio, but I was greatly relieved to hear that my sewing-machine was safely hidden.

"However, while the family treasures were saved from looters that time they were lost anyhow a little later when the house was burned down. The walls fell in on the underground storerooms and everything was ruined. I suppose what's left of it all, or at least most of it, may still be there.

"I was still in Del Rio when my brother was killed. What happened was witnessed by Old Buck, then my father's cook at the Diamond A. Buck had been kidnapped the day before by the same crowd and taken to Villa's camp. He was told that if he would cook for the bandits he would not be killed.

"It seems that when Arthur rode through the camp he seemed to be looking over the horses. He was studying the brands to see if there were any company horses there at the camp. He dismounted and went over to the fire where Villa was having coffee. Arthur shook hands with Villa, sat down on the ground and lighted a cigarette. Arthur had two other men with him, Bill Corbett and James O'Neil. They were all completely at ease.

"After a few moments of conversation Villa just said, 'I'm making war on the gringos, and I guess I'll just start right here with you.' One of his men then threw a rope around my brother's neck. Arthur thought it was a joke. He laughed and put up his hands to throw the rope off, but it was no joke. The rope tightened. Someone said it was a strand of barbed wire instead of a rope. The end was thrown over a tree limb, and Arthur was jerked off his feet.

"Buck said my brother was laughing when he died. He may not have realized even then that it was not all a rough joke. It took place so rapidly that Corbett and O'Neil didn't realize what was going on till too late. They tried to escape but the Villistas ran them down. They roped them and pulled them from their horses, then dragged them to death over the ground. Buck says they were so mangled that there was no recognizing them when the guerrillas finally stopped.

"Buck escaped the next night when the Villistas rode toward Columbus for their sneak attack before dawn. He made his way afoot to the Diamond A. There he found my father and told the story. He took my father to where Arthur's body was still hanging. They buried Arthur at Columbus.

"My father rode at the head of General Pershing's troops,

as guide, when they went down into Mexico to get Villa. I'm sure he hoped they'd catch up with my brother's murderer. As I think about it it's hard in a way to realize that the sweets-loving, superstitious, friendly man who liked to visit at the ranch would turn into a killer, no matter what the provocation. Still, I'll always remember the fear I had of him when I was just a little girl."

25

Juan Favela

*Favela was working for the Palomas Land and Cattle
Company and living in Columbus, New Mexico at the
time of the raid on the town.*

Definite warnings of the raid on Columbus had started
several days before March 9, 1916. On March 2, three Villistas were captured by Federals near Casas Grandes and had
confessed that General Villa planned to attack either Hachita
or Columbus. Also it was reported in town that General
Gavira, Carrancista commander in Juárez, had sent word that
Villa was heading north to make trouble for the United States.
Everyone, including Colonel Herbert W. Slocum, in command
of the American soldiers at Camp Furlong, Columbus, knew
about it.

"So why," Juan Favela says "didn't those in charge pay
any attention and do something about it? Why did Colonel
Slocum brush me off when I told him that I myself saw those
bandits camped south of Palomas?"

On the morning of March 8, Favela was riding toward the
Boca Grande River to meet Arthur McKinney, riding boss for
the Palomas Land and Cattle Company. Topping a sandhill
he saw below a small band of Villistas. Juan turned and rode

back. He dismounted and tied his horse in the brush, then walked back to the hilltop.

He could see the camp clearly. He saw Villa and Mc-Kinney sitting by the fire, talking and drinking coffee. They were too far away for Favela to hear what they were saying but they seemed to be in good spirits. Bill Corbett and James O'Neil, two of McKinney's associates, were at the edge of the camp, sitting relaxed, sideways in their saddles, smoking.

Favela watched Villa and McKinney. Suddenly Villa stood and watched one of his men tie a piece of barbed wire around McKinney's neck. McKinney seemed to be laughing as though it were a joke. The man stepped back pulling the wire taut and McKinney was jerked forward. Then as the Villista threw the end of the wire over a branch of a large cottonwood tree the American was lifted clear of the ground, his legs thrashing in the air.

There came a blast of shots and shouting. Favela looked back at Corbett and O'Neil to see them spurring their horses, trying to get away. Bullets cut them down. It all happened so fast that the cup that McKinney had held was still rolling on the ground.

Favela fell to his knees. He knew that McKinney and Villa had been friendly for years. Favela managed to stumble to his feet and make his way back down the hill to his horse. As he rode away, he heard shouting behind him. He had been seen. Bullets hit the rocks around him. He lay low in the saddle and headed away as fast as he could go. Because he knew the ground so well he managed to get away safely. Back at the headquarters ranch, Favela told his wife, Petra, what he had seen.

Although his wife pleaded with him to warn everyone in Columbus, Favela decided to try and see first if Villa had other troops nearby. He sent Antonio Muñoz, a young cow-boy who worked for the company, to watch from a safe spot on the hill. From there Antonio could see and count the

Villistas as they passed through a narrow defile on their way to Columbus. In a short time Antonio came back and reported there was a large band of riders headed for Columbus.

Favela immediately rode into town and went directly to his friend, B. M. Reed, owner of a grocery store. Reed accompanied Juan to Colonel Slocum's headquarters. Slocum was in a meeting with several officers when Favela started to tell his story. Slocum stopped Favela until he had dismissed the officers.

"Then," Favela says, "he listened to me, but his mind seemed to be somewhere else. He told me, 'I have sent troops east to the Bailey Ranch and west to the Gibson Ranch. If Villa comes, he will come by one or the other. A reception will be waiting for him. Do not be concerned, Juan.' The Colonel seemed to be in a hurry to get rid of me.

"Later we learned that Colonel Slocum, after sending most of his men out of town, left with almost all the officers and their families. I'll always think that Colonel Slocum believed me all right, and that he took care of his own skin and that of his family."

Juan returned to the home ranch. He was upset and as he rode he wondered why he had been brushed off by Slocum. It had been rumored for a week that Villa was going to attack somewhere along the border, but no one could tell where. Maybe Colonel Slocum had information that the townspeople did not and was right in being so sure that the attack would not be at Columbus. After all, even Villa, would hardly dare attack a town protected by an army post.

The night of the raid Favela and Petra, pregnant with their first child, couldn't sleep and sat out under the stars and talked. As they talked Petra became more and more frightened. She felt that they must get away from the ranch, which Villa would surely raid on his way to Columbus.

Thinking of Favela's mother living alone in Columbus, the young couple got into their old car and drove into town.

Favela kept thinking that if Villa did not attack that night that maybe by the next day the people of Columbus might be more prepared. He felt sure that Villa would strike only at night.

He drove as fast as he could over the rough road. Petra held a lantern and they bumped along through the chaparral thickets by its shaky light. Juan worried about Petra. This rough riding was bad for her. He tried to drive carefully. Twice Petra asked anxiously if he didn't hear something. Once Juan stopped the car and listened, but there were only the usual sounds of the nightwind in the brush and the small scurrying of little animals. Petra shivered.

At the inspection point at Palomas, the gateway into the United States, three miles south of Columbus, Favela warned the officer in charge that he was sure Columbus would be raided by Villa not later than the following night. Since he had heard nothing, seen nothing on the way in, maybe it wouldn't be this night. The officer showed little interest.

The two drove on to their home in town, a small frame house in back of the Commercial Hotel. The night was quiet and everything in Columbus seemed normal. Favela decided to wait until morning to talk to Colonel Slocum again. He didn't know that Slocum had left Columbus that afternoon. Petra and Favela were very tired from the hard ride and they went to bed immediately.

It seemed that he had been asleep only a few minutes when he heard the whistle of the "Drummers' Special," the train arriving on schedule from Douglas, Arizona, and bound for El Paso. Favela dozed off again. He was dimly conscious of the train's departing. Its chugging sounds had hardly died away when the ringing of shots and wild yells of "Viva Villa, Viva Mexico," started.

Favela ran to the window. Petra sprang out of bed crying, "It is Villa. He did come." She broke into wild sobbing. Favela turned from the window. He pushed Petra down to the floor and under the edge of the bed. He pulled the mattress down and they crouched behind it.

Then he and Petra remembered his mother. "She hadn't even a gun to defend herself," Favela says. "We had to go to her."

They dressed in the dark. All around now were the shouts of "Viva Villa" and shots and even screams. Favela opened the back door cautiously. There was no shooting back there. They went out and ran as fast as they could through alleys and streets, staying in the shadows of brush and the few houses they passed. They made their way to Favela's mother's adobe house.

"My mother was very relieved to see us," Favela recalls. "She quickly pulled us inside. She had been afraid that we'd been killed. By this time several buildings were burning and shots came from all directions. There was a red glare all over town. I felt that I must go out and help. And even then I couldn't stop thinking that if my warnings had been heeded this might not have happened.

"Outside I found people running around half dressed. Most of them didn't even have guns. I told some of them to get back into their houses and not to light any lamps. The screaming and yelling grew worse and everywhere was that shout "Viva Villa." More buildings were on fire. The raiders broke into stores and shot out windows that showed lights. They had brought cans of kerosene tied to their saddles and now they emptied them over the frame buildings which caught and blazed high.

"In the horrible confusion I saw a young woman leaning over the balcony of the hotel. She was screaming and pointing at the body of a man on the ground below, in front of the hotel. 'That's my husband! Someone help him!' she cried over and over. No one could reach him then and by morning all that was left of Walton Walker, bridegroom of less than a month, was a burned, blackened torso. I heard that poor young Mrs. Walton went out of her mind for a while from the horror of it.

"Now there were dead people in the street. Mr. Miller, the druggist, died trying to protect his store. Mr. Ritchie, the owner of the Commercial Hotel, and my very good friend, was killed in the hallway, near the steps. I helped Mrs. Ritchie and her three daughters get away from the hotel and into an adobe building where they were safe for a time. The two story hotel went up in flames.

"It seemed to me that the Ravel Brothers Store, the biggest in Columbus, was the center of attack. Even while the front of the store was burning the bandits were plundering it, running out with their arms full of loot. Some were shot down in the street. Some escaped and rode away unmolested. Dean's Grocery caught fire and Mr. Dean made a wild dash toward it. He was riddled with bullets before he had gone sixty feet.

"I wondered where the soldiers were all this time. I learned later that the Cavalry were breaking into the locked guardhouse to get at their guns and ammunition. There had been some trouble between the soldiers and the townspeople, it was said, and so it was thought wisest to lock up the arms. Also it was feared some of the guns might find their way into the hands of the guerrillas across the border. When the soldiers finally got the guns and ammunition they fought fiercely to defend the town. They managed to catch the Villistas in a crossfire that really picked them off.

"Villa, cunning as always, had not come into Columbus from the expected way. He had circled the town and come in from the northwest. He cut the fence between the two countries. There is a wide, deep ditch dividing the town and Villa took advantage of this natural cover to ride undetected into Columbus. The guards at Palomas had been knifed so there was no warning from that direction.

"I didn't know until later that not only did Colonel

Slocum have my firsthand warnings, but a newspaper in El Paso stated that President Wilson's agent, George C. Carothers, had been informed of Villa's march northward. Carothers sent telegrams to Colonel Slocum on the sixth and seventh of March and again on the eighth. He called Colonel Slocum by phone about noon of the eighth of March, but the call was not completed until about six in the evening. It is said that Colonel Slocum assured Carothers that Villa was seventy miles below the border. That was a lie! I myself had just told Slocum that morning that Villa was only a few miles south of the border with hundreds of men. I had sure knowledge. I had seen what he did to Arthur McKinney."

"When daylight came about fifty soldiers and citizens were organized into a pretty good fighting group. We were doing all right when Villa's bugler blew retreat and the raiders fled toward the border. More than sixty of them were killed as they rode out. They left some one hundred and twenty-five of their own dead around town.

"The people of Columbus were devastated. The town was a smoldering ruin. My own home back of the hotel had burned down. We men wanted to follow the raiders right into Mexico but Colonel Slocum had returned to the town and he forbade it. He threatened to put the town under martial law if we did such a thing. Major Frank Tompkins, with about thirty troopers, was the first to come to our aid. He followed the Villistas into Mexico for a few miles, then as Villa met them with a rear guard, Tompkins, outnumbered, came back to Columbus and asked the Colonel for more troops, but Slocum refused his request.

"That morning Colonel Slocum sent for me and gave me a pass to go any place in the United States. 'Just get out,' he ordered me. 'I don't want you talking to the newspaper men who will be pouring into the town.' He gave me some money.

"I went to Deming. But in a few days I came back home. In June Petra gave birth to our baby, a girl. The baby died in convulsions, caused we always thought by the hard ride into Columbus the night before the raid.

"We don't need a park here in Columbus named after Panch Villa to remind us of him and what he did as though he was a hero. That I will never understand."

26

Frank T. Padilla

Padilla lived in El Paso before and during the Revolution and was living in Columbus, New Mexico at the time of the raid.

"My father, a United States Ranger, died when I was a boy. So I had to go to work when I was very young. I got a job chopping wood for a woman who owned a restaurant in El Paso. Many times I saw Pancho Villa eating there. He came especially for breakfast. Sometimes he had his wife, Luz, with him. I remember Luz wearing a white blouse and red skirt, and a grey Mexican shawl.

"In those days Pancho went by his real name, Doroteo Arango. You know he took the name, Pancho Villa, from a bandit who was executed by the Mexican government when Doroteo was two years old. The original Pancho Villa was said to be six feet four inches tall. A friend of my mother who owned a bakery on Second Street here in El Paso used to tell us tales about Villa. I grew up on them. One story we never tired of was about the treasure Villa cached on the other side of Anapra. It was said that Villa had his men bury a couple of mule loads of gold and silver there. Then he had the men and mules killed and all buried on the spot. No one knew if the treasure had ever been dug up.

"When they made that moving picture, *Viva Villa,* here on the other side of the smelter along where the race track now is, I acted in it as a soldier. The actor who took the part of Pancho Villa, Wallace Beery, had the same size body as Pancho. When he put on a moustache he looked just like Pancho Villa. So, it's easy to see how a person could make a mistake thinking he saw Pancho Villa when he really saw an impersonator.

"That might have happened when Columbus was raided. There was a leader there that looked like Villa. People expected to see Pancho Villa. They were sure they saw Villa, just like that. Now, as to his riding a mule up to the border. Well, it's a known fact that Villa did use pack mules. When he had his headquarters at the Dolores Gold Mines in the Sierra Madres in Chihuahua in 1908, Villa ran whole trains of mules, hundreds of them, packing freight into the mining camps. Also he took about fifty mules from a Columbus man, Juan Carreón, and his son, because they were trying to get the animals across the border a few miles south of Columbus shortly before the raid. Carreón was trying to save his mules from the Villistas, but ran right into them and lost the whole herd. Sure, Villa *used* mules, plenty of them.

"I knew many of the revolutionary leaders. There was General Francisco Madero, later president, and General Blanco. I knew Doctor Talamantes who was killed in November, 1913, near Bauche, when the Huertistas tried to take Juárez away from Villa. I also knew Mrs. Talamantes. She and her two daughters took her husband's place with the troops until they could reach Juárez.

"General Pascaul Orozco was another I knew and knew of. Orozco had many friends in El Paso, and some of his family is living here. I will never forget the circumstances surrounding his death—or murder.

"Early in 1911, General Francisco Madero's forces were camped across the Río Grande, just north of El Paso. His troops were made up of bands of guerrillas and their leaders. One of the most important was Colonel Pascual Orozco from western Chihuahua. He was much more important than Villa. I remember the ceremony near the Madero camp at Peace Grove when Orozco was commissioned Brigadier-General. That was April, 1911 or thereabouts. At the same time Villa's rank was raised to Colonel. Over two thousand El Pasoans attended. It was very impressive, with speeches and band music.

"Orozco always looked like an officer, Villa more like a peon. Orozco was tall, over six feet, slim, blue-eyed and freckle-faced, reserved in manner. It was said that his family was descended from the Basques. Pancho Villa was squat and awkward off his horse, dark and sloppy. Those two men hated each other.

"Madero's troops defeated the federals at Juárez in May, 1911, and General Juan Navarro, commander of the federals, surrendered to Provisional President Francisco I. Madero. At a conference of Madero's staff Orozco demanded that Navarro be court-martialed. Instead Madero had Navarro brought safely into the United States because he respected him. From then on General Orozco was in open revolt against Madero. Villa remained loyal to Madero and he and Orozco became bitter enemies.

"Orozco and his followers, known as Red Flaggers, caused a lot of trouble in the Casal Grandes area and around Parral, where he and Villa took the city from each other in turn. After President Madero's assassination Orozco served as a division general under Victoriano Huerta. When Huerta was forced to leave Mexico and took up residence in Spain, Orozco kept in touch with him.

"Huerta went to New York in April, 1915, and told newspaper reporters that he was only visiting and intended traveling in the United States. He said that he would never return to Mexico. Everyone in El Paso said that Orozco went to New York and met there with Huerta.

"Then Orozco came back to El Paso and began his work of notifying all the many Mexican exiles in the region of a coming revolution to be led by Huerta and Orozco. It was common knowledge. Arms and ammunition constantly went over the border into Mexico in huge quantities. A hoard of it was discovered in an El Paso warehouse, ready to be transported.

"On June 27, Huerta arrived by train at the railroad station in Newman, New Mexico, about twenty miles north of El Paso. Huerta's son-in-law and Orozco were waiting for him. They had planned to drive by car to the border from there, avoiding the federal agents at El Paso. Instead they were met at Newman by agents of the Justice Department. Huerta and Orozco were formally charged with conspiracy to violate United States neutrality laws and taken into custody.

"A large crowd of Mexicans cheered the two Mexican leaders as they were brought out of the federal building in downtown El Paso. After being placed under bond, Huerta and Orozco were kept under house arrest at Fort Bliss. But Orozco escaped. He had many sympathetic friends in the city and the Mexican border near, so he was never caught. Huerta remained in prison or under house arrest until he died.

"Orozco remained active and it was rumored that he was still plotting a revolution. He was often said to be in and around El Paso. On August 29, with four companions, Christófero Caballero, General José Delgado, Andrés Sandoval, and Miguel Terrazas, Orozco rode up to the Dick Love ranch near Sierra Blanca, and demanded food. Love wasn't there when they arrived but returned while the fugitives were eating. It was said that Love was tipped off that Orozco was at his ranch. Orozco and his men fled.

"Next day, Love, with a large posse, tracked Orozco and his men to Green Canyon. This posse was federal marshals, Texas Rangers, deputy sheriffs, ranchers, and even troops of the Thirteenth Cavalry. From the ridges on both sides of the canyon they fired downward, killing all of the cornered fugitives. Not one of the posse was hurt. Their victims were caught afoot and unarmed. After shooting the five men they dragged them along the ground like dead dogs.

"Orozco was buried here in El Paso, on September third. They had a big funeral with about 3,000 Mexican people there. His friends said that Orozco had been assassinated. Feeling ran high. No one believed that Orozco had raided the Love ranch and stolen horses and cattle as was reported. Orozco didn't have to steal horses. I know that friends furnished him horses from Juárez. There were a lot of outlaws around Juárez who rustled horses and beeves and who claimed to be followers of Orozco, but they weren't.

"I read that even Pancho Villa, who hated Orozco when alive, sent a telegram to Orozco's widow saying that the family was authorized to bury Orozco wherever they desired in the national territory. He was buried in El Paso, but some years later his body was moved to the cemetery in Chihuahua City.

"Many people in El Paso believe that Pascual Orozco was given the *Ley Fuga*. There was a lot of resentment about the way he was killed. The Spanish edition of the *El Paso Times* had stories about it, also the San Antonio papers. Well, as I say, I knew Pascual Orozco, and his is a story that's never been fully told. If there was even an official investigation of his death the results were never given to the public.

"There's a lot about the Columbus raid that hasn't been written, too. I was living in Columbus at that time, working for the United States government. My job was to help build a road from Palomas to Casas Grandes. The night of the raid everything in town was quiet. There'd been rumors for weeks that Villa was going to strike somewhere along the border. But there were also pretty good reports that he was up around Casas Grandes or a dozen other places than near Columbus.

"Anyhow the stores were all closed as usual that night. The town was dark and quiet. Some of the soldiers from the camp there had been sent to ranches out along the line where it seemed raiders might attack. The cavalry was camped in tents to the left of the depot. The town lay northwest.

"Then about 4 A.M. all hell broke loose. There was shooting and yelling, *Viva Villa!* and you could hear some *Mueran los gringos!* Hundreds of raiders, Villistas with big hats and bandoleros, had sneaked up an arroyo, going around the area where the soldiers were camped.

"They set those wooden buildings afire and they blazed like hell. All the time that yelling going on. I watched. I didn't have a gun so there wasn't much I could do. I saw Martín López on a big bay horse right in the middle of everything. He and his brother, Pablo, were commanding the Villistas. Everyone knows they led that raid. Pablo was wounded but got away. Later he was executed in Chihuahua City. When the soldiers from the camp realized what was happening they came right in behind the raiders. They managed to catch them in a crossfire in an open area. They just mowed the Mexicans down. The whole scene was lit up by those fires.

"Shots and yells and screams and burning buildings, all scrambled together. And dead people. Lots more Villistas were killed than townspeople and soldiers. Next day I helped bury them.

"Three days later we started building the road to Casas Grandes. It became a real important project in a hurry with United States troops going into Mexico by the thousands, moving tons of supplies and equipment. Columbus really boomed during the time Pershing and his men were chasing Villa.

"It was said on pretty good authority that an eighteen year old boy born and raised in Columbus had been spying for the Villistas and that he told them in full detail where everything was placed in town, and the best way to take it by surprise.

"I guess you know my name, Padilla, means little frying-pan, and I guess I get pretty hot under the collar when I hear some of the stories about the Columbus raid, things that I know can't be right. I'm sure that the lady who was kidnapped from that ranch near Pearson, Chihuahua, by Villistas after they shot her husband, and who rode with them for nine days before the raid, *thought* that her kidnapper was Pancho Villa, and that she saw him lead his men right into Columbus, after changing his mule for a sorrel and white stallion. But, I say, she saw an imposter. And the telephone operator who saw a uniformed Mexican officer giving orders that night in Columbus, and who was sure that from pictures she'd seen of him, that this was General Villa, must have been watching some other Mexican officer. There were many of them who could have looked like Pancho Villa at night. Villa didn't like to wear a uniform while campaigning or in battle. He only wore his uniform when he was ruling Juárez.

"Villa was no hero and he did go after women. But he didn't kill ranchers or allow his men to. There were bunches of cattle rustlers all over Chihuahua who had nothing to do with Villa's troops but who called themselves Villistas and did those deeds."

27

Ben Turner

During the Revolution, Turner was a soldier of for-
tune and railroader. He fought under Villa and later
served under Pershing in his chase of Villa.

As a young man, working in El Paso as a machinist,
Turner was ready for adventure when Colonel Eusebio Calzada, a Madero supporter, came to Juárez in 1913 looking for
volunteers to fight under Villa. Having lived for a time in
Mexico as a child and again when he worked for the Southern Pacific Engineers Camp, Ben spoke Spanish fluently and
had a liking for Mexico and its people. So he attended a
banquet Colonel Calzada gave in Juárez for the volunteers.

The speeches were fiery and very persuasive. Madero had
inspired his followers to work and fight to free the masses of
Mexican people from oppression. Swept up in the spirit of it
all, young Turner found himself heading south the next morning with the volunteer army.

Action was not lacking. At Lerdo, Turner had his chance
to fire a machine gun. At Cornejos, after a battle between
Federals and rebels, Turner was checking over the trains when
he found a young Federal soldier lying wounded in the village.
He kicked in the door of the nearest house and ordered the
frightened people inside to care for the man.

That act of mercy almost cost him his life. A Villista officer had Turner jailed and ordered him to be shot the next morning. Turner sat in the adobe room that night and, watching the flickering flame of a candle, considered his hopeless situation. He decided to put up a struggle for his life.

The next morning the door of his prison room was flung open. A bearded man approached him and asked, "Who is this Texan we are going to execute?" Then he grabbed Turner in a bear hug and shouted "Hallo, Benito!"

Turner says now, "I was never so glad to see anyone in my life. It was Rudolfo Fierro, Villa's feared 'Butcher.' He rescued me from that firing squad."

The next day Fierro introduced Turner to Pancho Villa on the railroad platform at Cornejos. Fierro told Villa that he wanted him to meet "The biggest American tramp I know, Ben Turner."

"Villa didn't really smile," says Ben now, "but his face sort of relaxed when he gave me a tingling handshake. I was to learn to respect this strong man and his ideals and courage.

"I had railroaded with Fierro on the west coast of Mexico during the building of the Southern Pacific line there while Villa was in control of the railroads in the northern part of Mexico. Rodolfo and I had become fast friends at that time. Fierro had been in charge but his management was poor and he had been replaced by Colonel Eusebio Calzada, my boss. Fierro was really a dangerous man. It was said that he once shot a stranger in Chihuahua City to settle a bet on whether a dying man falls forward or backward. Fierro won the bet as the man fell forward.

"There have been many stories about Fierro's death. I favor the story told to me by one of his men who I met in Juárez a number of years later and who knew that Rodolfo Fierro and I were friends.

"He said he was there when Fierro was killed. He said that Fierro and some others had come to a mountain stream which was in flood and Fierro said that they were to cross. Everyone else wanted to wait until it was less strong. But Fierro said, no, he'd show them. He had a big strong horse, for Rodolfo was a heavy man, and like a bull he rode into the stream. The horse went down and it and Rodolfo were carried off. As usual the saddlebags were loaded with bullion and Fierro with bandoleros of ammo. The horse was found in a canyon, but Fierro's body was never found."

It was in 1916, after the Columbus Raid, that Turner, back in El Paso, was hired by the government as an auto mechanic, accompanying the cavalry in the Pershing Punitive Expedition.

"I received a big salary for those days, $150 a month. We realized that the real reason for going after Villa was not to capture him but to train American soldiers for the war in Europe that was getting closer to the U. S. The wild mountains and plains of Mexico offered a good training ground."

"It was a great life for a little while, but a strenuous one, and I sure almost lost it down there at Cornejos. I still remember the most ruthless killer of the Revolution, my friend, Rodolfo Fierro, as being my saviour.

"But what was Pancho Villa like? Well he was truly a crusader who never gave up on trying to help his people. As a man . . as a leader . . as a soldier . . . HIM . . . I don't think I can answer that. I am like the man that couldn't see the forest for the trees. I was too close to see the greatness in the man, for you must see the *great in history* from a distance in years, in order to see the spark that motivates him. For Man is an animal and although a thinking animal, these thoughts are not always the purest, and sometimes he uses the motto, 'That the end justifies the means.' At the time these things happened I was a youth with, as the youth of today, bubbling mind, out to correct the world. But now as the years have passed I can see more clearly.

"The land, all of the State of Chihuahua, belonged to the

Terrazas family and also all the cattle on it. It was said that a group of wealthy Americans wished to buy 10,000 head of cattle and approached Terrazas to see if he could supply that quantity. They didn't think he could do it but Terrazas said, 'What color did you gentlemen want?' And it is believed that the number at that time could have been delivered in one color. At that time, in Chihuahua, if you ate beef you stole it from Terrazas for he was the only one who had cattle and unless you paid his price you didn't eat.

"Pancho and his group ate and were bandits. Yes, the man who wrote more pages of Mexican history than any other Mexican living or dead was once a bandit. Later he was a follower of that inpractical Madero. Madero was a dreamer who also had that spark in him that inspires other men. He was like Christ and his followers were like the disciples. He was almost like a god to them, preaching of the freedom of the poor of Mexico. Pancho Villa was like the disciple Peter to Madero's Christ. They were both crucified.

"Villa was not a religious man, but he had a belief in Deity, I am sure. Once I heard Villa say, 'When you give to the people you are closer to heaven than at any other time in your life, for you are being directed by the Hand of God.' "

28

Sergeant Thomas F. Smead

Smead was with General Pershing's Seventh Cavalry on the Punitive Expedition sent to stop the Villista raids.

"The first time I recall seeing Pancho Villa was in El Paso in 1914. At that time Villa was well thought of here. His picture was published taken with General Scott and General Pershing, and he was entertained at Ft. Bliss. Villa was riding high on both sides of the border. It even seemed like Villa would receive official recognition as the leader of Mexico by President Wilson.

"Villa often made the Hotel Paso Del Norte in downtown El Paso his headquarters on this side. One evening I happened to be in front of the hotel with a friend. We watched as Villa and some of his staff talked with several United States military officers. A young reporter came up to the group.

"The reporter said to Villa in a real smart alec tone of voice that carried all over the street, 'I hear that you're a regular S.O.B. with the ladies!'

"Everything got very still. General Villa looked the young reporter over from head to foot. Then he said, 'Yes, I'm what you call a son-of-a-bitch with the ladies, and what I'd call you is a son-of-a-bitch and leave the ladies out.'

"Villa's voice was dead calm. His eyes were full of contempt as he gave the reporter one more cold look. Then he turned and walked into the hotel. His officers, all silent, followed him. I tell you that young man's face was white as chalk. He just slunk away and disappeared into the crowd.

"At that time Villa was buying millions of dollars worth of merchandise from the United States. He brought big business to this region. Americans considered him a friend. Then, less than two years later, everything was changed. Carranza's *de facto* government was recognized by President Wilson as representing Mexico. There was an embargo placed on selling supplies to General Villa. Pancho's forces suffered defeats and loss of power from then on. Villa's former friendship turned to vengeance.

"The attack on Columbus in 1916 brought quick action from the United States, and the order went out for American troops to pursue and disband the raiding bandits. They followed them down into the State of Chihuahua.

"About two A.M. on the morning of March 16, 1916, just a week after the Columbus raid, General Pershing led the Punitive Expedition into Mexico. My outfit, the Seventh Cavalry, with the Tenth and one battery of the Sixth Field Artillery crossed the international border at Culberson's Ranch, near Columbus. The other troops had crossed at Columbus the day before. Each soldier had been issued emergency field rations of potatoes, bacon, coffee and hardtack. We were on our way.

"Colonel Selah Tompkins—everyone knew him as Tommy —was my commanding officer. He was the finest officer I ever served under. His men were so loyal to him that they would have followed him through the gates of hell. His brother was Major Frank Tompkins, who was stationed at Columbus at the time of the raid.

"Tommy Tompkins was a strong character, what you'd call colorful, a real Old Army Cavalry man. He understood his men. Many a time he talked to us about hard drinking. He said he knew we might need a drink at reveille to clear our throats, and another maybe at morning mess, and of course after stable duty a man had to clear out the stink from his lungs, and a sociable drink at dinner was all right, and along the march it was needed for stamina, and maybe a beer or two to relax in the evening. He always wound up by saying, 'But I don't want to hear any more about this constant nip, nip, nip, and sip, sip, sip. It's got to stop.'

"The Colonel took a real personal interest in his men. He never forgot them. I remember after we got back from Mexico, he came to see my family when our first baby, a boy, was born. He rocked little James Joseph and said he was the prettiest baby he ever saw. It made my wife very proud.

"But to get back to our invasion of Mexico. The cavalry, and we were well mounted, made such good time that we got ahead of our supply train. The first ten days were about the most rugged I've ever known. We slept on the ground rolled in our blankets. The pup tents weren't much protection. There were cattle all over the country, branded and unbranded. We'd kill a cow and roast the beef in hunks, held over the fire on a stick. We ate it half raw, with no salt. I've never been able to enjoy rare steak since. Believe me, we felt like celebrating when our supply train with hard loaves of bread, canned meats, fruit and milk, finally caught up with us.

"I remember once a small brown bear came out of the brush. I shot and dressed it and we cooked some of the meat. It had a musky, strong taste and smell. One of the men, Dutch Klice, took one taste and threw it down in disgust. 'Hell,' he said, 'that thing was spoiled when it was still alive.'

"There was quite a bit of rivalry and good-natured competition along the marches. There was a little encounter between Colonel Langhorne leading the Eighth and our Colonel Tompkins leading the Seventh. Langhorne cut in front of us and Tompkins yelled, 'Get those blankety-blank tin soldiers out of our way or the Seventh will run over them!' Langhorne graduated from West Point after Pershing did. He was a good German American.

"One time early in the campaign we had Pancho Villa trapped. That is we knew where he was cornered and holed in. This was near Socorro, in mountainous country. We were camped in the foothills there. Villa actually came into camp several times at night and played poker with our men. He never wore a uniform on those occasions. The men with him looked bedraggled. I and others saw Pancho at those times and recognized him. Then Pershing got the order from the top to withdraw and we moved on.

"At Guerrero, late in March, Colonel Tompkins led us in intercepting escaping Villistas. The Villistas and Carrancistas had had a bloody battle at Guerrero before we arrived. The Villistas troops had taken the town but Pancho himself was gone when we got there. He had been wounded—shot in the leg—it was said by one of his own men. The report was that it was done by one of the 'volunteers' forced to join up with Villa. But his loyal followers claimed the shot was an accident. Anyhow, Villa had been taken away in the night. We always thought we had just missed him. Our Seventh Cavalry gave good account of itself in that engagement, capturing Guerrero and machine guns, rifles, horses and mules that we needed and really crippling Villa.

"After leaving Guerrero we marched hard, a forced march, headed for a little old Indian village called Tomóchic. It was very rugged country and we reached the village by going down the canyons, taking advantage of the cover of rocky ridges. When we had crossed a little river to charge the settlement, many of the Villistas we sought were already taking to the hills. Quite a force of them gained high ground and then began firing down at us. The firing was heavy until it grew dark, then the enemy pulled back. The battle was over.

"Next day, Easter Sunday, April 23, all was quiet and

peaceful. The Villistas had gone, leaving at least thirty of their men behind, killed or wounded. We had lost two men. We heard later that after we pulled out the Tarahumara Indians living in the region gathered up all the guerrillas, alive and dead, poured pitch over them and set them afire. Those Tarahumaras were savage, primitive people.

"The conflicts with the Carrancistas at Parral in April and then later in June with the Tenth Cavalry at Carrizal were tragic. The Mexicans, especially the Carranza forces, had come to resent American troops being on their soil. They had flat out ordered General Pershing to move only northward even though Villa's trail appeared to lead south. Pershing was furious, but he had to follow orders from Washington.

"The Carranza *de facto* government agreed at first to our going down into Mexico after the guerrilla bandits but turned downright hostile. They didn't want the cavalry crossing the border and did everything they could to stir up anti-American feeling.

"The most pleasant part of the whole campaign was the seven months we spent at Camp Dublán before coming back across the border. This was where General Pershing established headquarters, near the Mormon towns of Casas Grandes and Colonia Dublán. Those Mormons are real fine people. They were very good to us. They sold us fruit, vegetables, milk and butter, chickens and eggs.

"While we were at Camp Dublán, Colonel Tompkins sent for me and another soldier called Mac. We went to his tent wondering what we'd done wrong. The Colonel said, 'I have a mission for you men.' He wanted an aparejo [a Mexican saddle outfit for pack mules]. There was one, he said, in Carranza's warehouse there, but he didn't want his stolen from the Mexican government. He wanted us to pay a reasonable price for the aparejo, wherever we found it.

"Mac and I rode upriver about seven miles without seeing anything promising. We dismounted and sat on the bank, smoking and resting a bit. We weren't in much of a hurry. As we sat there we saw a Mexican riding up to the river. He rode a big burro and led another. Mac and I looked at each other. The pack burro carried just what we were looking for, an aparejo.

"We got up and started toward the Mexican. That poor *paisano* took one scared look at us walking toward him, gave a sort of hopeless yell, and took off through the cedars on his burro. He dropped the lead rope on the other animal. We tried to call him back and tell him that we only wanted to talk to him, but he just kept going. Maybe he'd stolen the outfit. I don't know. Anyhow when we examined the aparejo we saw it was just what the Colonel had ordered. Also it was loaded. Well, the colonel hadn't said anything about wanting what was *in* the saddle pack. We led the burro off the trail, out of sight of anyone coming along, and opened up the pack.

"We'd made a rich find. The aparejo had a dozen buckets of honey and some slabs of bacon. We sneaked the stuff back to camp and hid it in a hole we dug under one of our pup tents. The Colonel was very pleased with his aparejo. It was just what he wanted. He said it was about the finest he'd seen. He didn't ask any questions about where we got it. That was one of the things the men liked about Tommy Tompkins.

"Well, we couldn't wait till we fried some of the bacon in our mess kits. Of course it smelled so strong and good that it brought the other soldiers on the double. They sniffed their way right to where Mac and I were wolfing down bacon and hard-tack with honey. A Captain Jones offered us twenty dollars gold for two slabs of the bacon. We took his offer and started selling bacon to the others for twenty-five cents a slice.

"Our regular rations were issued from Colonia Dublán, so much potatoes, coffee, hardtack. There was a little bacon, and I saw men trying to eat it raw because they couldn't slice and cook it very well in a mess kit. We sure appreciated the vegetables and apples and other fruits the Mormons sold us.

"The Mormons told us they never had any trouble from Villa, but the Red Flaggers, Orozco's followers, and other Mexican Revolutionists were hard on them. Villa always showed friendship for the Mormons, and the colonists sold him plenty of beef.

"Finally in January, 1917, the orders came for General Pershing to withdraw his troops from Mexico. By February 4th we were at Palomas, Chihuahua, a few miles south of Columbus, New Mexico. Next day we crossed the international border and were back home in the good old United States. We were really happy when we stood again on the soil of our own country.

"On June 15, 1919, Villa with 4,000 men attacked the city of Juárez. His forces drove Carranza's federal defenders, under General Francisco Gonzales, out of the main business district. General Villa again seemed to be in control of Juárez.

"However, bullets had crossed the Río Grande into El Paso from the time the Villistas camped outside of Juárez on the night of the fourteenth. Snipers shot directly into our Command Post, taking advantage of the bright moonlight. One shot killed Private Sam Tusco and one seriously wounded Private Burchard Casey.

"El Paso citizens wired Washington in protest. President Wilson ordered General Howze, commander at Ft. Bliss, to run Villa out of his threatening position if it was necessary to invade Mexico to do it. Villa's outfit was between Juárez and the river. Though Villa got credit for shooting into the United States I don't think he was responsible. All evidence points to Carranza's soldiers doing that shooting toward El Paso, hoping to bring on intervention.

"Our Seventh was still under Colonel Tommy Tompkins, commanding the Second Cavalry Brigade, and camped between El Paso and Ysleta. We were stationed at Stanton Street Bridge manning machine guns. We watched across the river toward the race track in Juárez and we had our guns ready for action. Cannons were set up on Scenic Drive. A test shell was fired which burst about 100 yards beyond Villa's outfit. Observers in a balloon basket called back to reduce the next shot. So the next shot was fired right in the midst of the rebel troops. Then all four of our cannons fired at once. Villa's men waited for no more. They took off south.

"Orders came for us to chase Villa away, so we followed ten or twelve miles south and east. There was no real engagement. We were all mounted, firing with pistols. Our planes, piloted by what were called the craziest fliers in the world, dropped harmless smoke bombs. The Villistas jumped off their horses and ran afoot, dropping their guns. I reached down from my saddle and picked up a Smith-Wesson one of them dropped. I took out the firing pin and took it home for my little boy to play with. There was discarded stuff all over the desert. Most of it was mighty poor equipment, makeshift and shoddy.

"Chasing Villa away from Juárez was all the foreign battle service many of the veterans ever got.

"Lots of us didn't know why we were down there. I always thought one of the main reasons was to get the desert cleared for the direct route from here to Mexico City that is now the Pan American Highway. That sure must have been the real purpose of the Pershing Punitive Expedition, because we could have taken Pancho Villa a dozen times.

"Another thing, I don't believe Villa led the Columbus raid. I think he had better sense. Carranza's federal soldiers pulled that deal to get our troops down into Mexico. Why, those supposed Villista guerrilla raiders were followed 100 miles down into Mexico, then their trail turned and came back to Juárez. They were tracked by Indian scouts who had plenty of savvy about what they were doing.

"Those were wonderful days with the cavalry. They are almost all gone now, the soldiers and the horses. It's a lost world. The Parade Ground and drills, the real, live bugle calls;

it's all gone. It was a good life, the best, and I wouldn't trade it for anything. When they substituted tanks for horses I was through. I wouldn't have served with them if it meant court-martial to refuse."

29

R. L. Andrews

Andrews was an early aviation pilot. In 1920 he flew the governor of Chihuahua, Ignacio Enríquez, to meet with Villa for the signing of Villa's surrender papers. Andrews is now an El Paso businessman.

Andrews' aviation career had its beginning in 1899 when, as a boy, he was living on the same block as the Wright brothers' bicycle shop in Dayton, Ohio. That year Wilbur and Orville began experimenting with kites. "All of us school kids," says Andrews, "were out in the commons when they were flying those man-carrying kites. They were studying air currents."

Andrews learned to fly by the crack-up method. When his plane crashed he simply picked himself up, repaired his plane with whatever means were at hand, and went up again. "I always carried baling wire and tape," he says.

In 1910 he paid the Glenn Curtiss Company $500 for blueprints and patent rights, built the plane himself and went on from there. That first plane never got higher than ten feet in the air. "The motor would cut out," says Andrews, "and down we would come. But I learned a lot of aerodynamics in those grass-cutting flights." A year later, in his second plane with a motor capable of thirty to forty miles an hour speed with a tail wind, Andrews began giving exhibitions at the fairgrounds in Coffeeville, Kansas.

Andrews recalls a demonstration he gave in Bolivia. "We couldn't fly at La Paz as the altitude is about 14,000 feet and the Curtiss Pusher would not fly over seven or eight hundred above sea level, so we disassembled it and packed it by llama train down the east slopes to the Gran Chaco country where it was low enough to fly." To prove the biplane's maneuverability and military value, Andrews hedge-hopped over the trees carrying dynamite. He had cutting pliers fastened onto his wrist and was nonchalantly smoking a cigar. "We only made about forty miles per hour so I could easily smoke the cigar. I wired two boxes of dynamite to braces next to me, one on each side, in such a way that when I cut a looker wire the boxes would fall. They all went off either in the air or when they hit the ground. At seven hundred fifty feet altitude I lit one of the dynamite fuses from my cigar and when it was burning cut it free with the pliers. Then I lit the fuse on the other load of dynamite. The explosions landed on target, and so I guess I became the first bombardier in history. I sure impressed the government officials and army officers watching the demonstration."

In 1910 when Andrews passed his tests and received his International Pilot's License, Number 78, he became one of the first licensed pilots in the country. He enlisted in the American Air Force in 1917 and became a photographic officer. Using a box camera with telephoto lens he took pictures roped to the cross wires of his plane.

"I sold some oil leases that the Reverend Fuller Swift and I had in Kansas," Andrews recalls. "I had known him there, and when I arrived in El Paso in 1919, he was Pastor of the St. Clements Church. I took the money I had from the sale and bought a Hall-Scott 50 horse V8 motor which flew the ship fine."

Andrews was in the early Signal Corps Aviation Section

in 1908, and was stationed at the then Ft. Bliss Air Field at El Paso in 1919. That year he flew his first trip to Chihuahua City, in a J-I Standard.

There he performed a spectacular stunt of flying between the twin spires of the famous Cathedral. The Mexicans, knowing that the wings of Andrews' J-I Standard were wider than the distance between the spires flatly declared it couldn't be done. Andrews bet Adolph Krakhauer, a Chihuahua merchant, that he could do it. When his plane roared over the treetops around the church the plaza was filled with an expectant crowd. As he approached the narrow passage he simply tilted the plane and skinned through, barely missing the heavy copper cable that connected the spires, so winning the bet and thrilling his audience. Krakhauer paid the bill for the sumptuous banquet that followed.

Andrews describes the episode, "I just dove on the church and as I neared it I put the plane in a vertical bank and put one wing between the spires. I didn't know about the copper cable. When I got back uptown they told me I only missed it by about six inches."

The governor of Chihuahua, Ignacio Enríquez, was an enthusiastic aviation fan, and Andrews became well acquainted with him, flying the governor a number of times in Chihuahua. "One day when the governor was visiting in El Paso," Andrews relates, "we were having dinner and I suggested that if he would invite General Robert L. Howze, commanding officer of Ft. Bliss, to send a squadron of planes to Chihuahua on a friendly visit, Enríquez might be asked to fly down with them.

"I asked General Howze about it and he said, 'Do you think he might do that?' I told him I would feel him out about it. So the deal went through. General Howze sent down a squadron of De Havillands, two-seater, light, biplane bombers, known as 'flaming coffins.' We went down for a week's stay. When we arrived in Chihuahua the city was decorated all over with American and Mexican flags. There were many parties and banquets. We were not allowed to spend a cent as everything was paid for by our hosts. The day before we were to return home General Enríquez told us we had not been there long enough and that he had wired General Howze for a week's extension to our visit and had gotten it for us. Enríquez was a strikingly handsome man, six and a half feet tall."

Early in 1920 it was rumored that Pancho Villa had told friends that he was tired of fighting and killing and was willing to settle down if satisfactory surrender terms could be arranged with the government. In July of that year Villa held a conference at Sabinas with General Martínez, arranged by Villa's friends, Colonel Daniel Delgado, Attorney Michael A. Dolan and Don Elias Torres, all of El Paso. This conference resulted in the granting to Villa of Rancho Canutillo and 50,000 pesos in gold and a guarantee of personal safety for Villa and his Dorados.

For the final signing of papers Andrews flew his friend, Governor Enríquez, to meet with Villa and seal the pact.

"I landed on the banks of La Boquilla Lake with the governor. We met Villa there. He had a big smile on his face as he shook hands with each of us."

On July 20, 1923, Pancho Villa was assassinated. The story of his assassination was told to Andrews by Salas Barraza.

"Barraza was the head of a secret fraternity, the requirements for membership being that some female member of the member's family must have been mistreated by Pancho Villa. It was Villa's habit that upon seeing a pretty girl he would have his men bring her to him for immoral purposes. The object of this fraternity was the assassination of Villa, according to Barraza.

"Villa came to Parral every Saturday, driving from his ranch at Canutillo, and it was planned to get him on one of these trips. The street he always used passed a Plaza and

turned right, then crossed a bridge into town. At the turn
was what was called the haymarket. There were always
several loads of hay standing there. Salas Barraza and his men
hid in one of the loads.

"The first time they tried the assassination they could not
carry it off as the street was filled with children who just at
that time came out of a school on the other side of the Plaza,
and they could not shoot. However the next Saturday there
were no children present and as Villa turned the corner to
cross the bridge they let him have it.

"Villa was driving his old Dodge and had Colonel Trillo
in the front seat with him, with three soldiers in the rear seat.
They all died instantly, never knowing what hit them. Barraza
went to the car and using his 45 automatic almost cut Villa
in half with bullets. He and his men then mingled with the
gathering crowd as though they were innocent bystanders.
Later, however, Salas Barraza was tried and convicted of killing Pancho Villa. He spent some time in the penitentiary at
Chihuahua.

"In 1924 it was planned that I would fly Salas Barraza to
Durango where he would head a push to capture Villa's
ranch, but General Michel came down from Jiménez and
captured it so we didn't have to go."

Early in his career as a leader of the revolution, Pancho
Villa recognized the value of airplanes and their coming importance militarily. His army was said to be the first to use
planes in Mexico. Records show that he bought planes from
the United States and hired American barnstorming pilots.
U. S. Air Force records show that in May, 1913, Villa fliers
bombed Federal gunboats in the bay at Guaymas, being the
first aerial bombing in the Western Hemisphere. The Villa
fliers for this mission were Didier Masson and Thomas J.
Dean.

Records from the Air University at Alabama show that
Villa had four planes: two Wright-B's, one early Christoffer-

[margin handwritten, right side, vertical:] His chauffer Rosalio Rosales, Capt. Daniel Tamura, Int. Dot. ... i

[margin handwritten:] Miguel

[handwritten note at bottom:] April 1914 - Rebel plane piloted by Capt Gustavo Salinas bombed Federal defenders in Mazatlán, Sinaloa "Revolution!" p. 184, Ronald Atkin

son Curtiss Pusher, and a Martin T model. Villa used a small park at Monterrey as a landing field, as well as a rough airstrip near town and at Matamoros.

Andrews knew many of the pilots of the eight original planes of the First Aero Squadron, sent to and based at Columbus, New Mexico, immediately after the Villista raid on the town. Those Curtis J-N3 biplanes made of linen and spruce were called "Jennys" and were shipped from Fort Sam Houston to Columbus on a special train. Their pilots, under the command of Captain Benjamin D. Foulois, were Captain Dodd and Lieutenants J. E Carberry, C. G. Chapman, H. A. Darque, R. H. Willis, T. S. Bowen, A. R. Christie, W. G. Kilner, E. S. Gorell and Ira Rader.

Supporting General Pershing's Punitive Expedition they scouted, delivered messages, took pictures, and made the first successful aerial maps. By August 15 the augmented pioneer Aero Squadron had made 540 flights over 19,553 miles over the rough, unknown territory of Mexico. The pilots flew under almost impossible conditions, being attacked by hostile Mexican troops when forced down, stoned by villagers, with the pilot on one occasion being kept in a local "juzgado" until freed by the American consul.

Andrews served with L. Gordon Cooper, father of Astronaut Cooper, in the Army Air Corps at Ft. Bliss. The young fliers would fly along the border, using bombs, machine guns and any weapon at hand to kill Mexican bandits operating along the Río Grande in 1919–1920.

Their most important mission, the Second Punitive Expedition, was to hunt down Jesus Rentería, a Villista bandit leader. Rentería had captured Air Corps Lieutenants Harold G. Peterson and Paul H. Davis and was holding them for $15,000 ransom. Their plane was forced down in Mexico, across the border from Candelaria, Texas on August 10, 1919. Andrews was with the rescue expedition that went after them. On August 19 a cavalryman, Captain Leonard F. Matlack, paid half the ransom which had been raised by ranchers of the Big Bend country, and the pilots were freed. The next morning the Eighth Cavalry troopers crossed the Rio Grande in pursuit of the kidnappers. Pilots Lieutenant Cooper and his partner Lieutenant Estell, flying ahead, found Rentería in a mountain canyon, strafed and killed him.

Andrews became Major Andrews of the Mexican Air Force in 1924. He and Charles Mayse, an ex-Oklahoma cowpuncher, bombed and strafed rebel troops led by Villa's brother, Hipólito. On one occasion they laid a trap for Hipólito and caught him as he was about to burn a railroad trestle. One night in Jiménez, the twenty Mexican soldiers guarding Andrews' J-I Standard drained the plane of the cane alcohol Andrews used as anti-freeze and drank it. Andrews found them lying on the ground next morning, completely passed out.

"Moon-hopping may be glamourous," Andrews says, "but flying a home-made, crack-up and patch-up crate in 1910 was a real challenge, too, and so was flying in Villa territory."

Soledad Seanez

Soledad Seáñez is officially recognized as Villa's widow.

"Pancho told me he first saw me in 1917, in Villa Mata-mores, Chihuahua. He was wounded in the leg at the time and was passing through town in a carriage. I was sitting on a porch where I had taken some sewing to do in a good light. After seeing me on the porch Villa asked around town till he found a cousin of mine and became acquainted with him. I only knew Villa by name at that time. My cousin had a small picture of me which Villa asked for. It was very romantic. Villa carried my picture next to his heart till it was almost worn to pieces. He showed it to me when we finally met, two years later. He was still carrying my picture when he was assassinated."

They met in Valle de Allende, Chihuahua, Soledad's hometown and birthplace, through Villa's arrangement. Soledad was then a dressmaker and painting teacher. Villa had a party and, for the purpose of meeting Soledad, he invited her and her family and friends. At the party he put his hand on her head and said, "I am not going to leave you." He sang her a song and then announced in a loud voice that he had come to marry Soledad. From the first he called her "Chole," pet name for Soledad, and insisted that everyone else do so.

Soledad and Pancho Villa were married on May 1, 1919, in Valle de Allende, having both civil and church ceremonies. Present at the wedding were Generals Felipe Angeles and Nícolas Fernández, Colonels José Jaurieta and Baltasar Piñones, and Francisco Alvarez and other officers. Some of Villa's cousins also attended. A picture taken three days after the wedding, and which Soledad now keeps on her bedside table, shows her a slender, idealistic, dainty bride. Villa is pictured as rather subdued looking but with a proud expression. After the wedding there was a fiesta to celebrate.

Villa married Juana Torres on October 7, 1913, in Torreón, Coahuila. On December 17, 1915, he married Luz Corral in Chihuahua City. Juana Torres died in October, 1916. When Villa married Soledad Seáñez in 1919 he was then a legal widower and therefore his marriage to Soledad was legal. He married Austreberta Renteria in June, 1921, in Parral. Records show that Villa had two legal marriages, first to Juana Torres, second to Soledad Seáñez. He was never divorced from any of his wives.

"I was not recognized as widow of Pancho Villa until December 30, 1943, when the Senate in Mexico City formally approved granting me a pension as widow of General Francisco Villa. At first the government would not recognize me because the crime of my husband's murder was too fresh. Also I couldn't go to Mexico City to make my claim and straighten things out earlier because I had promised to stay and care for the children. I couldn't leave.

"After we were married I stayed for some months with my parents at Valle de Allende. It was my husband's decision that I come to El Paso for the birth of my baby. One of his colonels brought me to El Paso. I rented a house there with some cousins from Valle de Allende. My son was born there in our rented home at 816 North Oregon Street, with a midwife, the widow of a general, in attendance.

"Immediately after I had left my parents' home at Valle de Allende, Federal General Miguel Acosta took my mother, Manuela de Seáñez, and two nieces there, prisoner. It was fortunate that I had gotten away and across the border. They did these things to harass my husband.

"My son, Antonio, was born April 17, 1920, at that house high on the hill in El Paso, looking west across the Rió Grande. He was Pancho Villa's only recognized legitimate son, and from the first greatly resembled his father both in voice and appearance. I was always very proud of Antonio.

"I stayed in El Paso altogether ten months, seven months before Antonio was born and three months afterward. I was of course very homesick for my home and to see my husband. When Antonio was three months old I went back to Valle de Allende to the home of my parents. While there I received two letters from my husband. I cherish these letters, for they show the love in his heart for me and that he was thinking of me."

Canutillo, Dgo.,
July 10, 1920

Mrs. Soledad Seáñez de Villa:

Your letter is in my possession and I am replying to it. I cannot go to town because I don't want to and this deprives me of seeing you soon, but soon I will come by auto for you. Wait till the time is better and less rain. If you are short of money I will send someone from Canutillo that you can trust with a note for you. Let me hear from you quickly if you want me to send money. You are my life. Good-bye, yours,

Francisco Villa

Hacienda del Canutillo, Durango
November 25, 1920

Mrs. Soledad Seáñez de Villa,
Dear Chole:

I salute you because I don't want you to think I have
forgotten you and at the same time I tell you I'll go after
you the fourth day from now, and you will see all that I
have for you. Do not be discouraged, the trough lacks
water and I have not gone because I have lacked money.
Have patience, do you hear, my life?

Your humble servant,
Francisco Villa.

"My husband came himself after the baby and me on December 12, 1920. He took me straight to the home he had built
just for me in Cantuillo."

This began Soledad's few years of marriage and her real
acquaintance with her husband.

"My husband had worked hard and greatly improved the
large Rancho Canutillo which he received from the government in July of that year, 1920. There were many buildings
all together like a village. There were buildings for the telegraph, telephone, post office, grocery store, shoe shop, tailor
shop, room for sewing in general, rooms for the escort, dining
room for all.

"The school was separate, two or three miles away from
the big house. My husband was greatly interested in education
and always realized his own lack of schooling. He was determined that every child possible should learn. One school he
opened in Parral was named for him. In Chihuahua City one
school hadn't paid any teachers for a whole year and when
Villa learned about it he paid their salaries in full. He even
sent some children to the United States to school. He was
very strict about his ruling that every child on his land have
an education. He formed a band for the school. Two of his
nephews, Raúl and Pedro, and two others, and even college

boys, formed a band for the schools. He finally had 150 boys in the school bands.

"I remember it all like a song. The ranch at Canutillo was so white and so pretty. My husband had built a home apart from the big house just for me, on a road that he named Calle Soledad, for me. The others, including Luz Corral when she came to Canutillo, lived together in the big house. We all, Austreberta, Luz, and the others, took care of all the children. Everyone loved the children.

"Juana had one daughter, Juana Maria. Austreberta had two sons, Francisco, born while Villa was still living, and Hipólito, born after his father's death. At Canutillo, my first real home after I was married, I had three children to care for, my own litle Antonio, and two of my husband's other children, Miguel and Micaela. All were very dear to me. I have kept in touch with all of them and they have visited in my home, and still do.

"Miguel was like my own child. He was only one month younger than Antonio and I nursed him along with my baby. He grew into a fine young man. My Miguelito was killed in a plane accident in August, 1950.

"My husband was interested only in developing his wonderful farm at Canutillo, and in educating his own and the other children, and the school he had built. He was an affectionate, loving husband and father.

"Pancho Villa was not cultivated in the art of letters but could never be called ignorant. He had almost no chance at all for schooling when he was a child. He and all his people had to work like slaves from daylight to dark on the hacienda where he was born. He grew up suffering the cruelties and injustices of a brutal *patron* system under a wealthy Spanish don. All his life he hated those aristocratic *patrones*.

"He told me all these things, of his early life, and the later years, in the evenings that we spent together, in my own little home on Calle Soledad. My husband despised those dons and swore vengeance on them. In later years he persecuted and finally completely ruined the greatest cattle king, *grandero rico,* in the world, Luis Terrazas of Chihuahua. Terrazas was rich because he robbed the poor. Villa was going to put a train from Canutillo through Rosario, Durango, right to the Don's hacienda. He had a telephone put in and wired for that and a general store.

"Even more than he hated dons Villa hated the ignorance that kept the Mexican people crushed and hopeless. That's why he tried so hard to build schools and keep them going. When a powerful, ambitious, brilliant man like my husband is held down to slavery, is tied to a post and flogged when he tried to run away, hunted down and sent to rot in jail as a teenager, when his father dies from overwork, then is when hate grows. He promised himself vengeance. There seemed no chance to better himself. There was hardly hope of enough tortillas and beans to keep his mother and younger brothers and sisters alive. So what does Villa do? He rebels.

"Very young he steals what he cannot get any other way. He becomes defiant and daring and the first chance he had he took to make money the only way he could, by stealing. His mother was very strict and honest. When Villa brought her money he stole she felt very bad. She cried and wouldn't accept it, though there was no other way for a boy like Villa to survive. He was not a thief by nature, but there was no other way to live.

"He told me of the terrible hardships of those days. There was never any rest or peace. He suffered from dirt and lice. He had not even a handkerchief. No one knew how he suffered. Villa joined a group of men in similar circumstances. Being a natural born leader, he was soon leading the bandit band.

"He had only two sisters, named Marianita and Martinita. Marianita married a Señor Flores and died two months before my husband was killed. Martinita married Juan Martínez and has been dead for several years. Villa had two brothers, Hipólito and Antonio. Both are now dead. My son was named for Villa's brother, Antonio.

"All the time he was forced to live as a desperado Villa was hoping and working to help his own people, plotting to overthrow the dictator, Díaz, who kept Mexico in poverty and ignorance.

"Because I was a teacher, I was able to help my husband in his constant search for learning. He was a good pupil and learned quickly. Those who say he mispronounced words and spoke with a strong accent were not telling the truth. Villa had a light northern accent and spoke without mutilating either vowels or consonants, even though he was so accused by some writers. I excuse them because they are ignorant of the truth. He was a natural mathematician, perhaps that accounted for some of his military genius during revolutionary maneuvers. He studied at every opportunity under Professor Jesús Coello, the Director of the school which Villa established at his Canutillo ranch.

"My husband was a great swimmer, having skill swimming on his back. He liked to ride and was a stupendous horseman. He also liked to garden. He rose early most every morning—often at 4 A.M.—and got woodmen up to cut wood. He was very fond of physical exercise and he would run on foot a long way, often covering the distance between Canutillo and Rancho Llorón. People thought he was crazy to do that. He kept himself in very good physical condition, never drinking and smoking only on rare occasions.

"In the evening we played a card game called *baraja*. He would tease me when I won too often by cheating me. He often retold the adventures and war experiences he had when taking Chihuahua. Torreón, Parral, Zacatecas, Juárez. Or when fleeing one jump ahead of General Pershing or the Carrancistas. He also spent much time studying now that he had the opportunity.

"But there was always danger to my husband. Even at Canutillo when he was living in peace with no thought but to improve his land and help the people, there were threats and attempts on his life.

"Sometimes we dared keep no lights on in the house at night. One time a plane hovered over the ranch with someone in it trying to shoot my husband with a machine-gun. Others came and offered to teach him to fly, but he knew they were not to be trusted. There was a would-be assassin who carried a rifle that looked like a cane. Villa was working hard loading hay out in the field one day when three men tried to kill him. They were caught and executed by his bodyguard. There were many attempts to ambush him on trips to Parral, but they failed.

"One time a man, pretending to be an *arabe* [Arab peddler] was caught stealing at the ranch. He was killed there. This was reported to the military. The incident became greatly exaggerated and we heard that it was said that there was great killing and stealing at Canutillo. After reporting theft of his cattle to the Federal authorities and being ignored by them, my husband had stated that the next time there was a robbery or killing on the ranch he himself would deal with the outlaws and rustlers. This statement of his was also distorted. From then on there was discord with the military.

"Of course, I did not know of most of these occurrences till later. And I am sure I did not know of all the threats and attempts on my husband's life. He did not want to worry me. I did see one frightening incident that happened in 1922. Pancho was sitting in a chair, relaxing in the yard, when a man came up on a bicycle. He had claimed to be my husband's son and somehow had got by the guards. When he got very close he pulled out a pistol and would have shot my husband down if he had not been so alert and quick. The man was seized and taken away. I was so frightened that I could not sleep that night, though Villa laughed and tried to make nothing of it.

"His enemies stalked him like a deer. There were even assassins hiding in the woods along the way he would have to follow when he left the ranch.

"On the day of the assassination, we were going into Parral on the train. We were going to attend a family baptism. Just before we were to leave home a little old man came to the house and warned my husband that killers were posted to ambush the train. Villa was afraid for me and decided that I had better not go. He and Trillo, his secretary, and his guards took the Dodge car and left. That was the last time I saw my husband.

"I was finally told of the assassination by a telegram from Parral. At that time I was quite fat and thought I might be pregnant. The others at Canutillo didn't want to frighten me and so tried to prepare me for the shock. First they told me that my husband was wounded. Then that he was going to be taken prisoner. Of course they were lying. I felt that something was very wrong, but I was helpless. I had to wait for information. There was nothing I could do. For three days after he was murdered I never knew that my husband was dead. When I found out the truth he was already buried in Parral. He was killed at 7:30 A.M. on July 20, 1923.

"I knew later that for more than three months Salas Barraza, congressman from Durango, and Melitón, a rich rancher, had plotted with seven other men to murder my husband. Their hands did the terrible deed, but others, higher up, were responsible and it was done on their orders. President Obregón and Governor Enríquez had Pancho Villa assassinated. My husband was still loved by the people and those in power were jealous and feared him.

"They took his poor body to Hotel Hidalgo in Parral, which he owned. There the people came to look at him, and mourn him. And I, his wife, knew nothing of what had happened.

"I stayed on in Canutillo for ten more months, in my little home with Antonio, then only three years old, and little

Miguel. I didn't know what to do. My husband's younger brother, Hipólito, had come from Juárez to take charge of things and run the ranch. Then one day, with no warning or explanation, Federal troops came and broke into my home. The government took everything. My father came and took me and the children back to Valle de Allende. I heard it said that the government feared that Hipólito would make trouble."

After some years at Valle de Allende, and then in Mexico City, Parral, and Valle Matamores, Soledad moved finally to Juárez. There she is highly respected both for herself and as Villa's widow.

Her son, Antonio, who had been working as a special customs agent, was ambushed and shot to death in his car, near Chihuahua City, in September, 1967. It is painful for Soledad to speak of this, "Pancho was a loving, good father and husband, an avenger of the humble, a man who was trying to help his own people to a better life when he was truck down by cowardly murderers. His countrymen will always remember him so, as a true hero." She is very aware of the comparisons made between her husbands and son's deaths.

"I try, as General Francisco Villa's widow, to propose humbly to the liberal and revolutionary groups that his memory be put before the Federal government in five points. First, the Avenida Ferrocarril in Juarez be named Francisco Villa. Second, the monument that is projected, that has his old Dorados, be erected on the spot where he was sacrificed. Third, the house from where they shot him should be bought by the Governor and converted into a museum and library in honor of Villa. Fourth, his name be written in letters of gold in the Congress of the Union. And last, Villa's remains should be transferred to the Monument of the Revolution to lie beside those of Madero, Carranza, and Zapata. I am keeping his medals and certificates and other belongings until I am able to donate them to the museum I mentioned."

31

Carl A. Beers

Beers lived in El Paso since 1904 and knew Villa after his retirement to Rancho Canutillo.

"From the evidence of the sincere loyalty of his workmen and their families that I saw in my short visit to Rancho Canutillo I would say that he had their best interests at heart.

"He was a gracious, considerate host with a lively sense of humor. He was very proud of the school he had established on the ranch and had great plans for the education of the children of his workers.

"I watched Villa at work with the people on his ranch and brought back an impression very different from the popular picture of a brutal, bloodthirsty guerrilla chieftain."

In September, 1921, Beers, representing the W. G. Roe Company of El Paso and accompanied by Miguel Ortiz of the same city, set out for Rancho Canutillo in the northern part of the State of Durango. Beers hoped to sell farm machinery and implements to Villa who had been furnished the 5,000 acre ranch and 500,000 pesos gold to equip and run it as terms of his retirement from revolutionary activities.

The two men, traveling in a 1921 Ford over unpaved roads and through rough country, arrived at the boundary of Rancho Canutillo with slight feelings of trepidation. They went through an unguarded gate in a barbed wire fence and drove on down the road. They were now in Villa territory, and stories of the fierce, vindictive nature of the former leader could not be altogether forgotten. Fifteen miles farther on they reached the ranch headquarters, a white-plastered, thick-walled adobe hacienda atop a hill. The front entrance was wide enough to admit a wagon.

The estate was extensive, containing a church, store, the school, and quarters for Villa and his staff, as well as the homes of the workers. Beers knew that more than $200,000 had already been spent on roads, new buildings, improvements, and machinery. He hoped to make a good deal for his company on the equipment still needed.

Beers and Ortiz were met and greeted by Villa's secretary, Miguel Trillo. He told them that the General would see them in a short time, and in about twenty minutes he showed them into Villa's office.

Villa sat at his desk, dressed in the loose shirt and baggy trousers of the Mexican ranchero.

Villa recognized Ortiz as having served with him in the revolution and greeted him affectionately. Ortiz introduced Beers and explained that his firm had already sold Villa some plows and that Beers now wanted to sell him more farm equipment. Villa's appraisal of the American was keen and swift.

"You are welcome to my ranch," he said, "and it will give me pleasure to show you personally what we are doing at Canutillo. I hope you can stay at least three days. I will not be free after that time, but I will be glad to have you stay as long as you care to."

Beers remembers breathing a sigh of relief. It was known that the ex-bandit chieftain was unpredictable. He was known to form strong and instant antagonisms, and his love and respect for Americans had turned to bitterness in the past few years. Beers credited his acceptance to his companion, Ortiz, but seemingly Villa himself was satisfied with Beers after his initial appraisal.

After supper that evening, Villa took his guests on a tour of the grounds. They stopped at the stables and Villa proudfully discussed the pedigrees of his horses. Beers admired a particular black horse and stopped to look at him while the others went on ahead. The next morning he was agreeably surprised when Villa gave orders to saddle the black horse for his guest; proof, Beers thinks, of Villa's keen powers of observation.

That first evening was also memorable for an exhibition of Villa's skill with a gun. One of the visitors mentioned that he had heard that Villa was an unusually good shot. Villa took that as a challenge. He put an ear of corn into the fork of a tree, took out his six-shooter, stepped back about twenty paces, turned the gun upside down and blasted the corn to bits.

Ortiz talked with Villa of the Revolution and mentioned General Felipe Angeles, the famous strategist who in 1919 was captured and executed in Chihuahua City by Carranza's orders. Mention of Angeles evoked an emotional outburst from Villa. Tearfully he praised Angeles as a man of highest character and qualities; he cursed Carranza.

"I felt no weakness in Villa then," Beers says. "Rather, my respect for the man increased. His sorrow seemed to spring from an elemental strength of character, a nature endowed with a capacity for unusual affection."

Back at the ranch house Villa insisted on giving up his own bedroom to his guests. It was a neat room, furnished with a heavy brass bed and a dresser on which was an array of perfume bottles, mostly unopened. Beers feels that this is another inconsistency in Villa's complex character.

As Villa visited with them in the bedroom, Beers remembered that he had left his rifle and camera in his car. The more he thought about it the more anxious he was about losing them. Villa noticed his increasing nervousness and asked if there was anything wrong. Beers explained. Villa promptly informed him that his possessions were as safe on the grounds of Canutillo as they would be in an El Paso bank, but if it would make Beers sleep any better he would have them brought in. In a short time, the precious camera and rifle were in the room. Beers was grateful but embarrassed, but Pancho Villa didn't seem bothered.

Villa lounged back while he and Ortiz discussed old days, battles and campaigns of the Revolution. Beers listened with interest, following their Spanish as best he could. Suddenly Villa's hand dropped to his pistol. Beers' heart skipped a beat.

"Perhaps you would like to see this pistol, Mr. Beers," Villa said. "It is the one I carried with me through the Revolution."

Beers took the gun from Villa, admired it, and returned it while his heart slowed down to normal.

When hearing of the incident later, Villa's secretary, Trillo, said, "You are the first man as far as I know, Mr. Beers, that Villa has ever allowed to touch that pistol."

Breakfast the next morning—and every morning at Canutillo—was between 5 and 6 A.M. Beers observed again that Villa seemed to notice everything. Seeing that Beers needed fresh coffee, Villa told the mozo to serve him, pronto. Beers remembers welcoming the strong, hot drink, for in spite of the fine appointments and ready service at Rancho Canutillo he found the rooms too cold for his comfort.

After breakfast Villa proudly took his guests on a tour of the estate, pointing out what he had accomplished on the ranch and telling what he hoped to attain. He had harvested 35,000 bushels of wheat that year and planned to plant twice that much the next year. Enormous quantities of corn and beans were in the process of being harvested. The farmers worked on a sharecrop basis, being given receipts when they brought their produce to the warehouse.

Villa was strict and did not allow liquor on the ranch. He appreciated the efficiency of modern machinery and wanted as much of it as possible for Canutillo. He was said to fondly pet a baby tractor as though it were one of his favorite horses. About 600 men, including Villa's famous *Dorados,* were working at the hacienda, in the fields, commissary, in the shops where saddles and shoes were made, in the light plant, and in maintenance.

During the tour they came to one of the clusters of small adobe houses scattered around the ranch. With the greatest pride Villa displayed the school which he had built, and which was almost finished. It stood, clean, white-plastered, in a good sized play yard. Wooden blocks were imbedded in the concrete floor to provide bases for seats. It was Villa's idea to place the windows high in the walls so that there was good ventilation but at the same time were too high for the children to be distracted by looking out. He valued education and demanded that every child on the ranch attend school. He himself was studying economics and agriculture, though he never learned to write until he was twenty-five.

Beers asked if he could send something from the United States for the ranch school.

"Yes," Villa said. "You had two great men in the United States, Washington and Lincoln. I would like to have pictures of them to hang in my school room."

Beers agreed to send the pictures.

While inspecting the farm machinery and Villa's men at work, Beers noticed that the Mexicans had the belts reversed on a threshing machine so that the wheat was being thrown out instead of drawn in. Even though the machine had been sold to the farm by a rival company, he adjusted it properly and instructed them as to its use. Villa seemed grateful.

Villa ordered twelve turning plows from Beers' company, but the two men could not agree on which type was best for the job in hand. Villa finally said, "Well, Mr. Beers, perhaps you are right, though I believe I am. Let's do it this way. You send me six of the ones I want and six of the kind you think I should have. We will try them both out and when you again pay me a visit, we will know who was right."

The three days passed swiftly for Beers and he and Ortiz regretted leaving Rancho Canutillo and Villa's company.

Just as they were leaving, Villa beckoned a young man forward and introduced him as Captain Hernández.

"This fellow needs medical attention," Villa said, indicating Hernández' bandaged arm. "I would appreciate it if you could give him a ride as far as Parral where he can see a doctor."

Beers agreed to take Hernández.

Hernández, wearing a pistol and a belt of cartridges, climbed into the Ford and they waved to Villa and his staff.

Out of sight of the ranch building Ortiz started to go back the way they had driven in, but Hernández directed him to take the other fork of the road. The road was very rough and it took them a long time to reach Parral. After a pleasant farewell and a repetition of Villa's warnings about traveling that country at night, Hernández left them. Beers and Ortiz spent the night at Parral.

Late the next afternoon they arrived at Jiménez where Beers met with a man who wanted to buy some machinery. When his business was finished it was getting dusk. They got off on the wrong road, and found themselves lost in the rough country. In the darkness they were fortunate enough to find a farmer's home and spent the night there.

The next morning they learned that bandits had held up and taken quite a sum from a mine paymaster on the road they would have been on had they not taken the fork out of Canutillo as directed by Hernández. The narrowness of their escape struck Beers and Ortiz forcefully. Also it seemed more than coincidence that they had been guided out of danger.

The road on to Chihuahua City was very rough and no speed could be made. However, it was well-traveled and when darkness overtook them they weren't really worried. Contrary to the warnings they'd received about traveling this country after dark they began to relax as they realized that it was less than twenty miles to Chihuahua City. They were driving up out of a deep arroyo and onto a mesa when they heard the sound of gunfire ahead.

They pulled off the road. Before they shut off the car lights they saw a group of wagons down the road coming from Chihuahua City.

"Farmers coming back from market in Chihuahua, where they sold their corn," Ortiz said. "They're being held up."

Running footsteps approached from the direction of the wagons. One of the farmers reached the car. He said their six wagons had just been halted down the road by a group of masked, armed bandits.

"Have you guns?" he asked. "Will you help us?"

Beers and Ortiz had a rifle and a shotgun and they agreed to help. When they joined the farmers they learned that another ten wagons were expected to join their party in a very short time. About a dozen shots were exchanged before the reinforcements came down the road. At this the bandits withdrew, riding off into the shadows.

The grateful farmers placed their sixteen wagons in a circle around a campfire along with Beers' car. The drivers slept in their wagons with an armed man on guard. Two other men guarded the horses and mules in a makeshift pen of ropes strung between mesquite bushes.

The next morning the farmers, showing their gratitude to Beers and Ortiz, escorted them for several miles on the way to Chihuahua.

When they arrived in Chihuahua City they parked near the Plaza, at the Casa Myers. Hernández was standing there, smiling.

"Bueno dios, amigos!" he greeted them. "Did you have any trouble last night?"

"We certainly did," Beers said. He explained about the hold-up.

"But you must never drive in this country at night, señor," Hernández said.

After Hernández departed, Beers and Ortiz traveled on to Juárez where they stopped at a roadside grocery store for food and gasoline. There, to their surprise, was Hernández again, bandaged arm and all, standing on the steps of the store, white teeth gleaming in a smile of welcome. After a warm greeting he said he'd decided not to go to the hospital in El Paso as planned but instead would remain in Juarez for treatment.

A short time later a Mr. Soloman, Villa's broker in El Paso, had a letter from Villa advising that Beers and Ortiz had been of much value to him in connection with his farm machinery and that he wanted to be assured of their safe arrival home.

Before Beers was able to deliver the pictures of Washington and Lincoln to Canutillo for the school there, Villa and Trillo had been assassinated. The pictures were finally given to a school in the nearby town of Canutillo, Texas.

"I recall Villa," Beers states, "on that last day at Canutillo. The sun was bright and warm. All around were the sounds of a busy ranch at work. I remember hearing a team driver singing *La Cucuracha*. That was one of Villa's marching songs of the old days on the war trail. I asked Villa what he thought might be the solution of Mexico's problems. He said, 'Work and education.' "

BIBLIOGRAPHY

Atkin, Ronald. *Revolution: Mexico 1910–20*. New York: John Day Co., 1970.

Bailey, Harry H. *When New Mexico Was Young*. Las Cruces: Citizen, 1946.

Barron, Clarence W. *The Mexican Problem*. Boston and New York: Houghton-Mifflin Co., 1917.

Beaulac, Willard L. *Career Ambassador*. New York: Macmillan Co., 1951.

Beals, Carleton. *Mexican Maze*. New York: Book League of America, 1931.

Braddy, Haldeen. *Cock of the Walk: Legend of Pancho Villa*. Albuquerque: University of New Mexico Press, 1955.

Brenner, Anita, and Leighton, George R. *The Wind That Swept Mexico*. Austin: University of Texas Press, 1971.

Bryson, Conrey. *The Land Where We Live, El Paso Del Norte*. El Paso: Guynes Printing Co., 1973.

Bulnes, Francisco. *The Whole Truth About Mexico, President Wilson's Responsibility*. New York: Bulnes Book Store, 1916.

Bush, I. J. *Gringo Doctor*. Caldwell: Caxton Printers, 1939.

Carman, Michael Dennis. *United States Customs and the Madero Revolution*. El Paso: Texas Western Press, 1976.

Case, Alden Buell. *Thirty Years With The Mexicans*. New York: Fleming H. Revell Co., 1917.

Cervantes, Federico M. *Francisco Villa y La Revolución*. Mexico City: Ediciones Alonso, 1960.

Chase, Stuart. *Mexico*. New York: Macmillan Co., 1935.

Clendenen, Clarence C. *Blood on the Border*. Toronto: Macmillan Co., 1969.

Cumberland, Charles C. *Mexican Revolution: The Constitutionalist Years.* Austin: University of Texas Press, 1972.

Dils, Lenore. *Horny Toad Man.* El Paso: Boots and Saddle Press, 1966.

Foix, Pere. *Pancho Villa.* Mexico City: Editorial F. Trillas, 1950.

Franke, Paul. *They Plowed Up Hell in Old Cochise.* Douglas: Douglas Climate Club, 1950.

Freudenthal, Samuel J. *El Paso Merchant and Civic Leader.* El Paso: Texas Western Press, 1965.

Garibaldi, Guiseppe. *A Toast to Rebellion.* New York: Gadren City Publishing Co., 1937.

Gibbon, Thomas Edward. *Mexico Under Carranza.* Garden City: Doubleday, Page and Co., 1919.

Guzman, Martin Luis. *Memoirs of Pancho Villa.* Translated by Virginia H. Taylor. Austin: University of Texas Printing Division, 1965.

Hadlock, Adah. *My Life in the Southwest.* El Paso: University of Texas Press, 1969.

Harris, Larry A. *Pancho Villa and the Columbus Raid.* El Paso: McMath Co., 1949.

Harris, Theodore D. *Negro Frontiersman: The Western Memoirs of Henry O. Flipper, First Negro Graduate of West Point.* El Paso: Texas Western Press, 1963.

Hathaway, Mary Lucille. *An Album of Memories.* Tucson: Old Pueblo Printers, 1972.

Hatch, Nelle Spilsbury. *Colonia Juarez.* Salt Lake City: Deseret Book Co., 1954.

Ibañez, V. Blasco. *Mexico in Revolution.* New York: E. P. Dutton & Co., 1920.

Hinkle, Stacy C. *Wings and Saddles.* El Paso: Texas Western Press, 1967.

————. *Wings Over the Border.* El Paso: Texas Western Press, 1970.

Jamieson, Tulitas Wulff. *Tulitas of Torreón.* El Paso: Texas Western Press, 1969.

Johnson, William Weber. *Heroic Mexico.* New York: Doubleday & Co., 1968.

Joralemon, Ira B. *Romantic Copper.* New York: D. Appleton-Century Co., 1934.

King, Frank M. *Pioneer Western Empire Builders.* Pasadena: Trail's End Publishing Co., 1946.

King, Rosa E. *Tempest Over Mexico.* Boston: Little, Brown and Co., 1935.

Bibliography 269

Knotts, E. Franklin. *Prisoner of Pancho Villa*. El Paso: Per/Se, 1966.

Landau, Henry. *The Enemy Within*. New York: Van Rees Press, 1937.

Lansford, William Douglas. *Pancho Villa*. Los Angeles: Sherbourne Press, 1965.

Liggett, William. *My Seventy-Five Years Along the Mexican Border*. New York: Exposition Press, 1964.

Link, Arthur S. *Woodrow Wilson and the Progressive Era*. New York: Harper and Row, 1954.

Lister, Florence C. and Robert H. *Chihuahua Storehouse of Storms*. Albuquerque: University of New Mexico Press, 1966.

Mangan, Frank J. *Bordertown: The Life and Times of El Paso Del Norte*. El Paso: Carl Hertzog, 1964.

Martin, Percy F. *Mexico's Treasure-House: Guanajuato*. New York: Cheltenham Press, 1906.

Mason, Herbert Molly, Jr. *The Great Pursuit*. New York: Random House. 1970.

Means, Joyce E. *Pancho Villa Days at Pilares*. El Paso: Guynes Printing Co., 1976.

Meyer, Michael C. *Mexican Rebel: Pascal Orozco and the Mexican Revolution, 1910–1915*. Lincoln: University of Nebraska Press, 1967.

Middagh, John. *Frontier Newspaper*. El Paso: Texas Western Press, 1958.

Millon, Robert M. *Zapata*. New York: International Publishers, 1970.

Moats, Leone B. *Thunder In Their Veins*. New York: Century Co., 1932.

Neal, Dorothy Jensen. *The Lodge*. Alamogordo: Alamogordo Printing Co., 1969.

O'Shaughnessy, Edith. *Diplomatic Days*. New York: Harper and Brothers, 1917.

———. *A Diplomat's Wife in Mexico*. New York: Harper and Brothers, 1916.

———. *Intimate Pages of Mexican History*. New York: George H. Doran Co., 1920.

Parkes, Henry Bamford. *A History of Mexico*. Boston: Houghton Mifflin Co., 1938.

Pettus, Daisy Caden. *The Rosalie Evans Letters from Mexico*. Indianapolis: Bobbs-Merrill Co., 1926.

Pinchón, Edgcumb. *Viva Villa!* New York: Harcourt, Brace and Co., 1933.

Rak, Mary Kidder. *Border Patrol*. Boston: Houghton-Mifflin Co., 1938.

Rascoe, Jesse, Ed. *The Treasure Album of Pancho Villa.* Toyavale: Frontier Book Co., 1962.

Romney, Thomas Cottam. *The Mormon Colonies in Mexico.* Salt Lake City: Deseret Press, 1938.

Ross, Stanley Robert. *Francisco I. Madero: Apostle of Mexican Democracy.* New York: A. M. S. Press, 1955.

Rouverol, Jean. *Pancho Villa: A Biography.* Garden City: Doubleday and Co., 1972.

Schuster, Ernest Otto. *Pancho Villa's Shadow.* New York: Exposition Press, 1947.

Scott, Hugh Lenox. *Some Memories of a Soldier.* New York: Century Co., 1928.

Seymour, Charles. *The Intimate Papers of Colonel House.* Boston: Houghton-Mifflin Co., 1926.

Smith, Cornelius C., Jr. *Emilio Kosterlitzky: Eagle of Sonora and the Southwest Border.* Glendale: Arthur H. Clark Co., 1970.

Smith, Randolph Wellford. *Benighted Mexico.* New York: John Lane Co., 1916.

Sonnichsen, C. L. *Colonel Greene and the Copper Skyrocket.* Tucson: University of Arizona Press, 1974.

————. *Pass of the North.* El Paso: Texas Western, 1968.

Stevens, Louis. *Here Comes Pancho Villa.* New York: Frederick A. Stokes Co., 1930.

Thord-Gray, I. *Gringo Rebel.* Coral Gables: University of Miami Press, 1960.

Torres, Elias L. *Twenty Episodes in the Life of Pancho Villa.* Translated by Sheila M. Ohlendorf. Austin: Encino Press, 1973.

Trowbridge, E. D. *Mexico To-Day and To-Morrow.* New York: Macmillan Co., 1920.

Turner, John Kenneth. *Barbarous Mexico.* Austin: University of Texas Press, 1969.

Turner, Timothy G. *Bullets, Bottles and Gardenias.* Dallas: South West Press, 1935.

White, Owen P. *The Autobiography of a Durable Sinner.* New York: G. B. Putnam's Sons, 1942.

————. *Out of the Desert.* El Paso: McMath Co., 1924.

INDEX

Index

275

276 *INDEX*

Villa, Juana Torres, 12, 48, 111, 112, 113, 128, 250, 253
Villa, Luz Corral, 110, 188, 189, 190, 192, 197, 198, 203, 222, 250, 253
Villa, Pancho (Doroteo Arango), 3-15 *passim;* and Agua Prieta, defeat at, 16, 17, 34, 55, 73, 88, 143, 148, 208; appearance of, 4, 20, 45, 50, 111, 179, 224; assasination of, 48, 153, 192, 201, 245, 246, 257, 266; as bandit, 232; at Canutillo, 68, 192, 200, 201, 245, 252, 253, 255, 256, 259, 260-64, 266; and Celaya, defeat at, 142; Chihuahua State controlled by, 5, 27, 50, 91, 111, 134, 179, 189, 190; children of, 192, 251, 253, 255, 257, 258; Chinese persecuted by, 7, 31; and Columbus raid, 12, 14, 15, 16, 20, 28, 29, 34, 55, 65, 129, 146-50 *passim,* 154, 166, 191, 208, 219, 220, 221, 223, 226-28, 240; cruelty of, 11, 33, 68, 118; as crusader, 231, 232; education valued by, 252, 263; in El Paso, 27, 89, 178, 186, 187, 222, 233; firing squad faced by, 26-27, 91, 92; friendly side of, 32, 89; hardships during boyhood of, 253, 254; honesty of, 190; Juárez captured by, 27, 32, 93-95, 97, 179, 180, 181, 188, 191, 239, 255; Knotts kidnapped by, 58, 61-67 *passim;* and León, defeat at, 142; letters of, to Soledad Seáñez, 251, 252; Memoirs of, 94; and Mexico North Western Railway, 73, 77, 78, 79, 80, 81; and Mormons, friendship for, 164, 165, 167, 168, 171, 172, 210, 239; nephews of, 252; planes used by, 246-47; prejudices of, 7, 31; propaganda against, 16, 129-32 *passim,* 136, 141, 146, 147-48, 149, 153-54; as Robin Hood of Mexico, 102; in Sabinas pact with government (1920), 245; and Santa Ysabela

massacre, 8, 9, 10, 28, 55, 56-57, 65, 77, 129, 147, 148, 150, 154; Scott's impressions of, 153; as sharpshooter, 65-66, 261; *soldaderas* slaughtered by, 33-34; threats on life of, 256, 257; Visconti shot by, 108
Villa Ahumada (Mex.), 62, 63, 65, 66
Visconti, Arcangel, 103, 104, 110
Visconti, Enrico, 105, 106, 107
Visconti, Vincenzo, 103, 106, 107
Viva Villa (film), 223
Von der Goltz, Horst (Bridgeman Taylor), 138, 139, 140

Walker, John Walton, 207, 218
Wallace, Pearl McKinney, 210-13 *passim*
Washington, George, 24, 263, 266
Watson, C. R., 28, 56, 77
Weber, Máximo, 94
Welland Canal Plot, 138, 139
Wertz (Witcke), Luther, 138, 146, 148, 149, 150, 154
West magazine, 15
Western Livestock Journal, 14
Wheeler, Sheriff, 86
Whole Truth About Mexico, The (Bulnes), 131
Wilhelm, Kaiser, 37, 42, 130
Willingham, Harry, 16
Willis, R. H., 247
Wilson, Guy C., 156, 158, 160, 161, 169
Wilson, Henry Lane, 39, 40, 99
Wilson, Woodrow, 8, 11, 22, 41, 65, 88, 119, 120, 131, 133, 140, 141, 143, 144, 145, 148, 150, 151, 169, 210, 233, 234, 239
Wiswell, Harry, 207
World War I, 31, 145, 149
Wormer, Mel, 72
Wright, Ed and Maude, 166
Wright, Orville and Wilbur, 242

Yaqui troops, Villa's, 16, 135
Young, William, 172, 173

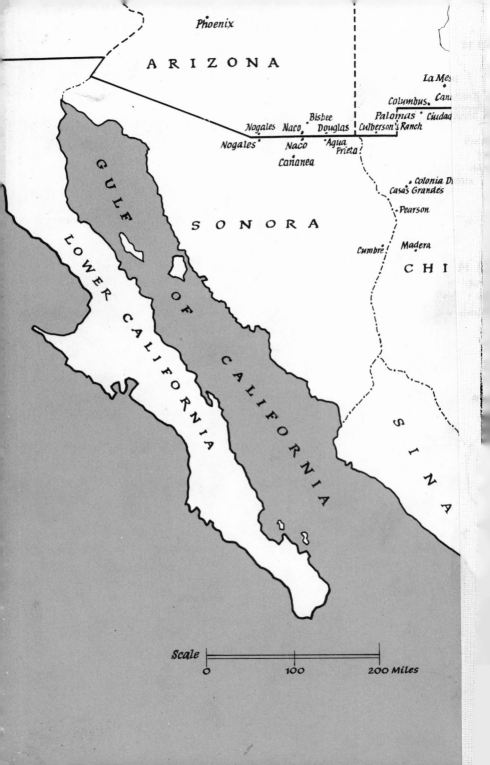

Phoenix

ARIZONA

La Mes

Columbus. Can

Nogales   Naco   Bisbee   Palomas   Ciudad
                    Douglas   Culberson's Ranch

Nogales   Naco   Agua
                          Prieta

         Cañanea

                                    . Colonia D
                              Casa's Grandes

                                 . Pearson

                           Cumbre   Madera

GULF

OF

LOWER CALIFORNIA

SONORA

CALIFORNIA

CHI

SINA

Scale

0   100   200 Miles